Silver Moon

HAVE A COLLECTION
OF 77 GREAT NOVELS
OF
EROTIC DOMINATION

If you like one you will probably like the rest

A NEW TITLE EVERY MONTH

Silver Moon Readers Service
109 A Roundhay Road
Leeds
LS8 5AJ
United Kingdom

http://www.electronicbookshops.com

If you like one of our books you will probably like them
all!

Write for our free 20 page booklet of extracts from early books
- surely the most erotic feebie yet - and, if you wish to be on
our confidential mailing list, from forthcoming monthly titles
as they are published:-

Silver Moon Reader Services

109A Roundhay Road

Leeds

LS8 5AJ

United Kingdom

http://www.electronicbookshops.com

or leave details on our 24hr UK answerphone
08700 10 90 60
International acces code then +44 08700 10 90 60

New authors welcome
Please send submissions to
Silver Moon Books Ltd.
PO Box 5663
Nottingham
NG3 6PJ
or
editor@electronicbookshops.com

The Girlspell
by
William Avon

PROLOGUE

IN ANOTHER PLACE..

"Gillianís ready now, Mr Platt," Alison said, putting her head round the door of Platt's office.

George Platt looked up from the account book he was working on and smiled at the bright, helpful face of his kennelmaid. "Thank you, Alison."

Platt took a medium weight cane from the selection hanging from a row of hooks on the wall and swished it experimentally through the air. Pocketing a couple of other items he followed Alison out into the yard.

The yard was a brick-cobbled square some twenty yards across enclosed by Platt's office and lodging, the stores and work rooms and the kennel block itself. Iron rings had been set at waist height in the sections of blank wall between the overlooking doors and windows, while from under the eaves above them projected heavy wrought iron angle brackets.

It was from one of these brackets that the only other occupant of the yard was suspended.

She was a woman in her early twenties, very slim and pale-skinned and, apart from a broad black studded collar fastened about her neck, completely naked. Her taut body hung from her upstretched arms so that her toes dangled two feet from the ground. Thick leather cuffs secured her wrists to a few links of chain and the ring that hung over the hook on the end of the bracket. A leather strap had been buckled about her knees, while another set of cuffs with a trailing chain bound her ankles. These constraints shaped her body into a slender arrowhead, twisting slightly from side to side as far as the chain that held her allowed. The stretching of her pectoral muscles exposed the pale hollows of her armpits and pulled her small high breasts into pointed pink-topped lozenges. Nervous breathing caused a rapid swell and contraction of the shallow double-dome of flesh under her navel that perfectly complimented her lean waist. Her

5

head, crowed by a mane of blonde hair tied in a simple pony-tail, hung forward between her upstretched arms as though in shame. Her eyes stared sightlessly down at the ground.

A flick of Platt's cane across her midriff jerked her back to her senses. Blue eyes wide with apprehension met his own stern gaze.

"Now then, Gillian," he said. "You know why you're here."

"Yes, Mr Platt," she whimpered. "To be punished. I'm so sorry. I'll never do it again, I promise!"

"No you won't girl," Platt said assuredly. "This session will make certain of that. Alison: lift her feet."

Alison grasped the chain trailing from Gillian's ankle cuffs and climbed the small stepladder placed beside the unfortunate girl, drawing the chain after her. Gillian bent in the middle like a jack-knife, the strap about her knees forcing her legs to remain straight, until her feet were almost level with her bound hands. Alison hooked the ankle chain over the bracket and then reached between Gillian's legs and chest. A snap ring dangled from her collar, and this Alison fastened to the strap about her knees so that Gillian's face was pressed against her shins.

Alison stepped down.

Now Gillian hung like the gourd of some exotic fruit ripe for picking, her hips almost at shoulder height, leaving her genitalia completely exposed. Her tightly bound knees squeezed her thighs together and forced her mounded cunt lips, from which the golden curls of her belly hair had been trimmed back, into an unwilling pout.

But it was the orifice below this that held Platt's attention. He poked the dark pucker of Gillian's anus with a stiff forefinger, making the girl jerk helplessly within her bonds.

"Now, girl," Platt said, "what's this?"

"My... my bottom hole, sir," Gillian said despairingly.

"And what's it for?"

"To void my excrement, sir."

"And what else?"

"To... to give pleasure to anybody I'm serving, sir."

6

"Good," Platt said. He took up a stance to one side of Gillian and rested his cane across her tight buttocks. "Now we're going to drive that message home so you'll never forget it."

The cane swished through the air and smacked into her flesh. Gillian yelped, twisting on her chain like a plum bob. A thin red weal burned across her bottom cheeks and the split peach of her cunt that rose between them. Platt let her come to rest, then asked:

"What can be put up your bottom hole, girl?"

"Cocks, fingers, dildos.. bum plugs... anything! sir," Gillian gasped.

Smack!

"And how often can these things be put up there?"

"As many times as my user wishes..."

Smack!

"And do you have any say in the matter?"

"No, sir... not my place, sir..."

Smack!

"What if it hurts you a little?"

"I'm... here to suffer, sir."

Smack!

"So will you ever refuse your bottom hole to anyone again?"

"No, sir... they can cram it full with whatever they want, sir..."

Smack!

"What are you?"

"A bondslave... a pack bitch..."

Smack!

"And don't you ever forget it," Platt said, lowering the cane.

As the girl hung sobbing and trembling he examined the results of his handiwork. Her bottom was criss-crossed with weals and scarlet with heat, but the skin had not been broken. Long experience had taught him just how much force to use on such occasions. Now there was one final detail and the punishment would be complete.

"You'll stay up here until lunch, girl," he told Gillian, "then

7

back to work. I'll see you later to make sure you've learnt your lesson. Understand?"

Gillian nodded as far as her bonds allowed and said faintly: "Yes, Mr Platt... thank you."

Platt took out of his pocket one of the items he had brought from his office. It was a hook set in the end of a length of inch-thick wooden dowel with a shallow screw thread carved into its surface. "Now, I need a place to hang a hook. Do you know of one, girl?"

Tremulously Gillian replied: "If it's convenient, sir... please use my bottom hole."

With the tapering wooden thread forcing her anal ring open, Platt screwed the dowel into the yielding tunnel of her rectum until only the hook end was visible. Then from another pocket he took an old tinplate alarm clock, checked it was wound, set the alarm and hung it on the hook protruding from its fleshy mount.

"That'll remind us when you're ready to come down, girl."

He turned to Alison, who had been watching the whole procedure in attentive and fascinated silence.

"Gag her. I don't want to hear a peep until the alarm goes."

"Yes Mr Platt," Alison said dutifully.

Platt returned to his office. Through the window he could see Gillian's pale, slender form dangling in the sun. He noticed she shivered occasionally, probably having a cry to herself now the worst was over, he thought.

Still he knew it had been necessary, and in the long run it would make her term of service easier. George wanted the girls under his care to be the very best, so sometimes he had to be cruel to be kind.

8

Amber Jones flitted through Hoakam Woods like a wraith, her black tee shirt and jeans merging with the shadows under the trees as her trim form moved with cat-footed sureness.

Reaching a large oak tree, its base half concealed by bushes, Amber halted and looked around her intently. Once assured she was not observed, she burrowed into the shrubbery and pulled back a fold of turf. From under this she withdrew a heavy sack wrapped in thick black plastic sheet which she opened lovingly. Within it was piled select small antiques, solid silverware, strings of pearls and assorted jewellery.

Amber smiled in satisfaction at the precious items, her attractive face lighting up as her lips parted to reveal white, even teeth. The set of her jaw was determined, her nose delicately square-tipped and slightly uptilted, while her cool clear hazel-blue eyes held a mischievous sparkle. Her eyebrows were boldly marked and her forehead smooth, high and intelligent, rising under a crown of short cropped brown hair.

Amber unzipped her black nylon holdall and the proceeds of her latest robbery joined the stash. She was about to add her pouch of trusty lockpicks when the puzzle box caught her eye.

It was a black lacquered box about six by ten by three inches deep, inlaid with mother of pearl and ivory in the design of an oriental dragon with a tail that ran all the way round the box, so that the beast appeared to be eating the tip. She'd acquired it two jobs back, but so far she had been unable to discover its concealed catch and didn't want to damage such beautiful workmanship by forcing it open.

But this time, as she handled the box, she felt one of the dragon's baleful pearl eyes shift downward slightly under her finger. Ahh, was that the trick? She felt across the lid. One of the claws also seemed to give slightly. She felt around further, finding a scale on the dragon's encircling tail was slightly proud of the rest. She pressed firmly down on all three elements at once. There was a tiny click from within and the box sprang open.

Amber gaped in amazement at the interior.

The inside of the lid was laid out with many small raised ivory buttons, resembling a calculator keypad, each marked with the characters of some oriental script. Other buttons were set apart, rather like function controls, on either side of a central block laid out in a five by five grid. This was strange enough by itself, but in conjunction with the items in the lower half of the box it was positively bizarre. Nestling in beds of white silk, were three ivory phallus heads, coloured red, green and blue, with three screw-topped handles resting beside them.

The heads were about six inches long and slightly curved. Each had the tiny carved figure of a nude woman at its base, her legs and arms embracing the shaft and chained together at the wrists and ankles. The figure's back and neck were arched, lifting the uptilted head away from the shaft as though in ecstasy.

Amber shook her head in wonderment. Though the 'keypad' had to be modern, both it and the phalluses had the indefinable aura of genuine antiques. Curiously she pressed a couple of buttons. Nothing happened. Perhaps the battery's dead, she thought wryly.

"You're under arrest," a woman's voice said behind her.

Amber froze in astonishment and dismay.

"Bring out your bag and whatever you've got in your hand," the voice continued. "We can collect the rest later."

Very slowly Amber backed out from under the bush, stood up and turned around.

A young black woman of about her own age faced her, dressed in a runner's shorts and singlet, with a small pack slung over her shoulder. She was holding out a warrant card for Amber to see.

"Constable Kingston, Hoakam police," she said, pocketing the card again. She stepped forward and took Amber by the shoulder. "Amber Jones, I'm arresting you on suspicion of burglary...'

Amber felt numb as her rights were read, only managing to protest feebly at the end: "Look, I just found this box under the

10

bush. I don't know anything about it."

"So your fingerprints won't be on any of the other stolen items I bet are hidden under there?"

They were, of course. She'd handled them without gloves after she'd stolen them. Careless!

Amber looked hopefully into Kingston's face. It was rather attractive actually; smooth coffee-dark skin, clear deep brown eyes, wide full lips, crinkled hair tied back in a thick ponytail. Unfortunately there was no sign of a gullible nature, just determination. In all not a combination of characteristics she normally associated with police personnel. Well, it would have had to have taken someone a little out of the ordinary to catch her.

Amber shrugged resignedly. "How did you find me?"

"By thinking for myself. There was a different style about these jobs, a touch of bravado. The boys from area crime -"

"I'm flattered to hear they were called in."

"Because you burgled so many influential people around here. Anyway, they thought whoever did it was heading back up the motorway to the city after each job. But there was no word on the street about it and none of the items were being fenced. So I thought maybe it was bolder and simpler than that. It was a long shot but I made enquiries and sure enough you'd rented a small cottage on the edge of Hoakam woods, almost central to the robberies. But you haven't got a record, so to prove my hunch I had to get you with the goods, and I knew you wouldn't keep them in the cottage. I've spent all my off-duty time since training here, and today I finally tracked you down."

"Now I remember seeing you about. Good disguise."

"I'm a serious runner."

"And now you've proved a local plod can solve the crime wave when the big city boys couldn't."

"A local black woman plod, yes."

"Ahh. I can see that would make you go that extra mile." She looked down at the puzzle box she was still holding. "Well, I suppose you'd better have this. Odd thing, isn't it -"

And she threw it into Kingston's face.

11

Kingston twisted aside to avoid the box and leaped on Amber before she had managed a couple of steps, catching her round the legs and sending them both crashing to the ground. Struggling and kicking they rolled over through the mud and leaf litter, Kingston trying to twist Amber's arm behind her back while Amber tried to land an incapacitating blow. But her opponent was faster and stronger than she was. This time there would be no escape -

Then they rolled over the puzzle box which lay open where it had fallen. Amber's flailing elbow rammed down on the keypad.

The air seemed to warm and thicken about them while the rustle of the breeze in the leaves grew muted. Their tussle took on a dream-like slow motion quality. Amber felt her nipples harden and her vaginal muscles contract as lustful desire replaced fear and anger. The fight also seemed to be draining from her opponent. As her grip slackened Amber pushed her to arm's length and saw the confused expression on Kingston's face, saw her nipples peaking through her singlet and knew she was feeling the same sensations as she was. Burning desire and desperate need that overwhelmed all else - but not for each other.

As one they turned their heads to the puzzle box. The simple functionality of the phalluses nestling so invitingly within it suddenly seemed irresistibly appealing. Amber didn't stop to wonder why, or how unlikely the sudden onset of desire was, she only knew she had to use one.

They both reached for the box together.

Amber kneed Kingston in the stomach. "It's mine!" she shouted.

As Kingston doubled over whooping for breath, Amber scrambled to her feet, snatched up the box and her holdall and sprinted away through the trees.

But she had hardly gone fifty yards when she realised her pants were wet with the thought of a hard, smooth rod of ivory thrusting up inside her. Her body was one big hole that needed filling. Though it was crazy in the circumstances, she had to satisfy herself immediately!

A little way above the meandering path was a slight hollow in the wooded slope where the roots of a fallen beech had pulled a great bite out of the earth. Amber scrambled up to it and threw herself down in the soft moss and old leaf litter, resting her head on her holdall. Feverishly she pulled down her jeans and pants, dragging them off over her trainers and kicking them aside.

She spread her lean and shapely legs; her glistening pubic lips gaping wide to the open air while leaves stuck to her bare bottom. Breathing faster, her hands trembling, she took a phallus head from the box, screwed a handle into it and without any preliminaries plunged it into herself, grasping it in both hands as though she was wielding some sacrificial dagger.

She gasped and arched her back, feeling her sheath contract around the phallus, trying to draw it deeper inside. How could mere carved ivory feel this good? It seemed to swell, fitting her perfectly, the upturned head of the chained figure at its base burrowing into her upper cleft and grinding against her already erect clitoris. She worked it vigorously up and down, feeling an inexorable wave of ecstasy rising within her... surging higher... cresting... bursting.

Still clasping her stomach, Melanie Kingston scrambled up the woody slope a few seconds later, drawn by the almost tangible wave of pleasure that had rippled out from the hollow.

On the ground lay crumpled jeans, a pair of pants and the black lacquer box with one phallus missing. The intimate scent of female discharge hung in the air, but there was no Amber Jones.

Melanie looked about her intently for any sign of the woman but there was nothing. Then she found her eyes drawn back to the box and its two remaining phalluses. A delicious knot of desire was tying itself inside her lower stomach once again. Her nipples were painfully engorged. Her body ached to be penetrated with one of the hard ivory horns.

She shivered and shook her head, forcing herself to think

13

calmly. What had caused that rush of intense desire that had overtaken both of them? Where had Jones gone half naked? The silent woods gave no answer. Whatever the reason there would have to be a search, and at least now she had her evidence she could get official help. She pulled her cell phone from her pack only to find it cracked and dead; a casualty of the fight. Right, it would have to be the nearest call box.

She put Amber's jeans and pants into her pack and tried to do the same with the black lacquer box. But she couldn't even bring herself to close the lid! It was too wonderful, too intriguing to be packed away. So, holding the box in trembling hands, she started off.

But with every step her arousal increased as the air grew warmer around her. Her pants were riding up into her cleft where they were being soaked by her juices. She couldn't take her eyes off the tiny figures chained to the phallus heads.

After a quarter of a mile her resolve crumbled. She had a healthy appetite for sex but had never felt the raw need for it so powerfully before. If she didn't relieve her desire immediately she thought she would faint. Her wet excitement was soaking through her shorts in a dark stain and glistening on her inner thighs. With a groan she surrendered to the inevitable and ran for the shelter of a rhododendron thicket.

Once inside its leafy shade she rolled onto her back and tore down her shorts and pants, which were actually sticking to her, exposing her bush of glossy black hair. Her pink inner lips, pouting from her cleft of darker flesh, were already swollen and glistening in anticipation. She twisted together a phallus and handle and rammed it inside her, heedless of bruising her delicate flesh.

Again and again she reamed her dripping hole until, bucking wildly as her brown buttocks clenched and flattened against the earth, she reached a climax. For a moment everything blurred. She felt a monstrous wrenching sensation and something seemed to snap exquisitely within her...

Then there was only the black lacquer box with its single remaining phallus lying on the carpet of leaf litter... waiting for

14

one last girl to fall under its spell.

2: Country Pursuits

Melanie recovered slowly from her orgasm. It had never felt so intense before, and she wondered if she hadn't momentarily passed out from pleasure shock.

When she did open her eyes she found herself staring up not into the sheltering rhododendron bush, but an interlaced canopy of high branches. She was lying in the open! She sat up with a jerk only to find the phallus was still lodged inside her. Gingerly she withdrew it, making an embarrassing sucking noise in the process, acutely aware of her still swollen nether lips. She really had used it hard, but how could she have got so excited about the thing? It seemed perfectly ordinary now.

She turned to put it back in its container. It had gone.

Her pack was beside her, a strap still looped around her arm, but not the black lacquer box. Dazed she looked around. Somehow the wood seemed thicker and greener than it had, and a clump of bluebells flowered just a few feet away. Surely that hadn't been there before. She twisted about to look further only to freeze in amazement.

A wall ran along a broad swathe cut through the wood behind her and disappeared from sight in either direction. It was about twelve feet high and made of brick, mottled with moss and lichen, and topped with a row of black iron spikes. It had obviously been standing for years, yet she knew for a fact there was no such structure anywhere in Hoakam Woods.

Trying to stay calm, she wriggled back into her pants and shorts, hoping the guilty stains on the crotch would dry quickly. She put the phallus in her pack, stood up and brushed herself off. The search for Amber Jones had to be postponed until she found out where she was herself.

As she headed away from the wall the trees thinned to reveal a stretch of open fields. Beyond them was a lake and a patchwork of ornamental gardens, presided over by a grand country house. It had symmetrical wings and a portico supported by a row of tall columns projecting from one facade. Melanie knew all the large houses in the area and was certain there was nothing like it for twenty miles.

Feeling slightly dizzy she leaned against the tree beside her. Slowly she fingered the bark and looked up at its tall trunk and heavy branches. It was a mature elm, one of several in view along the edge of the wood. But Dutch Elm disease had killed all the elms around Hoakam years ago. Only scattered pockets survived anywhere in the country.

Deep inside her the suspicion began to grow that she was now a very long way from home, in a direction she could not begin to measure or understand. She thought of the mysterious box, the powerful sensations its phallus had generated and her blackout. Could it have been responsible, and could the same thing have happened to Amber Jones?

Even as she struggled to make sense of it all, she heard the sound of voices and the gentle clop of horses' hooves. Quickly she crouched down in the shelter of a straggling laurel bush growing beside the elm, taking off her pack and holding it before her light singlet. Instinct told her to find out who was approaching before revealing herself.

Five riders appeared from between the trees, their mounts walking on at an easy pace. Two men and a woman came first with two more men trailing them. As they got closer Melanie saw the leader of the party was a vigorous ruddy-faced man in his fifties with a bristling moustache and greying sideburns. On his right was a smaller wiry clean-shaven man in a brown jacket and flat cap, while on his left rode the woman. She looked about twenty, pale-skinned, with blonde hair peeking from under her riding helmet as she glanced about keenly. She wore a long skirt or perhaps culottes, which Melanie thought looked a little dated. Then she noticed one of the men who took up the rear had a large moustache and both sported unfashionably long sideburns.

The older man's words drifted over to her as he addressed

16

the brown-jacketed man.

"... and see those dead branches are moved, Platt. We want a clear run through here."

"Yes, Major," he replied. "Perhaps they could go over to the stalking ground to give a bit more cover there?"

"Capital. Have the pack haul them. Give them a bit of hard exercise."

"Right you are, sir."

As the party rode on past Melanie wondered if she should reveal herself. They seemed harmless enough, but on the other hand how was she going to explain her presence?

Then the blonde woman leaned over and said something urgently to the man called the Major. He twisted round to look back and Melanie knew she had been spotted. Hesitantly she rose from her concealment. "I'm sorry to bother you, but I'm lost..." she began.

"What? A dashed trespasser!" the Major exclaimed.

"I say, tallyho, a bit of sport!" cried the young man with the moustache. He turned his mount about and headed straight for Melanie, flourishing his riding crop menacingly.

"Remember I saw her first, Gerard!" shouted the young woman to him, spurring on her own mount by a flick across the flanks with the springy switch she carried.

"Race you for her Arabella!" the other young man said, following on close behind.

With a cold shock Melanie realised she had totally misjudged these people. She didn't waste her breath on any more words but dropped her pack and took to her heels.

"Don't let her get away!" she heard the Major bellow as she disappeared through the trees.

Melanie ran harder than she had ever done before. She twisted between the trees, crashed through brushwood and leaped spreading roots. She knew she dare not try to escape over open ground or they would catch her in moments. Her only chance lay in keeping to the woodland where the horses' speed was limited, and hope she could find a gate in the wall or someplace low enough to climb. But the wall seemed endless, unvarying in height and without a sign of any opening. The air was still and close under the trees. Sweat began to sting her eyes and run down between her heaving breasts and the cleft of her buttocks. Despite her efforts the three younger riders were closing in, shouting instructions to each other to head her off.

"There she goes Thomas!" Gerard called to his companion.

"Nimble little vixen, isn't she?" Thomas replied.

"Yes.... and what a rump on her!"

Gasping for breath she ducked around a thicket and crouched down, letting the riders gallop past. Before they could turn about she was off in the other direction. If she couldn't outrun them perhaps she could find somewhere to hide.   But she had forgotten the Major and Platt. They thundered out from between the trees and rode straight at her. She leapt to one side but the Major caught her across the shoulder with his crop. She stumbled and fell heavily, winding herself and rolling over and over. Before she could recover her breath the whole party had surrounded her. They leaned down from their saddles and lashed out with their crops until she curled up on the ground in a ball, too shocked by the cutting blows to move.

The assault ceased. Strong hands hauled her to her feet, pulling her arms outstretched and holding them firmly. Blinking away her tears she found the two younger men were holding her while the Major and Arabella dismounted, handing their reins to Platt.

The Major's eyes gleamed as he looked Melanie's trembling form up and down in disconcertingly frank appraisal.

"What a remarkably fine specimen," he said heartily. "Such a turn of speed and agile with it." He took Melanie's chin between thumb and forefinger and turned her head from side to side. "One of our African cousins, it seems. I wonder how she got here?"

"She's obviously an outlander," said Gerard, twisting Melanie's arm a little to hold her still. "Look at her clothes."

"I've heard stories about outlanders," said Thomas, "though

18

I've never seen one myself before. But if they're all as pretty as this I'd like to see more," he added enthusiastically.

"I saw her first Uncle," Arabella reminded the Major, also looking Melanie up and down with disturbing interest. For a second Melanie read passion and hunger in her cool blue half-veiled eyes.

"All in good time, my dear," the Major replied. He dropped his hand from Melanie's chin to her still heaving left breast and experimentally cupped and squeezed it.

Melanie flinched and tried to pull away, finding enough breath to shout: "What the hell do you think you're doing!? How dare you!"

Arabella's horse switch flicked out twice, left and right, the tip bringing burning fire to Melanie's cheeks and fresh hot tears to her eyes. "You'll speak only when you're spoken to, girl, understand?" she said in a commanding tone. "Now what's your name?"

"M... Melanie Kingston," Melanie choked out, stunned by the suddenness of the blows.

"Melanie Kingston, Miss Arabella," Arabella corrected her sternly.

"Miss Arabella," Melanie added wretchedly.

"Well, Melanie," said the Major, "you've been caught trespassing on my land - and we have ways of dealing with trespassers." He smiled. "But first let us see what you're hiding under these clothes. Strip her, gentlemen."

"What?" Melanie gasped in disbelief even as the men began pulling at her singlet. Fear lending her renewed strength, she twisted about and kicked Gerard in the stomach. He let go of her arm and staggered backwards, doubling up and wheezing. Swinging round on Thomas, she grasped his shoulder, hooked her leg behind his knee and pushed, sending him sprawling on his back.

Arabella's switch caught Melanie hard across the back of her knees, numbing her tendons. As her legs gave way the Major's weight bore her to the ground face first, flattening her breasts

19

into the grass. He straddled her torso and twisted her arms up behind her back. Thomas and Gerard recovered themselves and grabbed her thrashing legs.

"Platt," the Major grunted as he rode Melanie's struggling body, "fetch some restraints - we're obviously going to need them."

"Right you are, sir." Platt remounted his horse and rode off.

"Our little brown vixen needs to be taught a lesson before we go any further," the Major continued. "Bare her rump."

Keeping her wrists crossed and arms pulled up towards him, he shifted around until he straddled Melanie's head; ignoring her shriek of protest and trapping her facedown between his knees. Gerard and Thomas pulled her wildly kicking legs straight, brought her ankles together and Gerard knelt across them. Thomas hooked his fingers over the waistband of Melanie's shorts and pulled firmly, dragging them and her pants down over her hips, exposing the swelling fullness of her brown buttocks and the deep sweat-bedewed cleft between them. Arabella knelt beside Melanie's pinioned form and ran her hand over the fleshy curves, sliding a finger between her cheeks to tease the crinkled tightness of her bottom hole, setting Melanie wriggling frantically and adding to the excitement of the spectacle she presented.

"Finest pair I've seen in years," exclaimed the Major appreciatively.

"They'd certainly look splendid in harness sir," Gerard agreed.

"Or with a tail dividing them," Thomas suggested.

"Indeed," the Major agreed. "One for the pack with any luck. Six strokes, please Arabella. Then we'll give her a chance to decide."

Cheeks flushed and nostrils flaring slightly in anticipation, Arabella laid the length of her thin springy switch across Melanie's bottom to measure the swing, then lifted her arm and brought it down in a smooth arc. There was a smack of leather, a shockwave shiver of flesh and a stifled squeal from Melanie. A fine, slightly darker line appeared in the olive skin, bridging the cleft between the two hemispheres across their upper curves just below the base of the spine. Arabella swung a second time, aiming lower and angling sideways slightly, lifting the swelling flesh just above the crease where buttock met thigh and making it tremble with the blow. Another muffled squeal. Melanie's hips wriggled as though she was trying to burrow into the ground to escape the punishment. Having scored parallel lines in the resilient flesh, Arabella changed her stance slightly and delivered two shorter cracks with the tip of her switch diagonally between them and across the curve of each cheek. Then she rose, stepped across Melanie's outstretched form and knelt on her other side, turning so that she delivered the next two swings backhand. They neatly crossed the previous diagonals in the centre of both buttocks. Arabella paused for a moment to admire her symmetrical handiwork.

"The only trouble with darker skin is that it doesn't show the marks so starkly," she observed mildly. "You have to be a little firmer -" And she quickly delivered a seventh blow right across the middle of Melanie's trembling bottom, joining the two "X's she had marked in her dusky flesh.

"Arabella!" her uncle said sharply. "I said six strokes!"

"What does it matter, uncle?" she said impatiently. "She's only an outlander, a tramontane! It's her fate to be used."

"I promised her only six, then she'd have a chance to speak. Would you have me break my word?"

Arabella got to her feet scowling and stood flicking her switch petulantly across the grass. The three men turned Melanie over onto her back, the Major pulling her arms in front of her then stretching them firmly up over her head to prevent any further escape attempts.

But Melanie was temporarily beyond any thought of resistance. She had been subdued not only by the pain of the switching that burned her buttocks, but also by the total self-assurance of the strangers. It was as though she had been wrong to resist them and had been casually chastised for her error. Her world had been turned upside down and she felt hopelessly confused.

21

Keeping hold of her wrists with one hand the Major grasped her hair and pulled her head straight again so she had to look him in the eye. His face loomed upside down over her as he spoke earnestly.

"Now, girl, listen to me very carefully. I don't know how it is in your land, but here you've broken the law. I'm the local Justice of the Peace, and I promise you'll get six months for assaulting Thomas and Gerard. Then there'll be charges for trespass, being a vagrant with no means of support or proper abode and illegal entry into the country. Not a day less than two yearsí public servitude, all told. That is, unless you decide to behave sensibly."

Melanie blinked back her tears. "What... do you mean?"

"If you voluntarily join the Hall pack for, say, a year, you'll have legal abode and gainful service. Then if you apologise to Thomas and Gerard and promise them some good sport in return, perhaps they'll forgive you."

"The Hall pack?" Melanie asked hesitantly.

"My girlpack, of course. You've already shown you have what it takes. I'm always looking for strong, agile girls with spirit. They must be quick witted and ready to respond to the discipline of training for the hunt. You should be proud of the opportunity. The Markham Hall bitches are the best in the south."

"You hunt women!" Melanie said, aghast.

"Of course," the Major replied simply. "A fine sport."

Melanie gulped, her mind spinning. "And... what happens when you catch them?"

The Major gave a rakish chuckle, making his moustache lift. "They're enjoyed in the usual way, of course. What better prize can there be after the hunt?"

Arabella spoke up: "You're not going to put her straight into the hunt, are you, uncle? I did see her first -"

"And you'll have a chance to compete for her with the rest in due course," he replied sharply. "Perhaps that'll teach you to obey me in future." The Major turned back to Melanie and slapped her cheek to regain her attention. "Well, girl? Do I call the constable and give you in charge, or do you choose the pack? It's one or the other."

As her captors looked down at her, eagerly awaiting her decision, a numbing sense of unreality descended on Melanie. She was genuinely being asked to decide between prison and a year of some bizarre form of sexual slavery! It could not be happening to her. It must be a crazy dream, a nightmare!

With a huge effort she focused her mind.

The hands that held her were real enough, as was the cool grass on which her hot striped bottom rested. It was reality, just not the one she had been born in. And if there was a way back to her own world it had to involve the phallus, which was in her pack back in the trees where she had dropped it. If she became part of this 'girlpack' (the thought made her shudder) she might get a chance to recover it. At least she would avoid being arrested like a common criminal. But did she have the nerve to see it through?

Summoning all her courage she took a deep breath and said: "I want to join the Hall girlpack, please, Major."

The Major beamed. "That's the spirit! Let her go," he told the others. "Stand up, girl, and take off the rest of those clothes."

Stiffly, her buttocks still smarting, Melanie climbed to her feet. Biting her lip she pulled her singlet over her head, and, after a moment's fumbling with the catches, unsnapped her sports bra. With a shiver she dropped it to the ground, baring her breasts.

"Wait," the Major ordered. 'Clasp you hands behind your neck."

Swallowing hard, Melanie obeyed, realizing how well the posture showed off her heavy breasts with their plump chocolate brown nipples. The Major reached over and squeezed Melanie's right breast, pinching the nipple and stretching it until she gave a little gasp, then let snap back. He ran his fingers down her deep navel, noting her trim and supple waist.

"Continue," he said.

Stifling a sob, Melanie dragged her shorts and pants down

the rest of the way and tossed them aside, leaving herself completely naked except for her trainers. Without being told she clasped her hands behind her neck again.

"By Jove... splendid!" Thomas exclaimed.

Her waist swelled to broad hips, full rounded buttocks and thighs. Between them sprouted a thick fan of glossy black curls. Her smoothly muscled legs ran down to strong calves. Years of intense exercise caused her body to radiate strength and vitality.

The Major knelt in front of her and inserted a probing finger into the moist folds of plump flesh under her belly curls. Melanie gasped at his touch and clenched her thighs together by reflex, but the Major's finger slipped inside her up to the knuckle. "Well, she's no virgin," he declared. He withdrew his finger and sniffed the glistening deposit that covered it with a smile. "And she's been aroused recently."

Melanie turned her head aside, her cheeks burning afresh in shame.

There came the sound of hoofbeats. Platt rode up and dismounted. Melanie saw he was carrying a bundle of buckled leather straps and a length of chain. With a thrill of alarm she realised they were meant for her. Surely she couldn't submit herself to such humiliation. Yet at the thought the tunnel of her vagina contracted and, incredibly, she felt her juices begin to flow. What was this place doing to her?

"On your knees and sit straight" the Major commanded, and Melanie obeyed. "This is Melanie," the Major told Platt. "She has volunteered to join the Hall pack."

"I'm sure she'll make a fine addition, sir."

"Secure her."

Platt fitted a broad leather collar about Melanie's neck. Leather cuffs linked by a short chain were fastened to a ring on the back and these he secured about her wrists, forcing her hands to remain in position. For a moment Melanie tugged against her restraints, but they were quite immovable. Platt clipped a longer and heavier chain to a ring on the front of her collar, leashing her like an animal. Her bondage had begun.

"Now," the Major told her, "crawl to Mister Gerard and Mister Thomas, kiss their boots and beg forgiveness for striking them. Properly - shoulders down and bottom up!"

As though in a dream Melanie lowered her shoulders until her face and breasts pressed into the grass. She was acutely aware of the air caressing her hot taut upthrust bottom cheeks and the pouch of dark flesh between them. Awkwardly she shuffled forward as well as her pinioned arms allowed, Platt walking beside her, allowing just enough slack on her chain to move. The humiliating thrill of her restraint and exposure burned within her stomach and flowed into her loins. She reached Gerard and kissed the instep of each of his shiny black riding boots, tasting leather and polish.

"Please forgive me for striking you, Mister Gerard," she said, forcing the shameful words out.

"And hope to give him some good sport," the Major reminded her.

"And I hope to give you good sport," Melanie added wretchedly.

Gerard patted her on the head. "You're forgiven, girl."

She crawled bottom high over to Thomas and repeated her apologies, then back to the Major. All the while Arabella looked on with frustrated desire contorting her fine features; angrily flicking her switch to and fro. The Major however seemed satisfied with Melanie's performance.

"Good girl. Take her away, Platt. I'll see her tested myself later."

"Right you are, sir."

The Major returned to the horses, which had been peacefully cropping grass, and Thomas, Gerard and Arabella - with one last lingering glance at Melanie - followed him. They remounted and resumed their interrupted ride. As they disappeared between the trees reaction set in and Melanie began to tremble. How could she have demeaned herself like that? She couldn't be a slave -

Platt reached down and squeezed her cheeks, forcing her

25

mouth open. Before she could protest he pushed in a hard rubber ball gag and secured it about the back of her neck with an integral loop of the same material. It pressed her tongue down making speech impossible, even as her lips were stretched and drawn back. Her bared teeth showed very white as they bit impotently on the gag separating them.

As she knelt shivering on the grass Platt walked thoughtfully about her, still holding the end of her leash, assessing her with an expert eye.

"Spread your knees wider," he ordered. "A packgirl is always on display, she hides nothing." Miserably Melanie obeyed until her thighs were parted almost at right angles.

Platt continued his silent examination for a full minute. Then he stopped directly in front of Melanie, reached down with both hands, pinched a plump brown nipple each between thumb and forefinger and lifted. Melanie scrambled to her feet with a choking squeal. Platt kept pulling until she stood on tiptoe and her eyes were level with his. Yet she read no malice in his face, merely masterful assurance and earnest intent.

"From now on my word is law to you," he said quietly. "The Markham pack are the best in the south and I want them to stay that way. Do what you're told and don't let me down, understand?"

And he continued to squeeze and roll her tender buds until, with eyes wide and glistening with tears, Melanie nodded her head vigorously.

Platt released his hold, gathered her discarded clothing and led her over to his horse. He mounted and started off, with Melanie walking beside him like a dog on a leash.

"Head up," Platt commanded. "Lift your knees and move proudly!"

Fearful, helpless, dazed, Melanie obeyed.

And so it was, with her breasts bouncing prettily in time with her steps, she was led across the fields towards the Hall.

Amber had been wandering through the woods for twenty minutes when the girl appeared. She was wearing a yellow pinafore dress and a large straw sun hat and was carrying a wicker basket half full of early spring flowers. Amber quickly hid behind a tree. This was partly from natural caution but mainly to avoid giving alarm - Amber was naked from the waist down.

She had recovered from an earthshaking orgasm to find her pack still folded under her head, but the tree root hollow she had been sheltering in had vanished. Also absent was the black lacquer box and her discarded jeans and pants. It was some consolation that there was no sign of constable Kingston either.

She had done her best to think constructively. Her holdall at best could only be held modestly before her. Her pouch of lockpicks also offered little aid, unless she could use them to break into a house and steal some clothes. She had scowled at the phallus once she had withdrawn it from her clinging orifice, suspecting it had something to do with the inexplicable alteration to the woodland around her. But she had no time to work out exactly what, so she dropped it into her pack. She wiped her still flushed and sticky pubic lips clean with a tuft of grass, then set off through the woods in search of answers and clothes, not necessarily in that order.

Now, as Amber observed the girl approach, she wondered what story she could give to explain her circumstances. Unfortunately the girl looked just the sort who might run when half-naked strangers accosted her. Her dress was distinctly old fashioned, falling almost to mid-calf, revealing white stockings and rather dainty black shoes. It was rather hard to judge her age, but Amber guessed at sixteen or seventeen.

Amber had just decided to speak up when a voice in the distance called: "Ernestine!"

A second girl appeared along the path, holding her skirts up to her knees as she ran. There was a brief interchange of words

27

between them, too low for Amber to hear, then they both turned away and disappeared between the trees.

Amber pondered for a minute then decided to follow the pair at a safe distance. They might lead her to some more responsible person from whom she could beg assistance.

She had taken two steps forward when there was a slight rustle behind her. Even as she twisted around a sack was thrown over her head and pulled down, trapping her arms.

Unseen hands wrestled her over and she fell face first into a clump of ferns which muffled her cry of outrage. Someone knelt on her shoulders as hands caught her wildly thrashing legs and held them together. Rope bit into her ankles. She bucked and wriggled but could not prevent her ankles being bound. The dusty choking sack was slid up to allow her arms to be twisted behind her and tied at the wrists. A hand grasped her hair and pulled her head back so that a strip of cloth with some small hard ball wrapped within it could be forced into her mouth and tied at the back of her neck. She gurgled and chewed at the material but she had been effectively gagged. The sack was pulled down again and its drawstring pulled tight about her thighs, leaving only her legs protruding.   "Grab her bag, Parsons," Amber heard a voice say urgently. "Get her away from the path... up that way!"

Hands grasped her bound ankles and Amber was dragged up the gentle woodland hill like a sack of potatoes. After a minute's bumping and scraping she felt herself dropped onto a soft bed of ferns. Rustles and excited breathing around her suggested her captors were also settling themselves.

"Let's have a proper look at her," a voice hissed.

"What about the blindfold?" another said.

"We don't have to worry about anything she sees," a third replied.

The sack was untied and pulled off. Amber blinked up into three faces hidden behind makeshift handkerchief masks. Even as she goggled at them the masks were hesitantly pulled down one by one to reveal the well-scrubbed features of adolescent

28

boys, sixteen or seventeen years old. They were breathing heavily and looked flushed and excited, their eyes riveted on her naked hips and belly and the fluffy hair at the junction of her thighs. Amber saw bulges growing in the fronts of their trousers. Not boys she decided, with a thrill of apprehension, definitely young men. They noticed the direction of her stare and suddenly looked embarrassed, shuffling awkwardly to conceal their erections.

"What do we do now, Jackson?" one with dark hair asked the blonde and tallest of the three.

"Take her to the pavilion the same as we planned for Arabella," he said. "Except we don't have to put her back again afterwards. We can keep her sort as long as we want."

"Can we do... everything to her?" the third boy with protuberant ears like pink seashells asked hesitantly.

Amber squirmed and made a muffled protest which they ignored.

"Of course," Jackson said confidently. "She must be an outlander. We don't have to be careful like we would with Arabella."

"But she hasn't been rotten to us like Arabella has," shell-ears pointed out. "So we aren't going to give her the same punishment, are we?"

Amber's eyes widened in alarm.

"We can if we want to, to make her behave," Jackson said. "She can be our own pet bondslave."

Amber struggled in growing alarm and shook her head.

"You mean we keep her through the term?" said dark hair.

"Yes."

"But where will we put her?"

"We'll work something out. She's a real woman. Think of all the things we can do with her."

As if to demonstrate, Jackson pushed her tee shirt up into her armpits until her neat cone-tipped breasts sprang free and pinched a pink nipple. Amber gave a little gasp of pain muffled by her gag.

Jackson laughed. "Look, they're going all dark and hard."

They took turns to pinch and tweak her swollen nipples, discovering how far they might be stretched and letting them snap back, making Amber's eyes water. Then Jackson placed his hand flat on her stomach and slowly slid it down over her mound, through the fleece of her pubic hair, and into the valley of her groin. Amber bucked and pressed her thighs together, but was helpless to prevent his intimate examination.

"What's it like?" the other two asked.

'Soft... and very smooth and warm. Feel."

They all felt Amber in turn. Curious fingers slipped into the folds of her cleft as far as her bound state would allow. Hesitantly they smelt the slickness she left on their fingers and looked at each other wonderingly, uncertain smiles on their faces. Their breathing quickened and the bulges in their trousers grew more pronounced. It was obvious what they wanted to do with her, and there was absolutely nothing she could do to prevent them.

"What about Harris and Gosset?" said shell-ears. "We agreed we'd do it together."

"That was about punishing Arabella," said Jackson impatiently. "This one's different."

I'm going to be gang-banged, Amber thought wildly, her panicky breathing rasping through her gag, then kept as a sex pet by a bunch of sixth formers. All right, she told herself, stay calm! After all there were worse things they could be planning for her. She'd played a few kinky games before. She'd simply have to co-operate with the inevitable and bide her time.

Blushing profusely, Jackson began undoing his trousers, fastened with old-fashioned fly buttons. "I'll go first - you hold her legs..."

Bicks and Parsons freed Amber's ankles and parted her legs with a heave as though pulling a wishbone.

The boys stared in fascination at the pale inviting valley now revealed between Amber's thighs. From its full fluffy crown at the summit of her mound, her lightly curled pelt divided about her cleft, thinning and spreading as it reached the inward curve of her buttocks about her bottom hole. There it formed a tangled clump about its wellhead before tapering off up between her rear crease. At the centre of this pubic forest her thick outer lips gaped, revealing between them the pink swelling inner labia, glistening with her secretions.

Jackson swallowed and dropped his trousers then tugged down his underpants. A well-developed and very hard erection sprang free over a scrotum that was tightly crinkled up with anticipation. He'll come before he even gets into me, Amber thought. Despite her situation the sight made her tingle inside and she felt her muscles contract about the sheath of her vagina even as her outer lips grew wet in anticipation. As far as her body was concerned, sex was sex.

She unconsciously twitched her thighs slightly. Thinking she was resisting Bicks and Parsons tugged her ankles even wider, stretching her tendons and making her sex gape. Amber felt an unexpected thrill at her helpless vulnerability. Right, she told herself, ride that feeling. Put on a show for them.

Jackson took a deep breath then lunged forward on top of Amber and clasped her shoulders. For a moment he looked into her eyes as though uncertain what to do. He was achingly well-scrubbed and smelled faintly of carbolic soap. Then he lowered his head and drove upwards. His first wild thrusts slid up her fold and rubbed her swelling clit. Then he found her hole and rammed in to the hilt, as though trying to drag his crinkled ball-sac in after his cock. Amber gasped at the suddenness of his penetration and groaned and bucked under him. He only had time to thrust a dozen times before he shivered and gasped. Amber felt hot sperm blossom within her. Then he slumped limply, head lolling across her breasts.

Parsons half pulled Jackson off her, dropped his own trousers and pants and frantically mounted Amber in turn. She grunted a little and lifted her hips to encourage him. He thrust wildly and spasmed even more quickly than Jackson, half of his come splashing over her lower stomach. After a moment he rolled aside and Bicks took his place, thrusting more easily into her now well-lubricated passage. He clutched at her breasts to pull himself deeper into her, working them as though he was trying

31

to draw milk and making her give a muffled yelp. Inside half a minute he had come as well and sagged limply over her.

Amber groaned with frustration. Her act had worked better than she planned and she'd genuinely begun to get turned on. If only the boys had taken a little longer she could have climaxed herself.

Bicks stirred and pulled out of Amber's hot, sperm-filled passage. He rolled off her, appearing suddenly embarrassed to be in close contact after such intimacy. His face was flushed and he glanced sheepishly at his companions, who looked as though they could not quite believe what they had done. For a moment there was silence in the fern hollow except for the boys' unsteady breathing.

They were too overcome to realise none of them were holding Amber down anymore.

Amber doubled herself up, rolled over backwards, came to her feet and hopped and slithered down the fern and ivy covered slope. From behind her came angry cries as the boys discovered it was impossible to run with trousers tangled around their ankles. She reached the path and headed in the direction the girls had come from, making good speed even with her arms bound. Her exertions caused the boys' sperm to begin oozing out of her: trickling over the inside of her thighs and slicking down her fine pubic hair.

She rounded a corner and for a moment was hidden from her pursuers. Quickly she darted sideways off the path and up into a thicket. Ignoring the scratches she rolled into a ball in the leaf litter and lay still, breathing heavily round her gag.

Ten seconds later the boys pounded past. She waited until their footsteps had faded, struggled out of her hiding place, slithered down to the path again and headed back the way she they come. This was the direction she had last seen the two girls take. She hoped they hadn't gone far. If she could catch up with them her current state should guarantee sympathetic treatment.

Then the path forked with no indication which way she should go, nor sign of anybody who might lend her some assistance. You'd think a bound and gagged half-naked woman would have had no trouble in drawing an audience, Amber thought ironically. She chose the right-hand fork. It wound between earth banks and was overhung by branches heavy with new leaf. After a couple of hundred yards it dipped and opened onto a deserted country lane, flanked on one side by a ditch and the green wall of the wood, and on the other by a tall hedgerow. A signpost indicated 'Shaftwell' lay half a mile to the right, while 'Lower Boxley' was four and a half miles to the left. Amber backtracked a few yards and scrabbled up the earth bank into a clump of tall grass, where she could keep both path and lane in view without being seen herself.

She curled up into a ball to drag her bound hands under her bottom and out in front of her, so she could pull out her gag and then use her teeth on the knots. But her wrists were so thickly tied that she just couldn't manage it. After much struggling and muffled curses she sat upright again and looked about for a sharp stone or a broken bottle to cut the ropes. But before she could find anything she heard the boysí voices and feet pounding down the path. Time to move on, she thought. She rose silently and stepped forward. A dry branch that had been buried in the long grass cracked loudly under her foot.

"This way!" Parsons called out excitedly.

Just then through the trees, Amber caught sight of a large policeman in an old-fashioned uniform wheeling a bike slowly along the lane towards her. For the first time in years she was glad to see an officer of the law. No doubt her appearance would embarrass a simply country bobby and it wouldn't be any joy for her, but it was preferable to becoming the pet of a bunch of rampant seventeen year olds. She slithered out of the trees down the bank and into the ditch, stinging herself intimately on a clump of fresh nettles in the process, scrambled up onto the lane and ran towards the policeman.

The constable's reaction, however, was not what she had anticipated. An expression of mild surprise crossed his solid red face, followed by an annoyed click of the tongue.

"What's this - a runaway?" he said.

As Amber blinked uncertainly he stepped forward, reached out a large hand and caught her by the ear.

"No collar," he continued slowly, twisting her round so that he could inspect her rear. Resting his bike against his hip he casually lifted her tee shirt that had settled back around her hips during her flight. "No owner's mark. That's unlicensed exposure in a public place, that is. Garments of foreign manufacture. You'll be an undeclared outlander, I'll be bound. I've heard about your sort. No passport I suppose?" He pinched her ear until she shook her head. "That's illegal entry into the country," he added. "No possessions, currency or..." he looked her up and down again and gave a fruity chuckle "...visible means of trade. That's vagrancy to boot. You'd better come along with me, my girl. I'm putting you under arrest."

Amber kicked him on the shin.

It was a reflex action triggered by the sickening realisation that she had just jumped out of the proverbial frying pan into the fire. She regretted it instantly, but by then it was far too late. The constable cursed, hopped on one leg and dropped his bicycle with a crash. But unfortunately he kept his hold on her ear. "And a further charge of assaulting a police officer in the course of his duty," he added, rubbing his leg. He pulled her face close to his, while his other hand closed over her right breast, and pinched her already tender nipple through the fabric of her tee shirt until she whimpered and her eyes watered. "You're going to regret that kick, my girl," he said ominously.

From a small case on his belt he produced a length of half-inch link chain, with a spring catch at one end and a leather loop at the other. Tucking Amber's head under one arm he lifted her tee shirt and looped and fastened the chain tightly about her waist. Standing her straight he drew the free end of the chain down over her navel and into the fleshy furrow of her tender and still dripping pubic mound.

"Who's been having their way with you?" he asked rhetorically, rolling a lock of her sperm-matted hair between thumb and forefinger. "Never mind, you'll tell me everything when we get to the station."

His large rough hand pushed the chain between her legs, up the cleft of her buttocks and through the loop about her waist. Then he pushed her face down onto the ground and knelt, straddling her thighs. With a penknife he cut away her gag, then the rope about her sore wrists, only to replace it with heavy handcuffs. Grasping her hair he pulled her to her feet again and experimentally tugged the chain trailing behind her like a tail. Amber felt it scrape around her bottom and groin, each link pinching and nipping into her flesh. She was suddenly acutely aware of how painful it could become if he tightened the chain any further. At the same time her clitoris, still aroused from her recent triple fucking, started to swell treacherously against the hard metal links that both teased and imprisoned it.

"Now you're going to walk ahead like a good girl showing me your pretty arse all the way," he told her in no uncertain terms. "If you give any trouble I'll give this a pull to remind you you're in official custody..." he jerked the chain again, making it bite deeper into her tender flesh, "...understand?"

Cheeks burning shamefully Amber nodded.

The constable picked up his bike and slid the loop of her leash over the handlebars. Amber obediently took up position in front of him so he could watch the roll of her chain-cleft bottom and they set off along the lane towards Shaftwell.

Platt led Melanie between the high wrought-iron gates and onto the oval acre of gravel that formed the central court of Markham Hall. An imposing columned portico rose the full height of the main building, flanked by many windows. Curving quadrant corridors linked it to two wings, each with its own smaller court-yard screened by high walls pierced by archways of different sizes. Rolling paddocks extended beyond them.

Melanie shivered as the gravel crunched under her feet. How many eyes were watching her from those tall windows right now? Out in the fields her nakedness had seemed less unnatural, but these grand surroundings only emphasized her humiliating situation.

"This is what you belong to now," Platt told her proudly.

He let her stand, trembling, exposed, helpless, for a full minute; as though knowing exactly how the sight was affecting her. Then he led her towards the right hand wing.

Through the archways was the stable court, a broad stone flagged space bordered by the walls of three smaller yards. Opposite was a set of large double gates through which she could see a row of stable doors, while the sound of dogs yapping came from the yard to the right.

A lad ran up as Platt dismounted and took his horse's reins. The boy looked Melanie up and down with frank interest, causing her to turn her head aside with a renewed blush of shame and clench her thighs in a vain attempt to conceal her pubic curls.

Platt's riding crop flicked across the front of her thighs. "Stand straight! Legs apart! Let the boy look at you. Packgirls aren't allowed any modesty here, so you'd better get used to it."

"Ain't she brown, Mister Platt," the lad said as Melanie displayed herself as she had been ordered. "Where's she from?"

"Somewhere far away in the south, Billy."

"She's got good legs. Bet she's fast."

"We'll see, lad; we'll see."

Platt led Melanie towards a green wooden panelled double gate set in the wall which formed the fourth side of the court. Beyond was a covered passageway with a wrought iron gate at the far end. Passing through this she found herself in a brick-cobbled yard overlooked by the windows and doors of its enclosing block. Suspended from a bracket projecting from under the eaves of one of these buildings was a naked woman.

She hung with the backs of her legs facing outwards, concealing her face which was pressed up against her shins. From the front all that was visible were her cuffed hands and bare feet, soles facing upward and outward, and the stretched length of her legs, broken only by a strap about her knees. There was something dangling beneath her...

Platt stepped over to the captive, dragging Melanie after him.

Appalled and yet fascinated, Melanie's eyes trailed down the bunched muscles of the girl's calves, the tight tendons behind her knees, the gentle pear-like swell of her thighs and hips and the fleshy undercurve of her glossy taut buttocks. It was here that the girl's tender exposed groin took on a rosy hue, her pale skin criss-crossed by the scarlet stripes of a cane or whip. Swelling from between her thighs was the blushing furry peach of her pudenda and below, like the dot of an exclamation mark, was the round pucker of her anus. Protruding grotesquely from this orifice was a glistening metal hook on which hung a ticking alarm clock. Its weight had pulled on the shaft of the hook embedded within the girl, distending the ring of rubbery flesh and opening a dark crack above it. Platt checked the clock and gave it a little tug. The girl twitched and gave a gag-muffled moan, her body swaying from the bracket.

"This is Gillian," Platt explained. "She put on a foolish display of tight-arse and disappointed one of the Major's guests. Now she's learning better. Do you want to be hung up like this?" Melanie shook her head vigorously. "Then you'll try hard to please, won't you?" Melanie nodded.

37

Platt led her across the yard and into an office. It was cluttered with a couple of plain wooden chairs, a heavy roll-top desk and chests of drawers and shelves, their dark brown varnish scratched and worn. As they entered a girl of about Melanie's own age was filing papers into one of the drawers. She had short blonde hair and was wearing jodhpurs and a white shirt with rolled sleeves over her neat sturdy figure. A switch topped with a spray of leather thongs hung from a loop on her belt. She turned a bright rosy-cheeked face to them, displaying the same look of frank and open interest in Melanie as the stable lad.

"Oh, is this the outlander you went off in such a rush about, Mister Platt?" she asked.

"That's right, Alison," Platt confirmed with a smile, handing Melanie's leash over. "Go on; assess her properly. It'll be good practice for you."

Alison turned Melanie's head critically from side to side, as though examining a prize animal, causing Melanie's eyes to pass over the walls of the room. What she saw made her start in disbelief.

The walls were lined with rosettes and photographs of the sort normally associated with horse trials and county shows. But instead of horses, dogs or prize livestock, they featured naked girls in bridles and muzzles, some harnessed to carts or ploughs in teams, others poised on all fours.

"Well, she's very exotic and pretty, isn't she," Alison said. She dropped her hand to run it over Melanie's lower stomach, causing her to squirm and drag her incredulous gaze away from the photographs. "Thick fluffy bush and a plump cunny... trim waist, and lovely smooth skin." Alison cupped and squeezed Melanie's breasts. "Good heavy titties... plenty of bounce." She rolled a full dark nipple between her finger and thumb and Melanie groaned in embarrassment as her flesh treacherously responded. "Oh, look: nice big stand-up nipples." Alison examined Melanie's back. "Strong full hindquarters and lovely round bottom cheeks. I see Miss Arabella has already paid her some attention there..."

Melanie did not take in the rest of Alison's assessment of her attributes as a curious detail penetrated her dazed senses. Platt's eyes rested not on her own exposed body, but on the tight seat of Alison's jodhpurs as she bent down to examine Melanie's calves and ankles. In his eyes was an expression of unrequited longing. Then he suddenly looked aside as though with a firm effort.

"That'll do, Alison," Platt said, sitting down hastily at the desk and drawing out forms and record books. "Remove her gag, will you."

Alison pulled the ball from Melanie's mouth, still keeping hold of her chain. Platt had her spell out her full name and give her age. He wrote for a minute, then turned the copies of the form and pen towards her. Alison released Melanie's right arm from its cuff.

"Sign or make your mark," he told her.

Melanie read the neatly printed document framed with crests and flourishes. Strangely it gave her some slight reassurance. It confirmed there was law and order here, if of an outrageous kind.

DECLARATION OF VOLUNTARY SERVITUDE

I Melanie Kingston, aged twenty three (23) years, resident of (no fixed abode)do this day Monday 12th April 1999 freely give my person into the ownership of Major James Havercotte-gore and his rightful heirs, of Markham Hall, Shaftwell, West Wealden, England, as a Class Three (III) servant for the period of One (I) calendar year(s). During this period I accept and submit to whatever lawful duties, functions, restraints or punishments may be imposed upon me, according to the Female Public Servitude (Bondslave) Act of 1769. (And as amended 1782, 1788, 1795, 1811, 1837, 1890, 1936).

She took a deep breath and, with a shaking hand, signed. Platt and Alison witnessed her signature in the spaces provided below. As they did so, Melanie noticed Platt had labelled a foolscap-sized folder and a slim red-bound book with her name and a number 9. On the book was embossed: Record of health and punishments. The documentation completed, Platt led the way through an inner door and along a short corridor to a door bearing the sign: ëExamination and Sick Roomí

The room within had whitewashed walls, fitted with more tethering rings, and a quarry-tiled floor. Dangling from the ceiling were chains supporting crossbars with padded cuffs on the ends. An old fashioned wood and brass tripod-and-bellows camera stood beside a glass-fronted cabinet with cluttered shelves, together with a stand-on weighing machine and a fixed wall scale for measuring height. The back of the room was closed off by floor to ceiling bars, enclosing a couple of utilitarian iron frame beds. In the centre of the room was a heavy table surfaced with white porcelain tiles and fitted with ominous looking straps and polished metal implements.

Alison removed Melanie's collar and cuffs and Platt ordered her to take off her trainers and socks. Melanie obeyed mutely, eyeing the switches dangling from her captorsí belts. Totally naked, she was measured and weighed, Alison entering the details in Melanie's record book as Platt called them out. Not only her bust, waist and hips, but also the circumference of her neck, wrists, upper and forearms, thighs, calves and ankles were measured. A set of numbered thin wooden boards with circular holes of varying sizes cut in them were slid over her breasts until the snuggest fit was found. Her mind raced wildly as she tried to imagine to what purpose they would put such an intimate detail.

From the cabinet Platt took a rubber stamp with a head some three inches square, together with a tin box holding a felt inking pad and a sheet of paper. He adjusted a dial on the back of the printer, inked it and pressed it to the paper, then showed Melanie the result. It was the Markham Hall crest surmounting a bold number 9 framed in chain links.

"This won't wash off," Platt explained, "and it'll be overstamped every month to keep it sharp. If you move while I'm marking you and make a smudge, you'll be joining Gillian out in the yard."

Melanie could see the girl's trussed body through the window. "I'll be very still, Mister Platt," she promised sincerely.

"Face the wall, brace yourself with your hands, legs spread," he commanded.

Melanie obeyed. With a towel, Alison wiped the upper curve of Melanie's right buttock until the skin was dry and clean. Platt re-inked the stamp and pressed it carefully against her, holding it in place for a count of ten, then lifting it cleanly away. Even on her brown flesh it left a clear bold mark.

"Stay in that position while you dry," Platt said.

While she waited Platt set up the camera and old-fashioned flashgun with a large polished reflector. Portrait shots of her face square on and in profile, then full-length shots of her body front, side and back were made.

"Shall we test her responses now, Mister Platt?" Alison asked.

"We'll wait for the Major. Meanwhile let's get her into a harness."

Melanie was led through another door bearing the sign ëHarness Room.í

She smelt metal, leather and polish. The walls were covered with hooks and racks, all neatly labelled, on which were held all manner of rods, straps, buckles and chains; fashioned into every type of harness and restraint imaginable for the female body. In the middle of this Aladdin's cave of bondage Melanie was ordered to kneel, spread her knees wide and clasp her hands behind her neck.

On a bench were a hammer, anvil and a set of chisel-like letter punches. Platt used them to stamp her name onto a small ringed metal disk. Then he took a thick glossy black collar from a rack and clipped the disc to it like a dog's nametag. He held the collar before Melanie so she could read what was inscribed on the metal strip riveted to its side.

'GIRL 9: PROPERTY OF MARKHAM HALL HUNT PACK'

"Nine's been free since Linda left. This will be your number from now on. You'll answer to it just as though it was your name, understand?" Melanie nodded meekly. "Head back, neck straight".

The collar itself was four inches broad with rounded padded edges and hung front and back with large fastening rings. It closed about her snugly with a very secure sounding click, its constraining pressure forcing her neck straight and lifting her chin up.

"Sit on the edge of the table," Platt ordered.

From a shelf Alison took down a pair of black ankle boots with enormous wedge-soles at least six inches high at the heels. Slender shin pads topped with rounded knee protectors hung from their insteps, while metal rings dangled from the backs of the ankles. As they were slipped onto her feet and buckled into place, Melanie discovered they were surprisingly light; the wedge soles apparently made of cork and only surfaced with rubber. The most solid parts were their stout toecaps, evidently designed for heavy wear.

"Hold your arms out straight, fingers together," Platt commanded.

They fitted her with black fingerless and thumbless mittens, buckling them about her wrists. As she tried to flex her fingers she found the mittensí thick padding made any dextrous activity impossible. More rings dangled from the inside of the wrists.

"Get down, girl," Platt commanded.

Sliding awkwardly off the table Melanie found the wedge heels on her new boots made it impossible to walk upright, forcing her to drop onto all fours. Suddenly she understood the function of the gloves, shin pads and the broad collar that braced her neck. This was how she would move about from now on.

Platt rummaged in a box and then withdrew what looked like a curving, foot long foxhound's tail, made of hair as black as her own. Attached to its root was a cone-shaped rubber plug an inch across. As Melanie watched in growing dismay, Platt opened a small tin and smeared the plug with petroleum jelly.

"Dip your back and spread your legs," Platt ordered.

But the thought of what he was going to do so appalled Melanie that her nerve failed her. "No... Please don't..."

"Brace her Alison" Platt ordered crisply.

Alison straddled Melanie's head and trapped it between her warm sturdy thighs, forcing her to remain on all fours with her bottom facing Platt.

"She's very new, Mister Platt," Alison said.

"That's no excuse, Alison," Platt replied, as he unclipped his switch from his belt and positioned himself. "She's been warned..."

There was a swish of air and Melanie yelped as a streak of fire seemed to sear across her buttocks. "Be firm with bitches from the very start and they'll respond quicker..." Another swish and smack of flesh, bringing forth a fresh gasp of pain from Melanie. "They respect it and it's kinder on them in the end..." Swish, smack. Melanie's buttocks trembled and clenched against the blows. "A few light flicks now may save them a harder session later..." Smack. Melanie's hindquarters bobbed and heaved but could not evade the remorseless switch. "You'll have to learn that if you want to be a head keeper one day."

"Yes, Mister Platt," Alison said dutifully.

With two final cutting blows across Melanie's now well-chastised bottom, Platt rested his arm and examined the marks he had made on her smooth brown flesh, feeling their heat. Satisfied he stood up. Alison released Melanie's head and stepped back.

Her bottom burning, Melanie swayed on all fours, blinking back hot tears of pain, mingled with those of shame and anger. Platt was right; she had been warned. She was a slave, the switch had driven home that fact very effectively. Now she must act like one.

Platt held the artificial tail in front of her face.

"Markham Hall packgirls all wear one of these," he said. "Now beg to have it fitted."

And Melanie found herself saying: "I'm sorry, Mister Platt.

43

I'll never do that again. I'll...I'll wear it proudly." She gulped. "Please put it into me." And on a sudden impulse she kissed the tip of the rubber plug at the tail's base.

Platt smiled approvingly. "That's better."

Melanie felt dizzy, yet paradoxically elated. She had surrendered to the inevitable and it had given her a strange thrill of relief, as though a great weight had been taken from her shoulders.

Platt examined the dusky pucker of her anus for a moment before sliding the plug into her, easily overcoming the final instinctive clenching of her sphincter. Melanie gave the softest of gasps as the plug bedded itself in her rectum. She felt the tail curving jauntily upright and clear of her buttocks, almost as though it was growing from the base of her spine.

"Now she's a proper Markham Hall bitch," Platt said with satisfaction. "Tether her in the yard so she can look at Gillian until the Major comes. It might remind her not to be so foolish in future."

Alison led Melanie away on a leash. Her new tail bobbed with the shuffling roll of her hips, the movement of its mounting plug teasing and stimulating her tender flesh, its continual penetration a reminder of what she had become.

5: In Custody

Shaftwell could have won first prize in any best-kept village competition.

It had a tree-ringed green with the traditional pond, hand pump and horse trough. On one side was a half-timbered pub and a row of small bow-windowed shops, while on the other were cottages with ivy-covered walls and tiny neat front gardens. Along the half dozen roads that radiated out from the green could be glimpsed a few grander houses of three storeys, with high roofs and heavy gables. There were no television aerials or satellite dishes to be seen.

Bailey marched Amber across one end of the green and down a side road, in sight of a handful of villagers, mostly women. The cut and length of their skirts was reminiscent of thirties fashions. Some carried wicker shopping baskets. An old man, wearing a smock and gaiters, called out: "Hallo Harry," to Bailey as they passed him. Amber, cuffed and chained and half naked, received some curious and quite unabashed stares from men and women alike but nothing more.

Then the illusion of dated normality was spectacularly broken.

A rattle of wheels announced the approach of a chaise, driven by a grey-haired man wearing pince-nez and sombre clerical garb. He waved cheerily to Bailey and drew the small cart up beside them.

But it was his transport that held Amber's astonished gaze. In addition to the two normal wheels it had a third smaller wheel for steering. This wheel was controlled by way of cogs and chains from a yoke mounted on a column rising from the footboard, and was set on the end of a single shaft that ran forward from the driver's seat. Secured on either side of this shaft, and providing the chaise's motive power, were two naked young women.

They were bent forward so their upper bodies were parallel with the ground. Broad padded leather collars encircled their hips and shoulders and were attached to the main shaft by short crossbeams. The hip collars had cuffs on their sides to hold the girls' wrists secure, while projecting forward from the shoulder collars were padded oval hoops in which the girls' heads rested face down. Their breasts hung pendulously in loose strap halters, bobbing as they moved. They wore high-laced sandals with thick wedge-shaped soles, apparently designed to give maximum traction for the angle their legs were constrained to move at by keeping their ankles straight.

The cleric pulled a lever on the side of the steering yoke, drawing in lines that ran through eyelets down the steering shaft and out to the padded collars. The halters tightened about imprisoned breasts, flesh bulging around the studded strapping. The human ponies obediently slowed to a halt, coming to a rest with their strong and shapely legs stretched out behind them at forty-five degrees, ankles neatly together.

"Ah, good morning, Bailey," said the cleric, eyeing Amber with mild interest. "What have you got here?"

"Morning Vicar," the constable replied, touching the brim of his helmet respectfully. "Some runaway outlander, I'm thinking. Er... I'm afraid she's unlicensed."

"Dear me," he said, looking away from Amber as though suddenly offended by her exposure. Her tee shirt barely covered her pubic bush, and the chain running from the small of her back lifted it clear of her bottom. "Well, you must get her inside as soon as possible then. I hope I shall see you at Evensong."

"Duty permitting Vicar," Bailey assured him.

The vicar tugged a second lever on the steering bar. Short spring-loaded canes mounted on the shaft drew back and then flicked across the smooth muscular roundness of the two naked bottoms before him. Legs bent and the cart started off again. Amber's eyes followed the rhythmic rolling of the girlsí buttocks about the dividing straps that secured them to their hip collars until they were out of sight.

Bailey flipped the chain that passed between Amber's legs so that it flicked across her own bottom and she quickly walked

46

on again, her mind a whirl. Naked girls pulling a vicar's carriage! Yet why had the vicar suddenly taken affront when he learned she was 'unlicensed'? This has to be a crazy dream, she thought. But the bite of the chain against her tender cunt flesh told her otherwise.

The police house was a small detached cottage with a more modern extension added to one side, over the door of which hung a traditional blue lamp. Adjoining this was a yard with high spike-topped walls and a solid wooden black double gate with a notice board mounted beside it. Bailey rested his bike against the door under the lamp, hung his cycle clips over the crossbar, and led Amber into a tiny lobby with a shelf and sliding frosted glass hatch in the wall. A second door gave access to the station room itself, taken up with a desk, a couple of chairs, filing cabinet and a large cupboard.

Bailey hung his helmet on a hatstand, holding Amber's chain tightly so she had to stand on tiptoe. Taking her chin in his hand he tilted her head back and looked her searchingly in the eyes.

"Outlander or not, I know your sort," he said. "Smart as new paint and a sight too wilful for your own good. Well you're already in enough trouble as it is my girl, so don't you give me any backtalk or strange foreign tricks while you're in my charge, understand? Remember," he added darkly, "I still owe you for that kick."

Through dry lips, Amber said faintly: "Yes Constable Bailey."

"Good," he said, unlocking her cuffs, "now get that top and those queer-looking shoes off. Can't have female prisoners improperly dressed inside the station."

Amber obediently removed her tee shirt and trainers and Bailey re-cuffed her hands behind her back. He then passed the end of her chain back between her legs and led her over to the desk, pulling the chain across it until the tops of Amber's thighs were pressed hard against the front. He looped the chain end back and forth about two drawer handles on his side until it was secured.

This left Amber's matted, damp, chain-cleft delta resting just above the desktop. Its edge, she now realised, was scored by numerous grooves in the same place her chain rested. How many other girls had been secured here before her? Unhurriedly Bailey seated himself in the worn leather swivel chair, drew out a sheaf of papers from another drawer, flipped open the top of the inkwell in the old fashioned desk set, took a stained dip-pen from its holder and started to fill in Amber's arrest form.

"Name?"

"Amber Jones."

"Date of birth?"

"Tenth September, 1973."

"Place of birth?"

"Epsom, but I don't think it's anyplace round here - ow!"

Bailey had picked up a long ledger ruler from the desk's pen tray, and with a casual backhand stroke smacked the flat of it across Amber's softly rounded lower stomach. "I didn't ask for your opinion, girl! I know you're from somewhere far away. I've heard tales of the place outlanders live. Great towers with thousands of people living in them, roads everywhere filled with horseless carriages with engines that foul the air. If they're true you should be thankful you've arrived somewhere decent. And now you're here, I've got to write a report for headquarters. Maybe they'll want you sent up to London for examination by those scientific types. But unless they do, keep your past to yourself, or else less educated folk might think you were a bit touched in the head, understand?" Amber nodded dumbly. He dipped his pen again. "Now, how did you come to be in the state I found you?"

Before she could answer the outer door opened and somebody came into the lobby and rang the bell. Bailey slid the frosted glass panel open to reveal an attractive thirtyish dark-haired woman, wearing a cape over a navy blue uniform.

"'Morning Sister Newcombe," said Bailey. "And what can I do for you?"

"Good morning Constable," she said briskly. "It may be nothing of course, but I just thought you ought to know. I was cycling down the long path through the woods near the Hall about half an hour ago when I heard some shouting, as though an argument was taking place. Sounded rather strident. Two or three men, I think. Then I caught a glimpse of somebody running through the trees, but I lost sight of them before I could follow on."

"Thank you, Sister," Bailey said. "That's most interesting. It may have something to do with this piece of baggage I've just come across."

He jerked a thumb over his shoulder at Amber, still tethered to the desk. Sister Newcombe regarded her with the same unabashed interest the rest of the populace had so far shown.

"I see. A runaway is she?"

Bailey lowered his voice slightly. "An outsider, I think Sister."

"Really. Well she seems to have a picked up plenty of dirt and scratches along the way. A couple look quite deep. They should be cleaned immediately. Would you like me to see to them?"

"If you can spare the time, Sister, thank you. Save me getting the doctor round to check her."

Sister Newcombe bustled in through the door, hung up her cloak and took a small, tin first aid box from a shelf. Her broad uniform belt with its wide scrolled buckle encircled a very neat waistline, Amber noticed. Behind small round steel-rimmed spectacles her eyes were a smoky grey-blue, set in a neat strong angular face. She drew up a spare chair and seated herself behind Amber.

"Don't mind me, you carry on," she said.

Bailey resumed his own chair and nodded at Amber.

While they had been talking Amber had been thinking about how much she should reveal. Nothing about her encounter with constable Kingston, of course, but as Bailey seemed to know something of 'outsiders' her story couldn't be an outright lie. However it might be useful to keep some details to herself for the moment. Besides, the truth was rather embarrassing.

"I was walking in some woods, where I come from, when I found a strange box," she explained. "It looked oriental in design. After some fiddling with it I got it open. Inside were what looked like three small statuettes. I handled one of them and felt dizzy. I think I may have passed out. When I woke up I was in a different sort of wood. I wandered around for a while trying to get my bearings. Then three men jumped me. I was tied up and carried off into the bushes... where they took turns raping me."

There was no reaction from Sister Newcombe and Bailey simply murmured as he wrote: '...multiple intercourse occurred...' Then he asked: "Can you describe the men?"

Even though the experience hadn't turned out to be that unpleasant, Amber felt she ought to protest on principle.

"Didn't you hear what I said - oww!"

Bailey had flicked the ruler across her stomach again. "I warned you before about speaking out of turn. Now can you describe them?"

Amber recovered herself. "Uhh... dark trousers and tops, handkerchief masks over their faces."

"Did they say anything - names or the like?"

"Nothing I remember. I wasn't exactly taking notes."

"I see. Then what?

"When they'd finished I managed to get away. I ran through the woods until I reached the lane."

"They let you go easy, did they?"

"First they were busy pulling their trousers up, then I hid while I was out of their sight and doubled back."
She heard a light chuckle from Sister Newcombe and even Bailey smiled.

"Said you were smart, didn't I? Still, it's a pity you can't identify them. They should be fined for what they did."

"Fined!" Amber flinched back as he reached for the ruler, jerking the chain painfully a little deeper into her tender flesh. Bailey chuckled.

"Not for having their way with you, girl, but for not reporting you like they should. I dare say that's why they wore masks.

They must have known what you were from your odd clothes. Probably intended to sell you on illegally afterwards." He saw her incredulous expression. "Forget any odd foreign ideas about what's due to you. Right now you haven't any say in how you get used until somebody takes you in, or you can earn your keep. We don't have any time for vagrants here, wherever they're from."

"But I'm no vagrant. I came here by accident."

"Did somebody make you open that..." he consulted his notes: i'oriental' box?"

"Well... no."

"Then it was your own fault for tampering with something that didn't belong to you. Everyone knows queer things come out of the East. Anyway, you've broken the law here and now you've got to face the consequences."

"But I didn't know I was breaking - oww!" the ruler had smacked across her stomach again.

"Hold still girl," Sister Newcombe admonished.

"Ignorance of the law is no excuse," Bailey said. "We treat people properly once they've earned respect, but if they break the law they get punished. Are you done, Sister?"

"Yes, unless she has any other injuries."

Bailey loosed the chain from the desk, allowing Amber to step back. Sister Newcombe examined her front with quick professional competence, handling Amber with an easy familiarity and even slipping a finger casually into her still moist and sperm-rimmed slit.

"They certainly made good use of her," she commented. "Will you be looking for them, Mr. Bailey?"

"I'll keep my ears open, but there's not much to go on. Unless you can give a better description."

"Sorry, I only caught a glimpse. Assuming it was the same men." She looked Amber up and down again. "Hmm. I was wondering if I should invest in a bondservant. Will she go for auction?"

Amber shivered at the word but they took no notice, continuing as though her opinion didn't count - which of course it

51

didn't. The feeling of being carried along helplessly into the unknown closed over her; frightening and yet darkly exciting at the same time.

"I should think so, after her time in the yard," Bailey said. "But she'll need a firm hand."

"Oh I'm sure I could provide that," Sister Newcombe replied, with a cool smile.

For a moment her eyes met Amber's, and she saw steel in their depths. Yes, Amber thought, I'm sure you could.

"Well I'll be off, then," Sister Newcombe said. "I have my own charges to look after. Good day, Constable. Do let me know if you manage to track down those fellows in the wood."

And she gathered her things and swept briskly out.

Bailey put Amber's tee shirt and trainers on a shelf in the large cupboard, and brought out some new items in turn.

The first was a broad heavy leather collar with a lockable buckle, which he fastened round her neck. Then he produced a thin cotton shift and put it on her. Essentially it was just two rectangles of material tied together at the shoulders and waist, allowing it to be removed around any bonds the prisoner was wearing. It fell to her mid thigh and was patterned with bold black and white chevrons.

"That tells everyone you're in custody awaiting trial," he told Amber.

"I'm sure it's the height of fashion," she said lightly, though her stomach was churning. "Don't I get anything else?"

He grinned. "This is just to keep you decent for court tomorrow morning. I'll have it off you the moment you're sentenced. Now, be still while I take your picture for the records."

This he did with an old bellows camera, taking full face and profile shots. Then he fastened a chain to her collar and led her through the room's second door. This opened onto a narrow passage fronting a row of three small iron-barred cells, in the nearest of which a simple tubular frame bed was visible. Beside them was an outer door which Bailey opened.

"Have a look at what's in store for you," he said, dragging

52

Amber after him into the walled yard.

It was brick floored, about forty feet long by thirty wide, and overlooked only by a few trees and the police house itself. Along the back wall stood several wooden constructions, one of which looked like a treadmill. A low railing was set a little in from the street gate; crossing the yard and running part the way down on either side. By the gate an old man sat dozing in a chair with several boxes by his feet. In the middle of the yard facing the gate was a low wooden platform with small wheels at each corner. Fixed to the middle of this was a vertical board as wide as the platform and seven feet high, mottled all over with fading multicoloured stains.

Projecting from the board was a disembodied pair of pink naked female buttocks supported by slender widespread legs. Grinning, Bailey led Amber over to the device.

The vertical board was made in two sections, the upper sliding in grooves in its supporting posts. The girl's waist fitted through a hole about ten inches across cut out of the boards where they butted together. The toes of her feet slipped through small holes cut in the base of the upright and were held there with ankle straps. This left her bent forward with her legs spread wide and her slim, almost skinny hips, thrust provocatively backwards, exposing her lightly haired sex and the pucker of her anus at the base of her bottom cleft. Bailey reached out and slapped one of the rounded buttocks, which Amber noted were striped with fading cane marks, bringing forth a muffled squeal from the other side of the board.

"This is Sally Potts," Bailey explained, "a tarty little piece you might almost call one of our regulars."

He moved round to the front of the board, dragging Amber after him. For the first time Amber saw the upper half of Sally's body - and gasped in surprise.

Sally's arms were drawn up and behind her, secured with cuffs and short chains to eye bolts set in the upper corners of the top board. A longer chain hung from a bolt in the top centre of the board connected to a heavy coiled spring, which in turn was fastened to the curve of a 'D' shaped piece of moulded rubber some six inches from front to back. The bar of the "D" was clamped between Sally's teeth while the curving section enclosed her head so the spring fastening rested at the back of her neck. The tension on her arms and head had the effect of thrusting forward her naked breasts, which hung bulbously from her slim chest. Suspended in front of them by a chain attached to a broad collar that encircled Sally's neck, was a curious ornament the size of a cricket ball, covered in stubby spikes.

But what made Sally's appearance so startling was that her entire upper body, and the board behind her, were covered in numerous wide splashes of what looked like thick multicoloured paint. Even her hair was matted with it, so that it was impossible to tell its natural colour. Only her eyes were clear, staring defiantly at them over her gag.

Bailey smiled at Sally's helplessly displayed body in satisfaction. "When her face and tits have had enough I'll swing her arse round," he said half to himself, reaching up to one of Sally's dangling breasts and tweaking a blue-soaked nipple, causing her to glare at him and tug at her bonds in a futile attempt to pull away. "The little minx has still got a few days left to serve, so you'll be able to keep her company from tomorrow. Have a look at this."

The old man in the chair woke up as they approached the gate. "Afternoon, Harry." He blinked at Amber through rheumy eyes. "New girl, eh?"

"That's right Tom. Just showing her what's to come."

The boxes by the chair were filled with multicoloured rows of translucent waxed paper packets about the size of small apples. Bailey picked one out and showed it to Amber. "Regulation pillory shot: clay and coloured water. Bursts easily and gives you a nice firm smack. People like dirtying a bad girl up and watching her squirm." He slapped her rump meaningfully. "Penny a shot. Goes towards your keep like your auction money, or for any compensation due, or else to the public purse. But before that there'll be the lashing for assault on a police officer, which folk always enjoy." He drew on her leash, pulling her close. "I'll be taking care of that personally," he assured her ominously. "Then, while you're waiting to be auctioned, you can try out some other punishments," and he nodded at the assorted contraptions at the rear of the yard.

Amber swallowed heavily. Punishment was the word all right. She imagined the shot hitting the spiked ball hanging from Sally's neck and how it would feel as it was driven into her tender breasts.

Perhaps she should have stayed with the boys in the wood. Being their pet could hardly be worse than the fate the law had in store for her.

6: A Call of Nature

The silent invisible lure of the Girlspell radiated through Hoakam Woods unheeded all morning. A bird watcher passed within feet of the bush that concealed the puzzle box and sensed nothing. A local woman artist out with her sketchbook paused as she felt a sudden unexpected warmth within her, but the sensation rapidly faded, merely leaving her smiling curiously. She had a family waiting for her and that bond could not be challenged. A young couple walked by unaware, with eyes only for each other. The spell called only to a special few.

Finally Susan Drake came into its range.

Sue's broad hips and full rounded buttocks rolled rhythmically under slick thigh-length shorts as she pedalled her bike determinedly on. A mane of shaggy blonde hair, tied back into a loose ponytail, flowed out from under her cycling helmet. Sparkling deep blue eyes shone out of a heart-shaped face, the creamy skin of which was lightly flushed about the cheeks with her exertions. Her full breasts bobbed freely under her loose vest as her bike, laden with bulging panniers, bumped its way along the track. She looked the sort of girl who should have been stretched out on some Mediterranean beach, instead of dodging spring showers while cycling across the south of England.

A few weeks before her plans had indeed included a more exotic holiday destination. But then had come the final showdown with Dave. The break-up of that relationship had cost her both emotionally and financially. She needed to get away for a while but she could no longer afford a foreign holiday. Then a friend had suggested camping and had loaned her the bike and equipment.

After the first few days of minor upsets and a few intimate chafes and aches, she began to enjoy the experience. The break gave her an unexpected sense of self-reliance, apart from being healthy exercise. Privately Sue knew she was not very strong willed, and tended to be easily led by others. That was how Dave had first taken her in. But she was determined not to let memories of him spoil her little adventure as he had everything else. She still had a week to go and wanted to make the most of it.

The footpath forked ahead of her and she braked to a stop, resting with one foot on the ground while she pulled a map from her saddle pack to see which turning she should take. Crossing through Hoakam woods was saving five miles on the way to her next planned stop and was also a more pleasant route than the busy main roads.

It was only as she put the map away that she felt the air had suddenly grown warmer. She became acutely aware that the horizontal top tube of the bike's frame was pressing intimately up between her thighs and into the sweaty crotch of her shorts. The growing tingle this generated reminded her, reluctantly, of what Dave had been like in bed. It was his one genuine talent and her weakness. She became conscious of her thin cotton panties riding up into her crease, and of her nipples rubbing against her top and beginning to stand up. She felt her cheeks flush hotly as they always did when she was excited. Unconsciously she grasped the handlebars and worked her hips backwards and forwards, rubbing her crotch along the frame and feeling the hidden fleshy lips of her pubis divide.

Disturbing memories rose in her mind of a night over a year ago...

Up until then their sexual moods had matched well, but that night she was genuinely tired and only wanted to sleep. Dave, however, was pestering her to make love, sliding his hand up her cami top and under the waistband of her briefs. She kept pushing him away, and finally rolled over onto her side of the bed with her back to him.

He reached over, caught her wrist and pulled her roughly onto her back and straddled her waist so she could not turn away. She looked up into his hungry eyes.

"I said I'm too tired."

"You've never been too tired before," he complained.

"Well I am now - get off!"

She tried to pull away from him and prise her wrist from his grasp, but he was far too strong. He began to smile at her futile struggles.

"If that's how you want it!" he said with a grin.

He caught both her wrists in one hand and, still holding her down, reached out to her dressing table, not much of a stretch in the cramped bedroom of her small flat, and began pulling open drawers.

"Dave - what are you... mmmfff!"

He had found her underwear and had pushed a balled pair of panties into her mouth. She kicked and twisted, but her legs were trapped underneath the sheets. He lay across her and used a pair of tights to bind her wrists to the corners of the tubular brass bed head. Throwing back the covers he secured her ankles by the same means, leaving her struggling, spread-eagled and helpless.

Hard with desire, he knelt over her again reaching out for her cami top, when a glint of metal in one of the drawers he'd pulled open caught his eye. He picked up a small pair of scissors and held them so Sue could see, snipping them in the air. Sue's eyes bulged and she gave a muffled squeak of dismay, shaking her head rapidly.

Ignoring her alarm Dave slid the blades around the hem of her cami. Sue went rigid at the touch of cold metal to her skin.

Snip, snip, snip, the fabric parted from her navel up to her throat. Dave pulled the remains aside and bared her pale breasts shivering like jellies, her nipples standing up dark and hard with fear. He brushed them over with the scissor blades and watched them pop up again.

"These look awake enough," he said. "How about the rest of you?"

Two cuts released her panties and he tossed them aside.

He ran the handles of the scissors up and down Sue's deep fleshy furrow with its crinkled inner tongue, eliciting more squeals from behind her gag. He picked at her mat of dark blonde curls.

"Can't see the rabbit hole for the grass. I think you need a trip to the barbers."

He drew out a lock of hair until the skin stretched and then cut it off. Then tugged at another and another.

By the time he was done Sue's eyes were brimming with tears and there was a small pile of fluffy hair on the sheet between her thighs. Her plump cunt lips were now completely exposed and reddened. He reversed the scissors and rubbed the handle up and down, pressing deeper into her cleft, teasing her clitoris terribly and forcing it into painful erection. Her secretions glistened on the shiny metal.

"Getting a little wet in there," he said.

Suddenly he pushed the handle end up into her, stretching her passage like some medical instrument so that only the tip of the blades protruded from between her soft love lips.

"Now, would you rather have that inside you or me?" he asked.

"You, you!" Sue tried to shout through her gag.

He pulled out the scissors, lay between her gaping thighs and rammed his hard cock up into her, using her with careless vigour, his thrusts causing her breasts to jerk and roll. Despite herself, she climaxed with him, an intense explosion of pleasure that did a little to compensate for what she had suffered.

He lay still for a minute then rolled off her bound body with-

58

out a word, leaving her sticky and glistening with sweat, and went through to the bathroom to clean himself. When he returned his face was still dark, his mouth an angry line. He sat down on the bed and caught hold of her chin so that she had to look at him.

"No more nonsense about feeling too tired, all right?"

Sue shook her head wearily, feeling miserable and confused. No apology or even a word of praise. Why did he still seem to resent her for giving him pleasure? If he now felt guilty why didn't he say so? She could learn to please him that way if he wanted, it was his mean selfishness that really hurt.

They said no more about it. She hoped it was a one off. It hadn't been...

Sue came to herself with a start, looking around guiltily in case somebody was watching. Fortunately the woods seemed quite deserted.

Breathing heavily, she unbuckled her helmet and hung it over the handlebars, then shook out her hair. She took a drink from her flask and then dabbed some onto her cheeks. But the trickling water only triggered a sudden urgent need to pee, the sensation confusing itself with her arousal. She squeezed her thighs together and looked about for a suitable spot. For some reason she knew just any old bush wouldn't do.

She dismounted and wheeled the bike along, her need growing with every step until she was tottering along bent half over, her free hand clutched between her legs, in grave danger of wetting herself and coming at the same time. Why was she torturing herself like this?

Then she saw a rhododendron thicket and knew it was what she was looking for.

She dropped the bike beside it and frantically pushed her way inside, tugging down her shorts as she went. She got them off with a struggle but before she could drop her panties her control failed. With a helpless thrill she felt the golden stream squirt messily through their thin fabric and pool between her feet. A warm dampness flowed up between her legs, soaking

59

her pubic bush, even as the pressure within her diminished.

But her arousal was not relieved by the emptying of her bladder and only grew stronger. She fingered herself through her wet panties, feeling the mounting pressure of desire. With a groan she tugged them down her legs and tossed them aside.

Her delta of pubic hair was matted with sweat and urine, the pink plump outer vaginal lips reddened with her arousal and days in the saddle. She dropped to her knees, rubbing her fingers frantically into her wet cleft, feeling as though the swollen bud of her clitoris was ready to burst. But it did no good. She wanted desperately to come but something was stopping her.

Then she saw the puzzle box peeping out from under the leaves a few feet away. As though in a dream she reached out and pulled it towards her. She didn't think to wonder how such a thing had got there, all she knew was that the single remaining phallus cried out to be used.

Suddenly a flock of birds took off from a nearby tree. Had something disturbed them? It brought her briefly back to the reality of her position, reminding her that somebody might come along the path at any moment. Forgetting her discarded panties, she pulled her shorts back on and picked up the puzzle box almost reverently. Gathering up her bike she set off uphill away from the path into the trees. In a minute she came upon a massive oak. This would do.

Leaning the bike against it she squatted down in the hollow between the spreading roots on its up-slope side and rested her back against its gnarled trunk. Not thinking how strange it all was, Sue pulled her shorts down around her ankles, feverishly assembled the last phallus, and drove it deep inside her.

The pleasure was indescribable. The phallus belonged within her, as though it had been made for her and she for it. It was both better and worse at the same time than the scissors had been. She rammed it into her soft interior again and again, until she tilted her head back and gave a cry of sheer delight that echoed through the woods.

There was a snap within her and a moment of dizziness.

Then the oak tree was gone.

She fell backwards, tumbling down a steeper slope than the one she had climbed. Her bike, suddenly without support, had also toppled over and was now slithering noisily down beside her.

Her arms flailed about trying to break her fall, even as the phallus remained within her; locked in place by muscles still spasming with pleasure. One roll rammed it in painfully deeper, driving the figurine on the handle halfway into her. On the next tumble she hit her head sickeningly hard on something solid and unyielding and knew no more.

7: Examination

Melanie stared up at Gillian's exposed genitalia in helpless fascination. She literally could not turn her head aside. It was Platt's idea of a lesson to reinforce her recent switching.

A round ball gag filled Melanie's mouth. From it two feet of taut fine chain ran up at a sharp angle to a small toothed spring clip which was clamped about Gillian's delicate inner vaginal lips. If Melanie moved her head she would pull on probably the most tender part of the poor girl's anatomy, which was the last thing she wanted. She could not even move forward to relieve the tension on the chain linking them. A second identical clip was fastened almost painfully tightly to her own petal-like inner lips. From it another length of chain extended backwards to a ten pound iron weight placed behind her feet. Her paw-like gloves made it impossible for her to unfasten either clip. All she could do was hold herself rigidly upright on her hands and knees and wait to be released. It was an acute reminder of her new state of helplessness.

At first she had tried closing her eyes to shut out the image of the bound and helpless girl, but an almost perverse curiosity got the better of her. She could not help staring at Gillian's suspended body - especially those areas normally kept concealed.

61

She had never looked at another woman's private parts so closely or for so long, and yet strangely she had not seen Gillian's face. The girl was simply a pair of shapely dangling legs, marked by the livid slashes of her recent whipping. Melanie was close enough to count the marks individually. At least two cuts, she noticed, had crossed Gillian's pubic mound with enough force to leave finer but sharper crimson weals on the tender flesh. Her inner lips of pink crinkled coral to which she was so intimately bound, pushed gaping and swollen from their confining pouch, as though offering themselves up for more punishment. Melanie could see a sheen of moisture on their inner surfaces. Could the girl be getting aroused?

What did it feel like, Melanie wondered? She herself had suffered two switchings but Gillian had obviously undergone something much more severe, followed by this prolonged exposure; unable to touch the parts of her that had been abused, yet knowing they were on show to all who cared to look.

After what seemed an age, Melanie heard the clatter of several pairs of boots enter the yard and pass through into Platt's office. A minute later Alison came out to her. The fine chains were released and she was led, on hands and knees, back into the Examination Room.

The Major, Arabella, Gerard and Thomas were all waiting inside expectantly. The younger men were grinning. The Major's face showed a keen, hearty interest. Arabella fixed her with piercing hungry eyes. With a shiver Melanie saw Platt was setting up the camera tripod at the foot of the central examination table.

The table had a shallow depression running down the middle to a drain hole, where there were brass taps with rubber hoses trailing from them. Chain clips and leather straps hung from the sides of the table, while mounted at the foot end were a pair of raised stirrups such as might be found in a gynaecologist's examination room, except they were also fitted with straps. Between them was a short metal bar carrying a set of clinical looking spring clamps and spatulas on sliding mounts and adjustable arms.

Even as she took this in, Alison pulled the tail from her rear, the plug coming free with a sucking pop. Platt grasped her collar and lifted, and she found herself half-sitting on the cold tiled edge of the table. Before she could slide off Platt lifted her legs up and around while Alison pulled her gloved arms backwards and down. In a second she was lying on her back in the middle of the table.

There were metallic clicks as Alison fastened her paw rings to the corners of the table on either side of her head. Meanwhile Platt was lifting and spreading her booted legs and placing them in the stirrup cups. More clicks and they were similarly fastened. Alison buckled a broad strap across Melanie's ribs, just under her breasts, flashing a brief encouraging smile as she did so as though to say: 'This is perfectly normal and you're doing fine.'

Another strap went across just above her hip bones. Then Platt adjusted the stirrup support arm pivots, bending Melanie's knees still further upward, spreading her legs wider and turning her feet outward until she felt the big tendons of her inner thighs standing out.

Then they were done and Melanie was completely exposed and utterly helpless, laid out for the pleasure of those looking down at her. A hand ran across the silky smooth skin of her inner thigh. Fingers pinched and rolled her nipples, testing their hardness. She tried not to meet their eyes but stared past them at the cracked plaster on the ceiling.

"Yes, her hindquarters are definitely her finest feature," she heard the Major say, picking up where he had left off his observations from earlier that morning. "Full, deep and well cleft."

"I wouldn't disagree with you, sir," said Thomas, "but I think her nether mouth is equally plump and delightful. I'm sure she'll juice well."

"She has really excellent proportions," Gerard said. "Full bodied but agile. A lucky find for you, Major. I can't wait for a chance to try her myself."

"She must be properly broken in," Arabella said firmly.

"Please let me see to it personally, Uncle."

"All in good time, my dear," the Major replied, brushing his fingers over Melanie's thick mat of pubic hair. "She needs a little clipping here, Platt."

Lifting her head against the resistance of her collar so she could look through the 'V' of her widespread thighs, Melanie watched anxiously as Platt trimmed back the growth with a pair of small scissors so that her furrow was completely exposed. When the Major was satisfied, Platt tilted the camera until it focused on her groin; exposing the now naked sooty band of darker flesh between her legs, with all its intimate folds and recesses, to the instrument's cold glass eye. She dropped her head back in resignation as the flash-gun popped and the shutter clicked and a picture was taken of her no-longer private parts.

"Wash her out, please Alison," Platt commanded.

Melanie's eyes widened in alarm and she lifted her head again, even as Alison picked up the end of a soft round headed rubber hose. She ran a few drops of oil from a can over the hose end, then bent forward between Melanie's widespread thighs. She felt her fingers pry apart her reluctant sphincter and slip the nozzle into her, smoothly feeding eighteen inches of hose after it into her rectum. Alison turned one of the brass taps and warm water hissed through the hose. Melanie gasped as it burst like a fountain inside her, swelling her bowels until it forced its way back out around the hose that plugged her, gushing out along the porcelain channel carrying her soil with it to gurgle away down the drain hole.

Only when the water ran perfectly clear was the hose withdrawn, leaving Melanie trembling in her bonds.

From the glass cabinet Alison brought a rubber probe with a rounded head and a ring handle. The probe was eight inches long, and grew in a series of stepped swellings and constrictions from half an inch across at its head to two inches at its flared base. Its length and each increment of its circumference were clearly marked on a scale down its side. Before Melanie's horrified gaze, Alison calmly oiled the probe and handed it to Platt.

Platt examined the faint starburst pattern of crinkles around her damp dusky bottom hole, then nosed the probe forward. Melanie moaned as the first section entered, despite her clenching buttocks and tightened sphincter. Platt slowly drove the probe deeper into her rectum. The second section of the probe opened her a little wider, then her anus closed over the neck of the swelling and slid down the smooth oiled shaft beyond. Another bulge, the stretching increased and she was impaled a little deeper. Her nipples swelled and lifted as though in sympathy. She was bursting! Surely she couldn't take any more! But another section entered her and another until she was corked as tightly as a champagne bottle, with only the flared base and ring handle visible within the ring of taut flesh between her legs.

"She's taken it to the hilt," the Major exclaimed. "Excellent!"

"A good deep bottom hole," Platt confirmed. "A full seven inches penetration and five dilations." Alison dutifully recorded the result in Melanie's record book.

With a series of slight sucking pops the probe was withdrawn from her rear. Melanie sobbed in relief, but they weren't finished with her yet.

Platt pivoted the instrument bar forward between her splayed legs and began adjusting its articulated tools about Melanie's gaping vaginal mouth which, she realised shamefully, had begun to lubricate in response to the stimulation of her rear passage. Her dark plump outer lips were spread by metal fingers and spring-loaded clamps pinched the crinkled edges of her inner lips and pulled them apart to reveal the glistening coral pink interior flesh. Her helplessness seemed to amplify every intimate contact. Never had she been so open, so intimately exposed. Her nipples had risen to bursting point again. More articulated fingers tugged at the elastic rim of her vaginal passage, stretching it wide. They were going to photograph her innermost recesses! With a muffled groan of dismay and disbelief, she felt her clitoris perversely but remorselessly hardening and lifting from its fleshy hood.

Arabella laughed at the unintentional display. "She's a sensual creature," she observed. "Oh, uncle, she could be magnificent if you let me train her."

The camera bulb flashed again and Melanie turned her head aside in shame. How could her body betray her so publicly? Surely it couldn't get any worse?

With a rattle of wheels, Alison rolled a wooden box mounted on its own small trolley up beside the table. On top of the box were heavy toggle switches, indicator lights and a couple of old fashioned black bakelite control knobs. To Melanie's horror she saw several wires trailing from terminals set into its back panel.

Melanie struggled futilely against her bonds as the wires were uncoiled and she saw what was on their ends. Alison caught her trembling left breast, squeezed so that the hard dark nipple rose clear of the curving mound of coffee-tinted flesh, and fastened a small spring loaded crocodile clip to it. Melanie whimpered behind her gag as she felt the tiny teeth bite into her. The operation was repeated with her right nipple, the wires trailing across her chest. Platt was bending between her legs and she felt two sets of tiny metal teeth clamp onto the spread lips of her inner labia. Then it was the turn of her erect exposed clitoris, as a fine collar of wire was slid down over it. Finally a slim metal electrode with a ball tip was inserted into her anus.

Platt turned a key on the side of the machine several times as though winding clockwork.

"Standard level of stimulation, sir?" he asked. The Major nodded.

There came a whir of gears from the box.

Melanie's body jerked as the electricity coursed through her, her gag muffling her cry of pain. But it was not quite the torture she had imagined. The stimulation ran down her body as the pairs of electrodes were triggered in sequence. Electric needles stung her nipples, her pectorals twitched and her breasts shivered. As the flesh of her nether lips burned, the gaping mouth of her vagina tried to close against the clamps that held it stretched wide. Her rectal muscles squeezed the slim probe as the current flowed between it and her pulsing clitoris. The most sensitive parts of her body were being forced into unwilling arousal.

Through misty eyes she saw her audience looking down at her with silent intense interest. At that moment she was the only thing on their minds. She had never had such close attention paid to her. The camera was still pointed at her. Platt had the shutter cable release in one hand while in the other was a large pocket watch. He was timing her response!

She moaned and tugged at the bonds, but the rhythmic stimulation continued relentlessly. Her nipples strained against the bite of the spring clamps. Her vagina was an empty void cruelly unfilled. Her rectal muscles worked against the smooth slender hardness of the electrode corking her rear. Trying to imagine it inside her front passage, she felt her gaping forward hole contracting desperately on thin air. She tried to cry out, biting hard on the ball-gag. Explosive contractions overwhelmed her and a flashbulb popped as she orgasmed, splattering the tiles between her legs with her expelled secretions. Then came the slow descent into blissful release and she went limp, twitching feebly as the current continued to pulse through her.

Dimly she was aware of hands clapping. The Major, Thomas and Gerard were applauding her unwilling performance.

"Bravo!" "Well done!" said the younger men.

"One minute and twenty three seconds," Platt noted, turning off the stimulator. "Allowing that she'd spent herself once already today, that's a quick response time and a good discharge. I think she'll make a fine pack bitch, Major."

"I'm certain of it, Platt," the Major replied. "Field trials this afternoon and I'll give her a ride tonight."

He led the others back out into the yard, leaving Platt and Alison to release Melanie.

Through misty eyes Melanie saw Arabella pause in the doorway and give her spread and bound form one final lingering look of unconcealed lust. There was no doubt Arabella wanted her, and Melanie shuddered at the thought of what her treatment would be like in her hands.

8: First Girl

Ten minutes later, Alison led Melanie, shuffling on her hands and knees, across the yard past Gillian's dangling form.

Melanie was confused after her recent ordeal. The pleasurable afterglow of her orgasm conflicted with the humiliating circumstances under which it had been extracted from her. The bobbing motion of her reinserted tail working the plug to and fro within in the newly sensitised sheath of her rectum made it impossible to forget what she now was.

Alison halted her before a door which had a pair of smaller hinged doors set within the frame of its lower half. They were just large enough to allow somebody on their hands and knees to pass through.

"Unless instructed otherwise, you will always enter or leave your quarters through here," Alison explained, "do you understand?"

"Yes, Miss Alison."

Alison's switch flicked lightly across her haunches. "Silly girl. You call me Miss Chalmers."

"Yes, Miss Chalmers."

"Now go in."

Melanie cautiously nosed aside the halves of the packgirl door. They were double hinged and lightly sprung and swung closed behind her.

Within was a room perhaps forty feet long lit by large barred skylights. It had whitewashed walls and a quarry tile floor partly covered by coconut matting. Filling its longest side from floor to ceiling was what looked like a bank of brick pigeon holes. There were three rows of nine alcoves, each about three foot high by three wide, the upper rows being accessed by short iron-work stairs and narrow landings. Each alcove was closed by an iron barred door hinging upwards. The wall opposite the alcoves was fitted with wooden lockers, hooks and racks from which hung harnesses and towels, airing bedding rolls and blankets.

Alison led Melanie along to an alcove on the ground level which had a brass plaque inscribed with a number '9' over its door. Melanie gulped as she looked into the bare interior, which was barely six feet deep.

"This will be your kennel," Alison explained. "When not in use, your harness and bedding is to be hung on the numbered rack opposite. The locker is for your brush, comb, soap and so on. You will keep it clean and tidy at all times, do you understand?"

"Yes, Miss Chalmers."

Alison led her back past an adjoining room fitted out with copper pipework that fed washbasins, ground level drinking fountains and a double row of open shower stalls.

"You'll learn about the ablutions later," Alison told her. "Until lunch you'll wait in the pound. There are a few girls in there already and the rest will be finishing work soon. Through there." Alison indicated a door opposite the yard door and tapped Melanie's bottom to send her on her way. Melanie shuffled forward and cautiously pushed her way through.

Beyond was a grassed yard planted with several shade trees and surrounded on three sides by high walls. The fourth side was closed off by a wrought iron railing fence, through which could be seen an open paddock. Five pack girls were sprawled lazily on the grass, all attired in collars, boots, gloves and tails as she was.

The slight creak of the door springs caused them to look round. Seeing a new face they scrambled upright and came towards her, moving on all fours with the grace of long practice. Melanie wondered if she would move as well after a year of similar bondage.

None of the girls were black, but otherwise they were of varied colourings, from a pale, freckled redhead to an olive skinned gypsy type with a mass of very dark wavy hair. Like her, each of their wagging tails matching the colour of their hair. What they had in common, apart from their costumes, was that they were all young, fit and attractive. At least pack girls seemed to be well cared for physically. As they advanced Melanie could not help staring at their bobbing, swaying breasts, noting how their posture accentuated their weight and mobility.

They circled slowly round her, looking her over curiously. She felt absurdly as though she had just started at a new school and had gone out into the playground for the first time.

"Brown all over," the first said.

"From somewhere foreign," said the second.

They peered at her dangling name tag.

"'Melanie'. She's the new number nine. Do you speak English, girl?"

"Perfectly well, thank you," said Melanie. At least she could talk to these women on equal terms.

"How did you get here?" a brunette with pale breasts and dark brown nipples said. Her name tag read Gail and the number on her collar was 5.

"What do you mean?"

"Did you ask for it, or did you do something bad?"

"You don't have to tell," another girl said quickly. "Nobody has to say if they don't want to."

Melanie subdued the impulse to explain everything. She hardly believed it herself anyway. She'd better be more sure of her ground before admitting too much. "Is it that important? Looks like we're all equal here."

A couple of the girls chuckled.

"Don't let Una hear you say that," Gail said.

"Who's Una?"

"First Girl in the pack. You'd better be nice to her."

"Is 'first girl' her official title, or just what she calls herself?" Melanie asked.

"It's not written down anywhere. She's first because she's the strongest. The Major and Platt don't mind who it is as long as we behave and give them good sport."

As Melanie digested this information she felt hair brush against her bottom and a nose nuzzle into the cleft of her buttocks. She twisted about, sitting back defensively on her

70

haunches, and glaring at the surprised looking blonde girl who'd been sniffing her so intimately. "Hey - stop that!"

The others laughed again.

"You're really new to this," Gail exclaimed. "Jill's only being friendly. The Major likes to see us sniffing at each othersí bums and cunnys like real bitches. You'll get used to it. What else can we do - shake hands?"

This was obviously an old joke, but it set them all off laughing, and Melanie found herself joining in. Jill and another girl pressed up to each other head to tail and made a great show of rubbing and whining, lifting their legs so they could sniff each other's crotches, which they did with theatrically loud snuffles and sighs of delight. Then they fell apart, rolling on the grass and laughing.

"You'll soon learn to put on a show like that - if you don't want a tickle from Platt's switch," Gail explained seriously. Then she smiled. "We've never had a brown girl here. Do you smell different from us?"

Melanie looked into a ring of expectant faces. After what had already happened to her today she hardly had any modesty left worth making a fuss about. She bent forward, lifting her bottom as Gail and Jill shuffled up until they were pressing gently against her on either side, heads facing to her rear, while the others circled eagerly about them.

She found herself closed in by warm female flesh, a surprising but curiously reassuring sensation. She felt hair brushing her raised bottom, and whispers of warm breath fluttering across the inner curves of her cheeks and tickling the dark curls of her bush. There came the fleeting touch of a nose or cheek across the soft skin of her inner thighs.

She realised Gail and Jill's bottoms were positioned either side of her head, waiting for her to reciprocate. She found herself peering over smooth softly curving hills of flesh to the deep valley between. The shining metal rods of their tail mounts running along the valley floors before curving over and plunging into the crinkled craters of their anuses. Below these were fluffy

71

forests of pubic hair, one russet, one golden, just visible as they curved away between their thighs. With a little thrill of excitement Melanie inhaled the warm intimate aroma that emanated from their crevices. Yes, they were distinctly different. Gail's scent had a slightly sharper tang, while Jill was more honeyish.

"She smells all spicy," she heard Jill say.

Then came a creak of springs from the pound door, and suddenly the warm friendly huddle of girls broke up.

Melanie sat back on her heels and looked round to see a dozen new girls entering the pound. At their head was a lean girl with collar length dark hair, who moved with the easy grace of a tiger.

"That's Una," she heard Gail say quickly. "Be careful."

Una had evidently seen Melanie at once, for she stalked proudly over and made circuit of inspection. She had an intense face with well-marked eyebrows, a strong straight nose and full slightly sardonic lips. Her shoulders were broad and muscular, with prominent collar bones. She had a deep athletic chest from which hung two heavy but taut and well-shaped breasts, crowned by prominent upstanding nipples.

"A new girl," Una said. She peered at her tag. "Melanie."

"And you're Una," Melanie replied evenly. "I've already heard about you."

"Then you know I'm the First in this pack. That means I get the best spot in the yard and the first pick of any treats. Also I have any girl I want, and I get respect all the time, understand?"

"And how do I show this respect?"

"You turn round, put you head down and bum up to me, so everyone can see. Then you kiss my cunt. Properly, with your tongue."

"And supposing I don't want to do that?"

It went very quiet in the yard. Melanie was aware of every girl watching them, but she kept her eyes locked on Una. Melanie had submitted to the Major, Platt and the rest because it was inescapable, but there was no reason to let Una dominate her. If there was going to be a confrontation then she might as well get it over with right now.

She saw Una tense. "Think you're good enough to fight me?" she asked.

"Only one way to find out," Melanie said.

Just then the pen door creaked again and a slender blonde haired girl entered. Another girl said: "Una, it's Gillian."

At first Melanie didn't recognise her as the faceless girl who had been hanging in the yard in punishment. Now she was kitted out as they were. She saw Gillian glance around uncertainly at the group, then quickly shuffle over into a corner and curl up against a wall, pulling her legs up, revealing the criss cross pattern of cane marks across her buttocks.

Una looked at Gillian, then back at Melanie. "I'll deal with you in a minute," she told her. Then she and a couple of other girls headed for Gillian.

Gillian shrank away from them in obvious fear, but they boxed her in. Una prodded her with a gloved hand, making the girl whimper.

"So, Platt warmed your bottom because you couldn't take a cock up it, did he?" Una said contemptuously. "Your airs and graces don't help now you're no better than the rest of us. Well I've been saving this up for you..."

And she cocked her leg over the trembling girl and sent a jet of urine splashing over her breasts and face.

"Stop that!" said Melanie, padding quickly over to the small group. "Leave her alone."

Una expelled the last of her flow, shook her hips to remove any drops from her dark wedge of pubic curls, and turned back to Melanie, her face dark with anger.

"What are you taking her side for? She means nothing to you."

"If she's been properly punished already that should be an end to it."

"She's had it coming," Una spat out. "She lets the pack down by not giving good sport. When that happens the Major gets angry with Platt and he gets angry with us."

73

"Have you tried helping her improve?"

"She hasn't got it in her!" She eyed Melanie narrowly once again. "Just like you haven't got it in you to take me. Last chance. Let's see your bum up an' hear you apologise for talking back to me."

"No."

"Then you're going to learn some respect the hard way..."

And she sprang, gloved hands swinging at Melanie's face.

Melanie knocked them aside and gave Una a blow to the ribs which sent her tumbling to the ground. Una was up in a flash and lunged again. This time Melanie gave her a stinging backhanded slap across the cheek. Una spun on her hip and lashed out with one booted foot. Melanie caught her ankle, twisted her over onto her front, and delivered a sharp smack across her hard smooth buttocks with her paw. She didn't want to inflict any serious injury on Una, because she didn't think Platt or the Major would be too pleased if she did. But she also had to win comprehensively, making it clear it was not due to luck.

And so they tumbled and rolled and punched, their sweating naked bodies intertwined. Una was tough but Melanie was just as strong and she'd also been trained in hand to hand combat. Melanie saw the anger in Una's eyes turn to despair as she realised she was outclassed and felt a thrill of power.

She forced Una face down onto the grass and twisted her arms. Una let out a yelp of pain and suddenly Melanie felt the fight go out of her. Breathing heavily she straddled Una's back as though riding her, realizing that her nipples were hard. Una's tail was doubled up between her legs, sliding between the unexpectedly slippery lips of her cleft. The fight had excited her, as did the feel of this strong and attractive woman lying submissively between her thighs. She'd only appreciated female beauty in an abstract sense before, but this intimate reality was something different - and disconcerting.

She looked about her, finding that she was the focus of a ring of intent faces. More girls must have come into the pen

74

during the fight, because there must have been nearly twenty of them now; all watching wide-eyed and expectant. She grinned at them, then bent over Una's head.

"Had enough?"

"Yes," Una said huskily.

"Don't give me any more trouble in future - and leave Gillian alone. Promise?"

"I promise."

Melanie climbed off her and sat back on her heels.

Una slowly levered herself onto her hands and knees. Her face was streaked with sweat and earth and her chest heaved. Melanie saw her nipples were also swollen. Una gave her one long uncertain glance, part of surprise, part of fear, then lowered her eyes. She turned about and bent her head and shoulders to the ground, arms stretched out to the sides, submissively presenting her bottom to Melanie. Quickly the two girls who had joined her in tormenting Gillian copied her gesture.

Melanie saw Gail amongst the watching crowd suddenly flash her a smile and turn her bottom to her, closely followed by Jill. One by one the rest followed suit until in a few seconds Melanie was surrounded by a ring of trembling tails and pairs of rounded bottom cheeks, each sheltering a furry split peach of flesh below. Several clefts glistened wetly, and the still air of the pound was scented with the excited secretions of almost twenty young women. A strange thrill of power coursed through Melanie, together with a dawning understanding of the pleasure the Major might feel in owning such beautiful creatures.

He owned her too, of course. But at least she was now the First Girl of the Markham pack.

Arabella burned with frustrated desire. She could not get the image of Melanie, spread and bound on the examination table, out of her mind. She recalled the exciting tremble of her brown buttocks and the crisp smack of resilient flesh when she had switched them out in the woods. What a delicious creature! How she would love to possess and dominate her. But Melanie was reserved exclusively for her Uncle's pleasure at least until her first hunt, and there would be no getting round Platt to gain even an hour's use of her.

Gerard and Thomas, who knew her moods well enough to recognize she would be poor company, wisely decided to take their leave that afternoon.

"Promised we'd drop in on the Wickley-Bassets for a couple of days," Thomas explained, "but we'll be back in time for the Ball."

"Meanwhile keep your chin up, Old Thing," Gerard said. "Don't fret over the Brown Vixen. You'll have your chance with her soon enough."

Arabella knew this was perfectly true. Her uncle would eventually tire of her and then it would be her turn. But patience was not one of Arabella's virtues. She was used to getting what she wanted immediately.

Still in a dark mood, Arabella saw them off.

Their carriage had just turned out of the Hall gates when Arabella heard somebody calling to her. She turned to see Penelope Hazeldine running across the gravel towards her.

Penny was one of a group of four local girls a few years younger than Arabella, who liked to think of themselves as her special friends, not realizing she found them rather immature. She knew the village boys called them the 'Snooties', which she thought properly summed up their respective families' social pretensions. They were absurdly flattered by any association with the Hall circle, and made much of the fact that their daughters could call there so freely. But Arabella had to admit they did sometimes provide innocent entertainment as they were so easily and amusingly manipulated.

Penny came to a halt looking flushed and excited. She glanced around conspiratorially before lowering her voice to a dramatic whisper. "Come and see what we've found!"

Susan Drake recovered her senses painfully slowly. Her head ached, she felt sick and it was hard to breathe. She could still feel the afterglow of her shattering orgasm, and the emptiness where the phallus had been. Where was it - and where was she?

She forced her eyes open. She seemed to be lying on her side on a musty rug. Beyond this a blur of light resolved itself into a small square-paned and rather grimy window, set in a wall decorated with yellowed and peeling rose pattern paper. Above, a low ceiling was crossed by dark beams. Her bike was resting in the corner.

There were voices. Several girls talking excitedly and interrupting each other. She listened, still feeling curiously detached from her surroundings.

"We were waiting for you,î one of them was saying excitedly, "and we thought we'd see if there were any better flowers in the woods inside the wall-"

"You did say we could go there as long as there wasn't a hunt on," another interrupted.

"Anyway, we heard this cry and a sort of rattle and crash from up ahead-"

"We were really frightened for a moment, but then Belinda said we should look-"

"And we found her lying at the bottom of a slope. And she was wearing such odd clothes - well, almost wearing them!" There was a group giggle. "And this bike was lying beside her with all these bags fixed to it."

"And she had this funny thing sticking out from her... you know, from between her legs."

"From her cunt, Jem."

"Belinda! That's rude!"

"We knew she must be an outsider from the things she had with her, and her bike was wonderfully light."

"So we gathered them all up, and found a barrow from behind the sheds-"

"And some old sacking to cover her so nobody would see."

"And some rope to tie her with-"

"And we brought her here."

"That was the right thing to do, wasn't it?" said the most doubtful voice. "Maybe we should have told Constable Bailey?"

"Don't be a silly goose, Jem," Belinda, the more forward sounding one, replied scornfully. "Bailey would only lock her up and that would be a waste, but here we can use her properly."

"But everybody knows you should report strangers," Jem persisted.

Belinda sounded exasperated. "Well we'll probably turn her in after we've had some fun with her, then. But it really doesn't matter if that's today or next week, does it? I mean it's not as though it's urgent, or anybody's going to be hurt if we don't do it right away?"

"Well... no," Jem conceded doubtfully.

"You did absolutely the right thing," said a cooler more incisive voice, speaking for the first time. "You've all done very well."

Certain words had finally penetrated Sue's confused thoughts and she didn't like the sound of them. She tried to turn over and only then did she register an alarming fact. She was gagged by a handkerchief balled in her mouth, her wrists were tied behind her back and her ankles were crossed and tightly bound.

"Oh, look. She's awake."

Sue struggled feebly and managed to roll onto her back.

Five girls were looking down at her. Four of them were wearing light one-piece dresses with skirts falling below their knees. Two of these wore sunhats, the others straw boaters decorated with ribbons. The last girl was really a young woman perhaps a few years older than the others. She was wearing a more maturely cut jacket with a dark calf length skirt, under which were leather riding boots. Unlike the loose hair and curls of the others, her honey blonde mane was tied back in a severe ponytail.

Her face was smooth and beautiful with a perfect creamy complexion, but it was not reassuring. The eyes that locked onto Sue's were of dark glacial blue, half veiled by heavy sensuous upper lids. They flicked up and down the length of Sue's trussed body, and as they did so a hungry smile grew on her shapely lips. Then she turned to her companions.

"Since she was found on Hall land obviously she's Hall property," she stated. Sue's eyes widened in disbelief and she gave a grunt of protest. "If you want to learn how to use her you'll have to help keep her," Arabella continued. "But above all, you're not to tell a soul about her being here, understand?"

The four girls shrank back from her stern gaze and nodded gravely. Arabella smiled coldly. "Now we'll begin by seeing what this pretty bitch has to say for herself."

She knelt down and took hold of Sue's jaw, twisting her head round so that she stared full into her eyes.

"I am Arabella Westlake," the young woman said, "niece of Major Havercotte-gore, squire of Markham Hall. You're an illegal outsider and you've been found trespassing on our land. The punishment for these crimes is enslavement. Whatever you were no longer matters. Now you belong to me, understand?"

Sue could only goggle at her in mute astonishment. With her free hand Arabella slapped her face hard twice until Sue nodded in desperate agreement.

"Good," Arabella continued. "In a moment I will remove your gag. When I do you will not waste my time making futile protests at your treatment, pleading to be released or calling for help. It will do you no good whatsoever and only result in swift and painful punishment -" she smiled wickedly and squeezed Sue's chin a little harder "- and believe me, I know how to deliver a punishment.

Of course, I will punish you anyway for amusement or instruction, but if you want to make your life as comfortable as possible, your only choice is complete and total obedience. You will begin by answering all questions promptly and respectfully, addressing me at all times as Miss Arabella. Is that understood?"

Sue nodded quickly. She was overwhelmed by Arabella's complete self assurance. She felt her own fragile willpower dissolving away under that cool dominating gaze. At that moment she could never imagine defying such a woman.

Arabella saw the look of surrender in Sue's eyes. The girl was a natural submissive. This would be interesting.

She pulled the wadded handkerchief from Sue's mouth. "First, what is your name, girl?"

"Susan Drake... Miss Arabella."

"Susan... that's quite pleasing. And what are you?"

"I... I'm your slave, Miss Arabella."

"A pretty and sensible little bitch," Arabella said to the others. "She's taken what I said to heart." She turned back to Sue. "Do you think that might save you a few strokes of the whip?"

Sue's eyes shied away from Arabella's for a moment. "I think... you will whip me as and when you please, Miss Arabella."

"Another good answer, girl - and quite true. Where do you come from?"

"London."

"How did you get here?"

"I'm... not sure where here is, or how I got here, Miss Arabella. I was cycling through some woods..."

They listened to Sue's account of finding the puzzle box and using the phallus. Arabella examined the phallus once again. It seemed a cold, dead thing to her, nothing like the font of pleasure Sue described. With a shrug she slipped it into her pocket. She might look over the rest of the girl's curious baggage at some later time. For the moment it was the lovely piece of flesh herself that mattered. They had a little time before lunch. They could make a start.

"Jemima and Penny, find a bucket and some rags. Draw water

80

from the garden pump. We need to clean her. Bel and Ernestine, you will help me remove her clothes."

Arabella saw Sue's eyes widen in alarm and her mouth open as though to protest. But she made no sound, only bit down on her lip. Her already beautiful face was made even more attractive by her distress, Arabella decided. Well, she could arrange plenty of that for her.

They untied Sue's legs and Belinda and Ernestine pulled her upright. Arabella drew a penknife from her pocket and unsnapped the blade; smiling as she saw the renewed alarm in Sue's eyes.

"Hold her tight," she commanded the other girls.

She slit up the front of her singlet, then cut the shoulder straps and pulled the tattered garment free. Sue turned her head aside as the girls stared in unashamed fascination at her exposed breasts.

"Isn't she big," said Belinda, comparing Sue's heavy breasts with their own slighter figures.

Arabella tweaked a full red-brown nipple that stood out proudly against the pale creamy skin surrounding it. "And they're here to be enjoyed," she said, stroking and squeezing the fleshy globes, weighing them in her palms. Sue whimpered and shut her eyes. Arabella laughed lightly.

Sue's boots and socks were removed, then her shorts were pulled down. Sue instinctively squeezed her legs together only to receive a warning slap across the back of her calf.

Jemima and Penelope returned with rags and a bucket full of slightly rusty water. They blinked for a moment at Sue's naked body, then set the items down. Arabella soaked a rag and rubbed it into Sue's dirt-streaked face, then down her body, the splash of cold water making her shiver. She ground the wet cloth into Sue's fleshy furrow, causing the girl to gasp. With the last of the dirt removed they dried her with strips of old curtain material. Sue flinched again as Arabella rubbed the fabric deeply into her crotch to dry her pubic hair.

Ernestine had a comb and used it to straighten the damp tangle of Sue's hair. When they were done and Sue was as clean

81

and fresh as a new pin, Arabella ran a critical eye over her.

"We'll keep her inside most of the time so she won't tan too much," she said. "Clear pale skin will show any marks we care to put on her to their best advantage. Her most striking features, apart from a delightfully open and innocent face, are undoubtedly her breasts and her bottom, which as you can see is full and fleshy..." she paused to caress the soft rounded buttocks thoughtfully. "I think we have time before lunch to give her a taste of what's to come. I have to fetch something from the garden. Tie her face down over the table."

When Arabella returned a few minutes later Sue was spreadeagled over the room's single low round table. Her wrists and ankles overhung the sides, and these had been bound to the table legs with strips of the curtain material. She was the very picture of naked helplessness.

As Sue's eyes fastened upon what Arabella was holding it seemed as though she was momentarily stirred out of her compliant state, gasping in dismay and tugging futilely at her bonds. There were a few gasps from the other girls as well, their faces filling with horrified fascination.

In Arabella's hand was a two foot length of freshly cut holly branch.

Arabella took up her position beside the table and looked down at Sue's trembling form, taking in shapely legs straining at their bonds, the curve of her dipping back, and the twin hills of her pale rounded buttocks. Sue's beautiful face twisted sideways to meet her eyes. It was contorted with alarm; silently pleading for mercy even though she must know she could expect none. A heady sense of power coursed through Arabella. Evidently Sue was no fighter like Melanie. Should she allow her the chance to avoid punishment by demonstrating her obedience? No, she was not begging aloud. Perhaps there was still a wilful streak that needed to be beaten out of her. And besides, Arabella was determined to break her completely and prove her methods.

She raised the holly switch and brought it down on Sue's bottom. With a swish and dry rattle of stiff spined leaves, a hundred pinpricks stung the creamy flesh. Sue gasped in pain, involuntarily bucking so that her body rose to meet the next blow of the switch. Tears filled her eyes. Now she began to beg, but it was too late.

"No! Please stop, Miss Arabella! Oww... Please! I'll do anything you want... Uhh!"

But Arabella ignored her moans and yelps and pleading. Systematically she lashed the heaving pink hemispheres until they turned to blushing scarlet, here and there spotted with deeper crimson. A few blows she directed into the dark valley between Sue's spread thighs, so she would know how vulnerable her most tender parts were. Only when Sue lay limply on the table sobbing and no longer responding to the switch, did she stay her arm.

"Feel her bottom," she told the girls, who had been watching with silent fascination. Hesitantly they did so, running their hands over the burning flesh.

"She's so hot," Jemima exclaimed.

"That's how she's meant to feel after a good thrashing," Arabella assured her.

"But will she be all right?"

"Of course. In a couple of days you'll hardly see a mark on her. Now turn her over. Let's see if she's learnt anything from her first lesson."

They turned Sue's limp form over onto her back and re-tied her. Her head lolled sideways and her tear-streaked eyes were half closed. Arabella splashed a wet rag from the bucket across her face to rouse her. Sue stared fearfully up into Arabella's eyes, causing her another frisson of delight. She had her slave's full and undivided attention. That was the first step to complete mastery.

"Inside two weeks I will have you taking a punishment like that in your stride, and thanking me for it afterwards," she told her sincerely.

"Yes, Miss Arabella," Sue replied in a tremulous whisper.

Arabella turned to the girls. "Go home and have your lunch. When you come back this afternoon, bring some food for her. And not a word to anyone, remember?"

The girls filed out, their feet clattering on bare wooden boards outside. Only when Arabella heard the door close did she look at Sue again. With one hand she grasped a fistful of Sue's thick blonde hair, while the other she ran up the inside of her thigh. Two stiff fingers stabbed through the curling golden pelt and between the folds of her cunt flesh and into the moist tunnel of her vagina. As Sue's mouth widened in a gasp of surprise at this sudden violation, Arabella swiftly bent over and kissed her fiercely, bruising her lips, thrusting her tongue deep into Sue's mouth. As Arabella's fingers worked away inside Sue, her thumb rolled and teased her clitoris into erection.

Skilfully, remorselessly, she masturbated Sue, stifling her moans and gasps with her own mouth. Unwillingly, helplessly, the confused and frightened girl began to respond; clenching her thighs as far as her bonds allowed and squirming about on the hand that was invading her. As Sue warmed and lubricated, Arabella introduced a third finger into her love hole, then a fourth.

Arabella briefly withdrew her lips from Sue's to lower her head and lick and nip the girl's hard, blood-swollen nipples between her teeth, until she gave forth tiny yelps of pain, which Arabella smothered with more fierce kisses. Sue's breathing quickened, and Arabella felt the hot rush of her exhalations on her cheek. Finally Sue climaxed; bucking wildly and tugging at the ropes, surrendering to the release of her orgasm, her sobbing cries echoing from the low ceiling. Only after long seconds of ecstasy did she slump back limply, eyes closed, chest heaving, a sheen of sweat over her groin and armpits and under her heavy breasts.

Arabella withdrew her glistening sticky fingers from Sue's passage and smelt them, then licked them urgently, cramming them into her mouth to savour her slave's most intimate offering. Then she dipped her head and buried her face between her spread thighs, lapping and sucking the exudation from the plump

84

love lips and the golden fur about them until they were clean once more.

Breathing tremulously, Arabella sat back on the side of the table recovering her composure, dabbing her face dry with a handkerchief and smiling in satisfaction. The girl was as responsive as Melanie. She would make a wonderful subject for training.

Arabella tucked the handkerchief away and lifted Sue's head by a fistful of hair, slapping her cheeks until her eyelids fluttered open.

"This is just the start," she told her. "A mild taste of what is to come. Now you know I control your pain and your pleasure. Next I will strip away your dignity and willpower as easily as I stripped off your clothes until you are totally broken in. You'll be a perfect slave, with no other thought but to please me. I'll show my uncle what a properly trained girl can be like." She paused, thinking once again of Melanie. "Then we'll see..."

10: Ablutions

Gillian emerged from the kennel block. She had been washing herself clean and her hair was still damp. She shuffled quickly over to Melanie who was sitting against a wall, flanked by Jill and Gail who were excitedly asking her questions about where she came from. The rest of the pack were spread around the yard, content for the moment to watch their new leader from a distance.

Gillian dropped her shoulders until her nipples were brushing the grass, crawled the last few feet with eyes lowered and spoke. Though her voice was tremulous her accent was cultured.

"Thank you so much for stopping Una and her friends from tormenting me further. I am indebted to you." She glanced anxiously across the pen to where Una was curled up against the opposite wall. "Can I stay by you. I'll... do anything you want." And she turned about until she presented her bottom to Melanie almost in supplication, her tail trembling.

Slightly embarrassed, but realizing something was expected of her, Melanie rolled onto her paws and knees and crouched beside the girl.

"It's all right," she reassured her. "Una won't bother you any more."

Gillian gave her a quick sidelong glance and smiled hesitantly, but she maintained her stance, reminding Melanie of a dog being displayed at a show. She was waiting to be approved of, and Melanie felt a renewed thrill of power as she looked Gillian over properly for the first time.

Gillian's hair was pale blonde, spilling across her shoulders in a mass of loose waves. Her eyebrows were sooty-dark by contrast, rising over deepset blue-grey eyes slightly shadowed by worry. Her nose was firm and delicately aquiline, complementing her good cheekbones and strong jawline. She had a lean figure with slender hips swelling to strong thighs. Neat, firmly rounded breasts were set high on her chest and capped by equally neat and rounded pink nipples. A bush of dark blonde hair nestled between her thighs.

Melanie's eyes could not help but be drawn to Gillian's poor reddened bottom again. It was the part of her that she was already most familiar with.

"Does it still hurt?" she asked the girl.

"A little," she admitted.

"Lie down. You don't have to stay like that."

Gillian obeyed, lying on her side. She watched Melanie alertly, reminding her of a dog at its Master's feet.

"Was it true what Platt and Una said?" Melanie asked. "Were you punished just because you didn't let a guest..." She hesitated.

"Sodomize me," Gillian finished for her. "Yes, it's true. I know it was foolish, but I couldn't help myself." Her eyes dropped. "There was a good reason."

"Too good to take it up her like the rest of us," Gail muttered, and Jill nodded.

86

"Yeah, she's too well bred to open her bum up to anybody."

Both were looking contemptuously at Gillian.

"Be quiet, both of you!" Melanie said sharply, putting a commanding edge on her words. If she had won a position of authority in the pack then she'd better use it.

The two girls instantly became contrite, bowing their heads slightly. "Sorry, Melanie," they said in unison.

"Do either of you know Gillian's reason for refusing the guest?"

"No, Melanie."

"Then wait until you do before judging her. Go on, Gillian. Was it the first time you'd had sex... that way?"

A tiny smile turned up the corner of Gillian's mouth. "No," she admitted. "There were other guests who used my bottom. It's not so bad when you get used to it. Once I even found myself, you know, coming. But this last time..."

"Yes?"

"I knew him!" Gillian blurted out in a rush. "We'd met about three years ago, before this..." she shrugged, indicating her collar, "...happened to me. It was just briefly at a party, we only spoke a few words. But I did remember him, and I was so frightened and ashamed that he'd recognize me, when it was time I just tightened up inside. When he couldn't get his thing into me he smacked me, but that only made it worse. Eventually he had me the usual way - I wasn't so tight there. But he must have mentioned it to the Major... and that was it."

"I see," said Melanie. She looked at Jill and Gail. "Now you know why Gillian behaved the way she did, what have you got to say?"

"Fine chance any one of our friends being invited here," Gail muttered.

"That's not an answer," Melanie said sharply. "What if they were and you met them like Gillian did. Could you be sure you wouldn't freeze up?"

Gail said nothing.

"But it's not meant to be easy, is it?" Jill said. "That's what

87

we're here for." She looked at Gillian. "She's paying her dues like the rest of us, so she's got to suffer the same."

"And that includes us giving her no sympathy or understanding afterwards, does it?" said Melanie, "Shall I tell the others the next time you get punished that you want them to make it worse by treating you like dirt?"

Jill suddenly looked anxious. "No, please!"

"Then don't treat Gillian the same way now. Understand?" They nodded. An idea came into Melanie's mind. "Right, on your knees, both of you," she said quickly. They rolled upright into alert postures. "Gillian, onto your tummy. Get on either side of her." The three girls positioned themselves quickly. "Now you, Jill and Gail, are going to kiss every one of those strap marks on her bottom better. Then you'll blow on them to cool them down."

And to Melanie's delight the girls obeyed.

Slowly Gillian relaxed under their ministrations and closed her eyes blissfully as the two planted kiss after kiss on her sore flesh. After a minute they started blowing on her injuries and Gillian let out a gentle sigh.

"Open your legs a little, Gillian," Melanie commanded. "Let them see to those inner thighs."

Gillian obeyed, and the girlsí heads bent down lower over her.

Gradually she began to squirm as the puffs of air whispered along her bottom crack and tickled her pubic hairs, and she let out a helpless giggle. Gail laughed at this and redoubled her efforts, closely followed by Jill. Soon all three were laughing, as Gail and Jill began kissing flesh that had not been marked by Platt's lashing.

Melanie found herself watching the trio with satisfaction and not a little pleasure. What had she started here?

Alison entered the paddock and rang a hand bell.

"Lunch time," she called out.

The girls scrambled to their knees as a large kitchen trolley was wheeled into the yard by one of the stable lads. From its shelves he and Alison took covered tin plates and laid them out on the grass in two rows. Melanie saw they were numbered to match the girlsí pack numbers. She found plate 9 and waited on hands and knees before it like the rest, who had formed two ranks facing each other across the line of plates.

When they were in place, the lad went down the lines removing the lids and releasing clouds of aromatic steam. Melanie suddenly realised how hungry she was. But how were they supposed to eat when they couldn't hold any utensils? Then she saw the food had been chopped and compressed by some means into small bite-size balls, covered with gravy. The whole pack was looking expectantly at her, even Una, while Alison was frowning in evident surprise. Resting her elbows on either side of her plate, Melanie cautiously lowered her head and took a bite. The others immediately began eating.

It was traditional meat, two veg and potatoes. A well cooked hearty old-fashioned British meal, unexpected yet obviously appropriate for her strange new surroundings. For dessert there were cubes of sponge pudding in custard. It wasn't exactly the diet Melanie would have chosen for herself, but the girls certainly looked healthy on it. She suspected any excess calories in the diet would be worked off them. Whatever privations she might have to suffer, starvation was obviously not going to be one of them.

They finished eating. A few girls licked traces of food from around each othersí mouths as the plates were gathered in. With a final curious glance at her, Alison pushed the trolley away. The pack spread out lazily around the yard again. Melanie went over to Gillian.

"Thank you for what you did," Gillian said quickly. "With Gail and Jill, I mean."

"That's all right. What happens now?"

"We've got an hour to rest before going back to work. They'll call your number when they want you. Then just do whatever you're told."

"What work do you do?"

"Pulling carts and other machinery for the gardeners. Sometimes a team will go out in the fields ploughing. The Major believes in getting his money's worth out of us, even when we're not being hunted for sport..." She faltered slightly.

Melanie asked: "Did you ever hunt girls yourself, before this happened to you?"

Gillian looked ashamed. "I did, a few times, when my people were invited down to the country. It just seemed such fun and so natural. It was exciting to ride the girls down and see them captured, all sweaty and panting. I remember how they squealed as they were bound and carried away, and wondering why they made so much fuss. Everybody knows they're there because they committed a crime or needed money and sold themselves. Why should they expect or deserve anything better? It's been done like that for hundreds of years. Of course, you never believe it could happen to you.

"How are your family coping with you being here?"

"Only the close family know. The rest think I've gone abroad for a health cure. My father managed to get me tried and sentenced away from home, so there's a chance nobody will find out. That was why I was so frightened about being recognized the other day."

"You don't have to tell me if you don't want to," Melanie said, "but what did you actually do?"

Gillian's face fell. "I don't mind telling," she said quietly, "though I am ashamed. Very simply, one day I became angry with my maid. She'd been careless and had broken a small ornament. It's strange, but if she'd been a bondslave I could quite properly have had her thrashed and nobody would have cared. But she was free and I could only scold her and threaten to take the cost from her wages. But she spoke back and I got angry and forgot myself and slapped her for being impertinent. But we were at the top of the stairs and she fell. She broke her arm quite badly. Other servants saw it happen. I received a two year servitude sentence. It's been terrible at times, but I've learnt my lesson. When I'm released I'll really try to behave better."

So the system did seem to work, Melanie thought to herself. And it was some comfort to know that, even here, nobody was above the law. She wanted to ask what sort of punishments men received, but suddenly realised she had a more pressing matter to attend to.

"I need to go to the loo. I haven't been for hours..." she frowned. "But how are we supposed to manage with these things on?"

Gillian smiled ruefully. "You'll see. Everything's taken care of for you."

She led the way into the kennel block and then right into the washroom.

Running the length of its far side was a row of nine small green-painted wooden hatches with arched tops, set about eighteen inches off the ground.

"You'd better learn how itís done at Markham," Gillian explained as they shuffled over to them. "First, find the hatch with your number over it. That's the one you must always use."

Melanie saw there were numbers painted over each hatch in sets of three. She went to the hatch marked 7-8-9.

"It saves long waits when itís busy and makes keeping the records easier," Gillian said.

"The records?"

"The Major insists all pack girls are kept regular. If you don't have a proper bowel movement at least once a day you'll be purged. Just sit down and you'll see how itís done."

Hesitantly Melanie turned herself about and backed against the hatch, lifting her bottom. Its lightly spring-hinged halves opened in the middle as her bare buttocks pressed against them, causing a small bell to ring somewhere in the dark void beyond. The arched and chamfered opening was just wide and deep enough to let her hips pass through as long as she kept her back bowed forward. She saw the front of a toilet seat and below it a white enamelled bucket half-filled with clean water. Pleased to be able to sit for the first time in hours she squatted down, only to find there was no rear half to the seat. She was supported only

91

under her thighs leaving her bottom hanging totally exposed. There was movement behind her and a long half-inch thick brass bolt slid out of the wall on her right. It brushed the curve of her stomach, passing over the top of her thighs, and locked into place on the other side of the hatch. Alarmed and surprised she tried to rise, only to find the bolt held her firmly seated.

"The pot boy will attend to everything," Gillian assured her.

"Who?" Melanie exclaimed. But she could already feel experienced hands spreading her buttocks and drawing out her tail plug with a sucking pop. She was expected to relieve herself whilst being watched by some unknown boy!

"He'll note your number together with how you've performed for the records," Gillian told her, even as a finger teased around the rim of Melanie's anus expectantly, causing her to squirm in alarm.

"I... don't think I want to go now - ow!"

The unseen fingers had pinched the fleshy underside of her bottom.

"Packgirls aren't permitted any modesty," Gillian said. "You won't be doing anything the boy hasn't seen hundreds of times before. Try not to think about it."

Unseen fingers tickled Melanie's anus again, while a hand slid round her waist and pushed in her lower stomach, causing her internal muscles to contract, confirming her need. She was completely at his mercy, Melanie realised. Even her natural functions were no longer private. A finger was inserted into her slit and expertly teased her pee hole. She lost control and water began to fountain into the bucket. Shutting her eyes, face flushed with embarrassment, she co-operated with the inevitable.

When it was over and she had been thoroughly wiped clean, front and rear, the nozzle of a hose was slipped into her anus. Melanie gasped as the water gushed from her.

"They want us to be perfectly clean inside, just in case anybody wants to use our bottoms," Gillian said.

The nozzle was withdrawn, Melanie's bottom wiped again, and her tail-plug, freshly oiled, was reinserted. The long bolt was withdrawn and Melanie unsteadily scrambled clear. The little door sprang shut behind her. Would she ever know the face of the boy who had tended her so intimately? Was there any other indignity left that she could be put through, she wondered?

11: Washing up and Washing Down

The big kitchen of Cranborough House School echoed to the clatter of plates and pans. Instead of its normal catering staff, five boys worked about the big enamel double sink and drainer in the corner.

"But will she tell on us to Bailey?" Bickley asked once again. "She saw our faces and must have heard our names."

"She's an outsider, so he may no take any notice of what she says," Jackson said. "We'll just have to wait and see."

"I'd have thought he'd have been round here by now if she had told him anything," Parsons pointed out hopefully.

"He might wait until Speers comes back," Bickley said.

"No, he wouldn't hold off that long," Jackson said. "If he suspects us he'd ask Sister where we were when it happened. But she'll say we were here. That was how we set it up to seem."

"Why didn't you just bring her straight back here as we agreed for Arabella?" Harris protested, flushing to match his ginger hair. "You all did it to her for real! You actually came inside her, but Gosset and I didn't even get a look."

"That's right," Gosset agreed, his freckled face full of righteous indignation. "If you'd been patient and brought her here, she wouldn't have escaped. It's not fair."

"Well at least Bailey won't be arresting you for not reporting an outsider when we should," Bickley retorted loudly.

"That's enough, you chaps," Jackson said sternly. "We'd better all agree what to do if Bailey does come asking questions. If we just stick to saying we were working about the school all the time, then it's her word against ours."

"But if she's given him our descriptions, how do we explain

93

how she knew what we looked like?" Parsons said.

They were silent for a moment. Then Bickley added: "And what should we do about her bag? That's evidence."

"Maybe we can say we thought somebody was spying on us while we were working, and when we went to look we found the bag," Jackson suggested. "That would explain how she knew what we looked like."

"But what about the way Bailey found her?" Parsons said. "Stands to reason she couldn't have done that to herself. I think we should get rid of the bag and say nothing."

"But what about that statue-thing inside it?" Gosset wondered. "It looks valuable."

Harris sniggered. "We all can see what it looks like."

Gosset persisted. "I know, but it's still valuable. And that little bag of tools. You know what I think they are -"

He was cut short as Sister Newcombe came into the kitchen.

"Come along, boys," she said briskly. "You should have done that by now."

"Yes, Sister," they chorused, turning back to their drying and stacking.

"As you finished clearing the pavilion," she continued, "this afternoon you can make a start on the old stable block."

"But Sister, that's absolutely packed to the roof with old lumber and stuff," Harris protested.

"High time it was given a good spring cleaning, then," Sister Newcombe replied with a bright smile. "You are here to work off your punishment, so you might as well achieve something worthwhile. Now, sort out the real rubbish for the gardeners' bonfire pile. Put any useful wood or metal aside in neat stacks, and make another heap of anything you can't decide upon. I'll be along to look it over later. All clear?"

"Yes, Sister," they replied unenthusiastically.

She looked at them severely. "Do you want to continue to be treated as responsible boys who will do a job properly without constant supervision, or will I have to watch you every step of the way because you can't be trusted? It may be menial work but it still has to be done. I assured the Headmaster you wouldn't let him down again. I wouldn't like to have to tell him I was wrong when he comes back."

"No, Sister," Jackson assured her hastily. "We'll make a good job of it."

"I hope so. You still have the spare keys to the outbuildings? Good. Then I'll be checking on you later."

And she swept out of the kitchen. The boys watched her go with relief.

"Doesn't she look fierce when her eyes glint like that," Harris said. "Wouldn't want to be around when she really gets angry."

"But she's a good sort," Jackson said. "She could've made this business pretty rotten for us."

"Yeah, she's a decent sort all right," Bickley agreed.

There was a pause as they caught each others' eyes and grinned knowingly.

"And she's also got a really cracking body," Harris added.

"Did the girl you found look like her?" Gosset asked Jackson.

"Her titties weren't as big - but she was a corker all the same," he admitted.

"And you corked her all right," Harris quipped despondently. "Wonder how Bailey's treating her?"

Amber watched as Sally Potts jerked helplessly at the bonds that fastened her to the pillory. Sally's hair was plastered with pillory shot, splatters of which had highlighted the outline of her torso on the vertical board behind her. The board was already streaked with dried mud as the shots of several of her earlier tormenters had been quite erratic and had often missed her altogether.

But now two brawny youths stood at the punishment yard rail. From the power and accuracy of their throwing, Amber suspected they must be members of the local cricket team. They had already paid Tom two shillings for twelve shots apiece (no decimal currency here apparently), and they looked as though they were enjoying themselves enough to invest the same again. Sally's out-thrust and provocatively dangling breasts were their targets, and they seemed intent on making them swing like bells.

The two men were now synchronising their shots. They drew back their arms together and let fly. Sally squealed from behind her gag bar as a parcel of blue-stained mud smacked into her left breast and then burst across it, while a spray of red mud exploded over her right. Between them the spiked ball jerked and bounced, adding a painful reminder of its own presence as it pricked her flesh.

Dripping with their new colours, her pummelled mammaries stopped swaying, until all that was left was the slight tremble imparted to them by her anxious breathing. Laughing, the two men reached for fresh shots.

Amber forced herself to turn away from the small barred window of her cell that overlooked the punishment yard. She had to admit there was a terrible fascination about watching an attractive girl being treated in this way, even knowing she was likely to be joining her in the pillory the next day. Ideally, of course, Amber would prefer to avoid the experience, but circumstances seemed set against her. If only her family could see her now, she thought wryly. Her pompous father would have a fit, and her fearfully correct mother would disown her - if she hadn't done so already.

Years before, feeling stifled by privilege, and dreading the prospect of a 'suitable' marriage and sinking into a meaningless round of parties, visits to the beauticianís and shopping, Amber Ffoulks-Jones had rebelled; leaving her home and her double-barrelled name behind her. She knew she had brains, just no idea what to use them for. After a year of low paid menial jobs and with her savings gone, she had made the gesture she fully expected would get her locked up: she stole an antique clock from the house of a particularly repellent old school mate. But she got away with it, and in doing so discovered a talent, and taste, for the more exclusive kind of cat-burglary. So she had begun her career; re-establishing her former contacts with the rich and privileged so she could best plan how to relieve them of their superfluous valuables. But she was determined it would not be another form of the self-indulgence she despised. So, after fencing and the deduction of her 'fee' as she thought of it, a variety of truly deserving causes found themselves surprised recipients of anonymous cash donations. Well, hadn't her mother always spoken highly of 'charity work'?

But now it looked as though her promising career had suffered a severe, not to say bizarre, setback. First constable Kingston, then the puzzle box, now this place... wherever it was.

Once again she examined her cell. It was clean and had a flush toilet of antiquated design in the corner adjacent to the outside wall. But above all it was very secure. Its lock was sound and she literally had nothing on her that she could use to force it. If only she had her set of lockpicks, she thought gloomily. But they were presumably still in her bag, together with that wretched phallus. She'd never steal curious oriental boxes again, that was for sure.

A rattle of bolts from outside caused Amber to return to the window. The youths and Tom had left, and Bailey was just shutting the gates. It seemed the midday punishment session had ended.

Bailey uncoiled a hose from a tap set in the corner of the yard, and walked over to Sally. "Can't take a mucky girl like you back inside my nice clean cells," he said, sending a fountain of spray over her.

A stream of multicoloured water gurgled away down a drain in the middle of the yard as the mud caking Sally was washed away. Her skin turned pink once again, and her hair hung in damp golden locks. Bailey adjusted the hose nozzle until it produced a narrow sharp jet, which he directed at Sally's breasts, setting them swaying once again as he blasted the last of the mud from them. Sally squirmed at the fresh assault on her already tender glands.

Bailey turned off the water and gazed at the drops falling

from her pink swollen nipples for a minute. Reaching out he tweaked one between his fingers thoughtfully.

"Maybe I can find some clip-on bells for these? Then next time the boys will know when they've hit their target."

Sally said something angrily that was so muffled by her gag bar that Amber could not understand it, but which brought a cold chuckle from Bailey.

"You won't half be sorry for that tonight, my girl," he told her.

12: To Heel

After lunch, the pack girls were called away to their various tasks, leaving Melanie and Gillian alone in the pound. Both girls lay on their sides. Sitting upright in the normal fashion, Melanie had discovered, tended to drive her tail plug further up inside her, which was simultaneously uncomfortable and stimulating. It was easier to sprawl with her arms and legs outstretched, rather like a dog. The effect was no doubt intentional; reminding bondslaves they were helpless animals. While they lay undisturbed, Melanie questioned Gillian about the alternate England in which she now found herself. She soon discovered that atomic power, jet engines and television were unknown, a King James the Fourth sat on the throne while the Prime Minister was one Grenville Russell, and England had never fought in a 'world war'. It was certainly a very different history to her own.

A lump formed in her throat as she thought of home. She couldn't believe she'd only been gone a few hours, so overwhelming had her experiences been and so easily had she slipped into a niche in this strange society. How long would it be until her absence was noted? She was on a couple of daysí leave and had nothing planned socially, so it might not be until she was due back on duty. Could she could get back there before then?

Oddly the idea of escape made her feel guilty and the image of her bondslave agreement came into her mind. Of course such

98

a document would be regarded as outrageous and totally illegal back home, and in any case she had signed it under duress. Or had she? The Major had made it clear what she would become and she had agreed, though she could have chosen arrest and then argued her case in court. Here her status was apparently quite proper, and if she escaped she would be a criminal, an idea that appalled her. But she couldn't possibly give her captors 'good sport' as she had promised, even though she hated to break her word under any circumstances... or could she?

Memory of the pleasure of having Una's body lying submissively between her thighs returned. She'd never felt anything like it before. Was she simply responding to the all-pervading atmosphere of sexual bondage around her, or did she have tastes and desires that were only now being revealed?

She put these confusing thoughts to one side for a moment. Eventually she would return to her own world, but how? Suppose she simply used the phallus again? Would it reverse the process and take her back to the puzzle box? The box had to be the key to her incredible transition, though it had apparently not come with her.

Sudden insight struck her; had what had happened to her already happened to Jones? That would explain the missing phallus and the discarded jeans and pants. If Jones was here as well then she was still on her trail, though hardly in a position to follow up her arrest. If she wanted to bring Jones to justice she might have to be patient - she had enough problems of her own to be going on with. Well, she would simply have to make the best of things.

Much of her life had been spent making the best of things, ever since she had to come to terms with the death of her parents when she was young. Then it had been overcoming all the usual sexual and racial prejudices in her chosen career. Perhaps that was why she liked running. It was an honest challenge: pitting herself against the vagaries of the ground underfoot, fighting to make it up the next hill, the eternal conflict between her endurance and the pain barrier, and the happy state of elation and exhaustion when it was over and she had set a new personal best.

She supposed she had already achieved a sort of breakthrough within the girlpack, though how much being First Girl counted outside it she could not tell. The thought brought a new question into her mind.

"Gillian; how did slavery and punishment ever get mixed up with sport?"

"That was early in the Eighteenth Century. The Earl of Avonbry sent out serving girls for his guests to chase when disease killed the foxes on his land. Finding it good sport, he began hiring and training girls specially for hunting. Gradually the fashion spread to any who could afford it. The old laws of bondslavery were amended to accommodate the practice as a common punishment for most crimes committed by young single women, or as a voluntary alternative to the alms house."

"It was accepted as easily as that?"

"Well, the government approves because it saves public money. Humanists approve because conditions for the women are actually better than prison, since they have to be kept healthy for work or sport. The church thinks public shame and exposure is a suitable penance for women and it serves as a warning to others."

"The church hierarchy here being all male, I suppose. How are men punished?"

"They're sentenced to hard labour camps or road and railway building gangs out of the public eye. Unlike us they need professional guarding."

"But you - we - are not just worked hard, we're being used for sex! Don't you think that's wrong?"

Una shrugged. "It's part of the punishment." She gave a quick slightly guilty smile. "Actually it can be quite... pleasant. Sometimes you find you can't help enjoying yourself. Of course, they don't use us every day - the duties are mostly shared out about the pack in turn. The Major usually has a girl each night, and so does Arabella."

"She's a lesbian, isn't she?" Melanie said, remembering the hungry looks she had given her.

Gillian looked puzzled. "I'm not sure what you mean. Most women who can afford it like to play with a pretty girl almost as much as men do. Or at least have one to keep them warm in bed at night. Just like any other sort of pet, really."

Melanie blinked. "I see. Well, who else can, uh, play with us?"

"Platt can try us anytime he likes for training, and any houseguests get a pick. The estate workers will always give us a pinch and squeeze when we're working in the grounds - and more if they can get away with it, and sometimes we're given to them for extra punishment. And of course we're the prizes in the hunts, and -"

The pound door opened and the Major and Platt appeared, the latter carrying a canvas bag.

Gillian immediately took up an alert posture. She half squatted with the wedge soles of her boots flat on the ground for the first time, her weight taken on her stiff arms. Her chin was tilted up while her back dipped and her breasts thrust forward. Just like a dog on display, Melanie realised.

"Do like I do," Gillian whispered out of the side of her mouth, and Melanie quickly adopted the same stance.

"Wiggle your bottom to make your tail wag," Gillian continued, already doing so herself with a practiced rhythm.

Melanie copied her, feeling the sprung tail begin to swing from side to side, while its securing plug seemed to pulse in sympathy within her. She tried not to think of the spectacle she was making of herself.

As the men approached, Gillian hissed: "If you can respond just by nodding or shaking your head, do it."

Then she was silent, looking up alertly at the two men, the picture of an exotic creature eagerly awaiting her master's attentions. Feeling a knot of anticipation and strange excitement growing in her stomach, Melanie did the same, aware of the warmth of Gillian's naked body by her side.

"And she fought Una?" the Major was saying as they came up to the two girls.

"Apparently, sir. Certainly Una gave way to her when they were fed."

"I said my new Brown Vixen was special, didn't I, Platt?"

"That you did, sir."

The Major circled the two kneeling girls thoughtfully, then bent and ran a hand over Gillian's red-welted flanks.

"You gave her a good striping, I see."

"She needed a sharp lesson, sir."

"Quite so. Well now she can show us, and Melanie, that she hasn't forgotten her basic positions and obedience training. She already seems to have taught her the sejant position. Gillian: beg!"

Immediately Gillian sat back on her heels with her back straight and knees spread wide. Tucking in her elbows she raised her pawed hands until their backs pressed against the underside of her firm breasts, lifting and squeezing them together. Her mouth dropped wide open, her pink tongue lolled out, and she began to pant rapidly; as though waiting for her master to toss her a titbit. Her nipples were standing up, red and hard, from the smooth domes of her breasts.

Melanie stared in dismay at this humiliating posture, but remembering the punishment for disobedience, made herself copy it. As she held the stance she found that her own nipples swelled rapidly into thick chocolate-dark cones under the eyes of the two men. She wanted to cover them for betraying her feelings, but she dared not move. The Major walked round her critically.

"Knees wider, girl, show yourself properly... that's better. Head up a little more... good. That is the 'Beg' position. Remember it well. Now, Gillian: Splay!"

Gillian rolled smoothly onto her back, arms crooked at her sides with the palms of her paws up as though she was surrendering.

Her back arched to lift her breasts. She drew up her legs and parted them, knees bent, until the big tendons on her inner thighs showed taut. The posture stretched open her mound of venus, revealing glistening crinkled lips of coral pink.

Melanie swallowed at the sight of such a beautiful body so blatantly displayed, then, biting her lip, assumed the same position. Platt and the Major looked down at her with approval.

"Lay couchant!"

Melanie didn't understand the command until Gillian rolled over onto her stomach, spreading her bent legs this time flat to the ground. Her supple back curved up as she rested her elbows on the ground, lifting her shoulders, her breasts jutting out proudly as she stretched her forearms neatly out before her. It was the pose of the Sphinx - or that of a dog before the hearth. Melanie matched her. The grass mingled with her pubic hairs.

"Display!" the Major ordered.

They moved onto their hands and knees, backs dipped, chins lifted, legs apart. Melanie had seen dogs on examination tables at shows in the same position. We are bitches being treated as bitches, she thought. But she could feel moisture oozing between her love lips. Whether through fear or expectation, there was a terrible sense of excitement about exposure and obedience. She caught a whiff of female scent in the air and realised Gillian was also aroused.

"Submit!" the major ordered.

Shoulders down until their breasts flattened to the ground, hard nipples pressed back into the soft mounds, faces buried in the grass, arms outstretched. That had been Una's posture, Melanie recalled, bringing a fresh tingle to her stomach.

They were left in the position for almost two minutes, while Platt and the Major walked thoughtfully around them, making comments about minor details of their posture. For Melanie it meant growing discomfort and acute shame. Though she had already had two orgasms that day, her sex urge seemed to be undiminished. She could feel her labia swelling and was horrified that the men would see how excited she was becoming.

At last, the Major said: "Good. Now let's see how well she

103

moves. Watch Gillian closely, girl. Sejant heel!"

They scrambled to take up position on either side of him, their naked flanks brushing the leather of his boots. Following Gillian's example, Melanie looked up at the Major's face, awaiting his next command.

"Walk to heel!"

He began walking and the girls shuffled along at his side, heads up and alert, hips rolling, tails bobbing, freely hanging breasts swaying with every stride. They made two circuits of the pound in this manner, then the Major suddenly changed direction and cut diagonally across the grass. Both girls had to twist nimbly and scrabble sideways to remain in step. They laughed. It had become a game. The Major smiled down at them benevolently and changed direction again. Slowly Melanie felt herself sinking into the comforting embrace of surrender and blind obedience as she scrambled to follow him. The glow of illicit excitement inside her was not to be resented, she thought dizzily, but welcomed. This was quite normal behaviour for a slave. He was her master, as her collar and the crest stamped upon her flesh proclaimed. What more natural than she should walk at his heel?

The Major halted and they squatted at the ready, tails wagging.

"She moves well. Let's try the double leash," he said to Platt.

Platt drew out a length of chain from his bag which he clipped to their collars. Two feet of chain linked them together, shoulder to shoulder. From its middle a single length ran up to a leather loop which Platt handed to the Major.

"Bottoms high!" he commanded.

Hands still on the ground they straightened their legs.

"Walk!"

Keeping in step, they began a new circuit of the pound. It was not as uncomfortable as Melanie had expected. Her bootsí wedge soles lifted her heels, making it feel almost as though she was placing her feet flat to the ground, and so reducing the strain in the tendons down the backs of her legs. It was quicker than

104

shuffling along on their knees because they could take longer strides. Then she realised the view their doubled-over gait was presenting to the Major as he followed on behind them holding their leash. He could see their crinkled bottom holes pierced by the anchoring pins of their tails, and below them two full pouches of flesh, one pink and one dusky, split by pouting inner lips. He could see their wetness. He might even be able to smell their excitement. The knowledge only made her arousal more intense.

The tip of the Major's riding crop flicked lightly across their bottoms.

"Faster. Pull a little. You're on the scent of your quarry."

They increased their pace, swelling thighs pumping, breasts jiggling and bouncing. Melanie felt the pressure of her collar against her throat as she strained eagerly on her leash. Gillian was snuffling theatrically at the grass and Melanie imitated her, very aware of the whisper of warm flesh as their naked shoulders and thighs brushed together. Gillian flashed her a look of playful delight. They scampered about the pound, noses down and bottoms up, almost dragging the Major after them, until they were called to a halt.

The Major mopped his brow, chuckling with pleasure.

"These bitches seem to have plenty of energy. Perhaps they need a little more vigorous exercise. Get out the sticks, Platt."

From his bag, Platt produced two pieces of roughly turned wood about a foot long, scarred about their middles with teeth marks. The Major showed them to Melanie and Gillian, then tossed them into the far corner of the grassy yard.

"Fetch!" he commanded.

So immersed was Melanie in her role by now, that she immediately bounded away after Gillian in pursuit of the sticks. Only for a moment, as she buried her face in the grass to grasp the stick between her teeth, did she wonder how she could be doing anything so degrading, yet at the same time feel so desperately excited at obeying her owner's commands.

They scurried back to the Major with their trophies in their mouths and squatted before him in the begging position. He patted their heads. "Good girls." He took the sticks from them. "Again!"

Three more times they retrieved the thrown sticks, until they both knelt before him lightly flushed with their exertions. Their breasts were trembling on swelling chests, sucking air about the sticks clasped between their white teeth. The Major accepted the sticks, patted them again, then withdrew some small things from his pocket and presented them on upturned palms. Chocolate drops. They swallowed the treats gratefully, delighted by this sign of approval.

"Well?" the Major asked, turning to Platt.

"She certainly has poise, sir, and she moves well. Seems to bring out the best in Gillian, to. They make a good contrasting pair. We might train them in obedience together."

"Just what I was thinking. Let's see how compatible they really are. Gillian: Splay, Melanie: display over her, head to tail."

Gillian lay back on the grass and splayed her legs wide, flashing a quick apologetic smile at Melanie. With a sudden numbing shock Melanie realised what the Major intended. How could she possibly do such a thing? The answer came instantly: because she had no choice. She was a slave whose only duty was to obey her master's orders. As though in a dream, Melanie straddled Gillian so that her head hung over the junction of her widespread thighs. Her heart thumped as she awaited the next, inevitable, command.

"Cover Gillian, Melanie. Tongues to cunts both of you and don't stop until you've spent."

Melanie gaped at the mound of Venus just inches from her nose. She'd never made love to another woman before!

Platt's crop flicked lightly across her bottom. "Get on with it, girl," he warned.

Melanie ducked her head and hesitantly kissed Gillian's bush of golden hair, and gazed down at the glistening crinkled pink inner lips pouting through the rounded cleft of her labia; flesh that she had been intimately tethered to only a few hours earlier. She thought of Gillian's suspended body and a new thrill of excitement coursed through her. They had both been helpless to change their positions then, they were both helpless now. All she had to do was surrender to the inevitable.

Platt's crop flicked her bottom again, and she heard the Major murmur: "Gently, just encourage her."

How well the Major already seemed to know her! The sting of the crop reminded her of her own exposure, of the blatant spectacle she must be making of herself before the two men. There was a thrill in the perverse, and she was succumbing to it as an instinct for animal pleasure took over, warming her loins. She could feel the heat rising off Gillian's body and ducked and kissed her bush again, noting her pouting lips glistening wetly, while the heady musk of her arousal almost overwhelmed her; the most intimate perfume, subtly different from the private scent of Jill and Gail.

She thought of Gillian looking up into her own swollen and excited sex, realising she was almost as wet as she had been before using the phallus. Was it dripping onto Gillian's face? Was she licking the drops up as they fell?

Another light flick of the whip on her bottom.

"Gillian is a beautiful little bitch," the Major said. "Enjoy what she has to give."

Yes, Gillian was beautiful, Melanie thought. All she had to do was let herself go...

She buried her face in the hot cleft of flesh under her, licking and nuzzling furiously, even as her own thighs closed about Gillian's head, and she felt her eager tongue burrowing into her own slit. This first penetration of her by a woman wrenched a gasp of delight from her lips, muffled by the enveloping flesh of Gillian's sex pouch. She jerked her hips up and down, grinding her cunt into Gillian's face, her tongue rasping over the hard nub of her clitoris even as her nose pushed into the mouth of Gillian's love hole. She was riding her in a race for pleasure, even as Gillian bucked and squirmed in mounting delight.

They climaxed together with a series of yelps and whines of pleasure that befitted two passionate young bitches. Still intertwined they collapsed and lay unmoving except for their ragged breathing.

After a timeless interval, Melanie felt her hands pulled behind her back and her paw rings were clipped together. Then Gillian's hands were drawn up about her waist and fastened to Melanie's bound wrists, so they were locked in a strange embrace. Their legs were pulled wide and spreader bars clipped to their ankle rings.

And so they were left alone for an hour in the empty girl pound. Their faces, still glistening with the juices of spent passion, pressed into the warm sweet split figs of flesh between each others' thighs.

13: Sue in the garden

Arabella was already waiting for the girls when they returned from their respective lunches. She had a long switch hooked onto her belt. Sue, now wearing a proper training harness, was resting on her hands and knees on the table so that her reddened bottom was facing them as they entered.

Arabella gave a tin of skin cream to Belinda.

"Put some on her rear," she told her. "We want to keep her smooth and tender. The rest of you look at her closely - feel wherever you want to. She must get used to being handled."

The new harness positioned Sue well for such examination.

Her wrists and ankles were secured by cuff rings fastened to steel rods a foot long. From the middle of the ankle rod a chain ran under her body up between her breasts to fasten to a broad leather collar, while from the middle of her wrist rod a second chain ran along to the ankle rod. Secured thus she could not straighten her body, and could only move by shuffling forward on her knees and palms.

As Belinda worked the cream into Sue's hot and sore bottom, the other girls, with many giggles and whispers, tentatively examined their new pet.

108

Sue's heavy breasts, hanging in bulbous cones with perfect hard dome-like nipples at their tips, were squeezed and fondled. The smooth curve of her belly was stroked, and fingertips run around the pit of her navel. Her broad full hips were admired. The girls' hands ran over the golden-haired red-lipped pouch of her sex. Daring fingers probed the folded flesh within, sampling its warm, slick wetness, then they were held out for others to sniff the intimate scent of her body.

Arabella looked on, smiling benignly, watching Sue's beautiful face strain to express her confusion and discomfort. Her blue eyes begged silently but hopelessly, as though she knew Arabella would spare her no indignity.

When the girls had satisfied their curiosity, Arabella said: "Get down, girl!" Sue obeyed awkwardly, constrained by her chains and almost falling to the floor.

"Did you remember to bring food for her?" Arabella asked the others.

They produced small packets of greaseproof paper which contained slices of bread, cheese, cake and a couple of apples.

"That'll do," Arabella said. "Sit down and hold out some pieces on your palms, the way you feed a horse. She'll come to you."

And Sue did so; shuffling from one girl to the next, delicately nibbling the scraps from their open hands, then, at Arabella's order, licking them clean like a dog.

"Good," Arabella said when she had finished the last crumb. "Now we'll take her into the garden." From the long canvas bag she had brought from the Hall with her she removed a leather leash and clipped it to Sue's collar. "We must get on with the next stage of her training."

"Is it safe take her outside?" one of the others asked. "Won't we be seen?"

"Not if we keep her round the back. Bring my bag, Belinda."

On her hands and knees, Sue was taken through a low wood panelled door and into the open air.

From outside it was apparent that the tiny half-timbered cottage, topped with a mildewed thatched roof, was not a proper dwelling at all, but an elaborate children's playhouse that had been recently neglected. Its back garden comprised a small rectangle of lawn badly in need of cutting, surrounded by overgrown flower beds and a shaggy box hedge some seven feet high. The single gate in the hedge was so smothered by growth from either side as to be almost invisible. With the playhouse closing off the fourth side they were completely shielded from the outside world.

Arabella unclipped Sue's ankle bar and gestured to the nearest flower bed.

"That is your toilet," she told her. ìScrape a hole in the earth and use it, clean yourself, then cover it in neatly after you."

The girls looked at her in surprise.

"Slaves cannot afford to have any modesty," she told them simply. "If I treat her like an animal, she must behave like one. She must also learn to obey immediately -"

She unhooked and raised her switch, but Sue was already scrabbling in the earth with her hands.

As they watched in embarrassed yet fascinated silence, she awkwardly squatted like a dog and relieved herself into the hole. When she was done she wiped her rear with a hank of grass, covered the hole again, then looked up at Arabella anxiously.

"Good," Arabella said. "Now we shall change her harness. I want to see how well she moves. Hold her upright."

She removed a bridle from her bag and held it by its training bit: an ovoid of hard rubber, slotted in the middle. Seeing this, Sue instinctively clamped her lips shut. Arabella pinched her bottom sharply. Sue opened her mouth to cry out and the bit was forced between her teeth and slipped into place, her tongue going through its slot. As the rest of the bridle was pulled over her head she found her tongue was trapped, making speech impossible. Her unintelligible grunts and moans of protest were ignored as her face was enclosed in a lattice of leather straps which buckled at the back of her neck. The bridle, just like a horse's, had blinkers, restricting her field of view to what was directly

110

ahead of her.

The bar and cuffs securing her wrists were removed, and at Arabella's direction, the girls pulled Sue's arms up behind her back so that her forearms were pressed together. Arabella took a broad 'T' shaped length of buckled leather from her bag. The base strap of the 'T' was fastened about Sue's forearms, encircling them from wrists to elbows, while the two side straps secured her upper arms, preventing her from slipping out of the main sleeve. The restraint pulled her shoulders back, thrusting her breasts forward.

Arabella walked round the trembling body of her new slave, slapping the crop she had brought with her thoughtfully against her thigh. Sue's eyes stared out fearfully from between the straps and blinkers that surrounded them. Her broad hips and full breasts made her waist appear deliciously pinched-in by comparison, while the dark leather of her harness contrasted dramatically with her pale flesh.

A smile played about Arabella's lips. "I think she needs decorating."

"What with?" Jemima asked.

"Flowers. The way we did for our sylvan dancing."

In a few minutes they were splicing buttercups and daisies into chains to be garlanded around Sue's neck. A platted crown of broom stalks was placed on her head, while the heads of two narcissus were tucked behind her ears. They stepped back to admire their handiwork for a moment, then Belinda's face lit up in a wicked grin.

"There are two other places we can put flowers," she pointed out.

Arabella smiled at her approvingly. "Well done, Belinda. You're getting the idea. You tell them how you want it done."

Sue's eyes widened in dismay and she moaned and shook her head in protest.

"We couldn't!" exclaimed Jem, blushing.

"Yes we can," Belinda said.

As the other girls laid Sue on her back and held her legs

apart, Belinda cut seven daffodils and trimmed their stems into a tight bunch some eight inches long. Sue squirmed and bucked her hips as Belinda knelt between her thighs, spread her outer lips and inserted the bunch. She gave a muffled squeal as she felt the cool sap oozing across the tender ribbed flesh of her forward passage as the stems were forced into her until only the cluster of yellow and white trumpet heads showed, as though sprouting from the dark golden moss of her pubic curls. The girls giggled at the novel display.

"You don't have to limit yourself just to flowers," Arabella suggested, and Belinda smiled wickedly.

"Get her onto her knees and bend her forward," Belinda commanded. The girls obeyed: pressing Sue's face and shoulders into the grass so that her bottom was raised.

In the hedge was the holly bush Arabella had cut her switch from earlier. Belinda cut a short stem and stripped it back until a crown of a dozen leaves remained.

Sue wailed behind her gag.

Belinda knelt between Sue's spread knees and pried apart her plump bottom cheeks to reveal a puckered hole, only slightly darker than the surrounding flesh. Belinda probed it with the end of the holly stalk, ignoring the Sue's frantic squirming and the contraction of the sphincter, and slid it into the reluctant anus until the spray of leaves rested at the junction of Sue's cleft and the folds of her buttocks.

Arabella jerked her leash and Sue stood up in an ungainly fashion, keeping her feet wide to prevent the holly pricking the soft inrolling flesh of her bottom. The girls sniggered at her evident discomfort.

"Being used as a vase is a good lesson for her," Arabella said. "A bondslave must learn to be decorative as well as functional. Once she's trained she'll learn to open herself to whatever you want to put in her." She examined the holly crown as it nestled under the curve of her buttocks. "It also provides just the right target to teach her how to move to order."

Arabella replaced Sue's leash with a long schooling rein and drew out a coiled springy whip from the bag. Positioning herself in the centre of the lawn she let out about ten feet of the rein.

"Walk," she commanded, flicking the tip of the whip across Sue's round fleshy buttocks and leaving a faint red stripe. Fearfully, Sue began walking stiff-legged in a circle constrained by the length of the rein, feeling the flower heads and holly crown planted within her brushing the insides of her thighs and bottom cheeks.

"Keep your chin up and chest out. Even steps," Arabella said, and Sue strove to obey.

"Trot," Arabella said, flicking the whip across Sue's bottom again. It struck the holly, driving the spines into her flesh and making her yelp.

Sue circled about the garden at a faster pace, aware of the flower stalks twisting within her. As her movements became more vigorous the holly spines began to scratch and prick in earnest.

"Run. High prancing steps, little filly. Make those breasts bounce!"

Sue pulled her knees as high as she could on each stride, horribly aware that she was being treated as though she was a show horse. Worse, she could feel the bunch of daffodil stalks in her vagina begin to grow slick as her juices mingled with their sap. The holly leaves were digging deeper into the soft flesh around her anus and making her gasp, but despite the pain her nipples were swollen and hard. Sweat began to sheen her body.

Arabella suddenly commanded her to halt.

"She's not putting enough effort into it. She needs more encouragement. Belinda. There are some canes in the bag. Share them out, please..."

Arabella stationed the girls, canes in hand, at equal points around the lawn outside the track Sue was beginning to leave in the grass.

"As she comes opposite you," she told them, "give her a flick across her bottom. She'll soon learn the faster she goes and the more she pulls her legs up the less it'll hurt."

Sue was started off again, and now the whip was joined by the stinging swishes of the canes. A heavy blow with plenty of follow-through from Belinda, a tentative flick from Jem, medium hard swipes from the two other girls. Then round again. A new criss-cross pattern of red stripes began to grow on her scarlet flushed bottom cheeks. Several of the blows struck the holly crown, driving the spines into her again and again. Drops of blood began to appear on the undercurve of her bottom cheeks and the plump tops of her thighs. Sue's eyes misted with tears.

Naked, bound and blinkered, breasts bouncing, bottom rolling, thighs pumping, around and around she went. Flower petals were falling about her feet or clinging to her sweaty body. She was panting for breath now, sucking air in around the bit in her mouth. When would this torture end? Stinging sweat entered the scratches and punctures about her anus. Her bottom was on fire. Her nipples felt as if they would burst. Her thighs were wet with her secretions and streaks of blood. She felt the terrible need and shame building within her and gasped in torment.

The garden seemed to blur. Her legs gave way and she fell forward onto her knees, doubled up and squeezing her thighs together, desperately clenching her inner muscles about the daffodil stalks and the holly stem; working herself up and down in spasms of pleasure even as Arabella's whip cracked across her back.

Then she collapsed onto her face and rolled limply onto her side, legs sprawling, slowly discharging the sopping stringy remains of the daffodils across her pale thighs.

Arabella stood over Sue's limp form, gazing down at her in wonder and delight, even as the other girls clustered round anxiously.

"We've killed her!" Jemima moaned.

"Nonsense, she's fine," Arabella assured them. "Get a bucket of water from the pump."

The cold douche brought Sue back to her senses, and she lay on the grass giving muffled sobs of shame.

"Stand in a line," Arabella directed the other girls. She exchanged the whip for a crop from the bag, then pulled Sue up onto her knees before them, holding her rein tight. "This is Belinda Jenkins," she told Sue, indicating the first girl in the line. "She has seen you relieve yourself like a dog and has used you for a vase. She knows you are just an animal to be trained. Kiss her feet."

Still dazed, Sue hesitated. Arabella flicked her crop across her out-thrust breasts, bringing forth a muffled yelp from behind her bit. Sue bent over hastily, pushing her abused bottom, still painfully plugged by the holly crown, out to balance herself. She lowered her head over Belinda's neat shoes and kissed them as well as her bridle allowed. Arabella smiled as Sue's large breasts flattened into fat pancakes on the grass and the wet and tangled matt of her pubic hair peeped between her thighs. Such an inviting target was irresistible and she flicked her crop across Sue's blood-flecked bottom, bringing forth another yelp.

In the same manner Arabella introduced Ernestine Chadwick, Penelope Hazeldine and Jemima Moncrief. Sue did not hesitate to kiss their feet but received a flick of the crop across her bottom each time anyway. Finally Sue knelt at Arabella's own feet, looking up at her fearfully with tears sparkling in her eyes.

Arabella felt a warm glow of anticipation surge through her as she looked down into those moist eyes. A lovely pliant outlander girl with a broad streak of masochism in her. Hers alone to master. Breaking her in would not provide the same challenge as Melanie, but it would have its rewards nevertheless.

"I am your Mistress and you are my slave, do you understand?"

Sue nodded quickly.

"Kiss my feet."

Fearfully, Sue obeyed. As she desperately covered her boots in kisses, Arabella flicked the tip of her crop from side to side across the flaming red twin hills of her buttocks and the miniature holly tree that sprouted between them.

Sue's second lesson in slavery had gone very satisfactorily.

Later that warm bright afternoon, Alison Chalmers strode back through the gates of the girlpack yard. All was quiet. Apart from the new number 9, who had been secured in her kennel following her training session so she would be rested for her duty that night, the other girls were out working. Even the pot boy had a few hours off at this time.

Alison's rosy-cheeked face wore its usual bright smile. She was a naturally cheerful and straightforward girl who liked to be useful, and enjoyed working at the Hall. In her hand she clutched the papers which Mr Platt had sent her to the Major to have signed. She had managed to catch him before he went out on his afternoon ride, and so had not needed to wait for him after all.

Her family were distant, slightly impoverished relations of the Havercotte-gores, and he had taken her on a few months ago mainly as a favour to them. She suspected Mr Platt had some reservations about her employment, but she had tried her best and worked hard, and gradually seemed to win his approval. Now, she allowed herself to believe, he had become quite fond of her, and trusted her with managing the pack whenever he was absent from the Hall.

Her only failing, which he was always gently correcting, was that she was too lenient with the girls when they had to be punished or corrected. A firm but fair hand, he told her, is kinder in the end. They'll learn that pain and pleasure mix here. It brings them alive and makes them respond better.

But Alison thought they looked so perfectly beautiful, harnessed and naked, that she could never accept that a few stripes on their breasts or bottoms would not spoil them. She was also acutely aware that they were valuable property, and was frightened every time she even flicked one with her switch that she would accidentally mark her too severely. What made it more complicated was that Mr Platt had also told her that it was not simply a matter of how many strokes a girl might be given, or how severe they were. Each girl was a unique individual, he said, and would respond best to different degrees and forms of punishment. He had made her practice on them, of course, but she wondered if she would ever learn to be as fine a judge of bondgirls' inner natures as he was.

Entering the office Alison put the papers on Mr Platt's desk. She was turning to leave when she heard his voice coming faintly through the connecting door to the Examination Room, which was slightly ajar. She went through but found the room empty. Platt spoke again, and she realised he was in the Harness Room. She went to push open its door, only to freeze in surprise and embarrassment.

Through the narrow crack between door and frame she saw Gillian stretched over a high trestle, facing slightly away from her. Gillian's wrists and ankles were spread and fastened to the trestle's feet, while her hips rested on its padded top. This presented her bottom at a convenient height for Mr Platt to examine, which he was doing with care: tracing the path of the whip stripes he had put on it with his fingertips to check for broken skin, lifting and kneading the pale flesh to test its pliability and parting the buttock cheeks to expose the cleft between them.

Normally none of this would have made Alison pause for an instant, as she had seen such examinations dozens of times before. What caused her to hesitate this time, however, was that Platt's naked penis was projecting stiffly through the open flies of his jodhpurs.

She stifled a gasp as she goggled at the thick rod of flesh. She'd seen her brothers naked when they were all young and understood the male anatomy and its functions perfectly well in theory, especially as they applied to the girls in her charge, but she'd never seen a mature erect penis with her own eyes. Her family situation and the need to find employment had limited her contact with young men. So far this gap in her experience hadn't troubled her. But now, though she knew she shouldn't, she felt an overwhelming need to observe the real thing. Guilty but excited she looked and listened.

117

"These will have healed in a week," Platt was saying to Gillian, as he concluded his examination. "I hope I won't have to give you the same again."

"No, Mr Platt," Gillian assured him. "I've learnt my lesson, really I have. You made me see how foolish I was."

"You were certainly willing enough with Melanie," Platt conceded, running a finger up and down the crease of her buttocks. "But then she wasn't using your rear for her pleasure."

"I know, sir. But I really do feel easier about it now. I won't get tight there ever again."

"Oh, there are times when you can have a nice tight arsehole. Men like that. But you've got to let them in to enjoy it." He took hold of the base of Gillian's tail and worked it gently to and fro. "You've learnt to relax when your tail's put in."

"Yes, sir. But that's not alive." Her voice dropped. "And it was a... particular person."

"A packgirl can't make distinctions about who uses her. She must serve one cock as well as another. Just learn to control your hole. Don't think of who's putting what into it. It'll make things easier for yourself as well. Try it. I'm going to take your tail out. Loosen up, let it ease out..."

Alison saw the ring of flesh around Gillian's anus bulge as the tail plug came free with a soft pop.

"There," said Platt, "that was easy. Now I'm going to put it in again." Gillian's anus crinkled, almost making the tiny hole in its centre vanish. "No, I can see you going tight again. It's a reflex with you, girl, but you've got to learn to overcome it. Let your whole body go limp."

Gradually Gillian relaxed as far as her bonds would allow.

"That's better," said Platt. Carefully he inserted the tail plug once more. "Now squeeze it as hard as you can for a moment, hold it inside you. Now loosen..." He pulled the plug out, then reinserted it. "Squeeze again... now loosen. Tight... open. Good. Keep repeating it. Learn what your bottom muscles do... that's fine."

Gillian's buttocks clenched and unclenched in a delightful

118

rhythm as the tail plug slid easily in and out of her rear. Then, without warning, Platt exchanged his index finger for the plug. Gillian jerked her head up in surprise.

"Continue as I told you," he ordered. "I want to feel how hard you can squeeze... now go loose. Good. Can you feel my finger moving inside you, giving you a little tickle? That wasn't so difficult to take."

"You... you've felt me there before, Mr Platt," Gillian replied with a tremor in her voice. "You're my trainer... I'm used to you."

"It could be anybody's finger, Gillian. Any guest you're given to has as much right to put their finger or their cock up you. All that matters is that you please them. Don't think of who they are, just what you are doing. Now once more: squeeze, loosen. Hold as I draw my finger out, release as I push in. Be easy to enter, but difficult to leave. Make a man think you want nothing better than to keep him inside you."

He withdrew his finger and pried her bottom cheeks apart so that the naked skin around her anus was stretched. "Keep going, I want to see you pinched tight, then gaping open. You're giving an invitation. Show how much you want to have your arsehole used. That's good..."

Alison was diverted between Gillian's bottom and Platt's penis, feeling an unexpected but pleasant tingling in her lower stomach. Platt's organ had grown even stiffer as he had coached Gillian until the veins were standing out on its sides, and the purple plum of its head began to peep over its taut foreskin. Suddenly he grasped Gillian's hips and thrust his rod into the centre her bottom hole and buried himself inside her up to the hilt.

Gillian let out a yelp of surprise and bucked, jerking at her bonds. Platt gave her a slap on the thigh to keep her attention.

"Now you can squeeze, girl. Give me something to work against!"

He rammed into her, lifting her hips off the trestle top with the force of his thrusts and making her gasp. The trestle creaked and its feet squeaked on the stone floor.

"Remember how this feels! From now on every cock put up inside you will feel like this. When you please a guest, you please me!"

Gillian replied brokenly, between his thrusts: "Yes... Mr Platt... I'll try... to remember!"

Platt grunted, gave a series of rapid jerks, then hunched over her pinioned body, clasping her round the waist and remaining still for almost a minute. Gillian, her hard-nippled breasts trembling, could only bear his weight patiently. Alison looked on at the silent tableau in wonder and fascination, hand over her mouth to stifle her excited breathing. She had seen a packgirl used properly by a man and for the first time realised how exciting it was.

Finally Platt straightened up and withdrew his glistening and somewhat limper member from Gillian's stretched bottom hole, which slowly closed after him. As he wiped his manhood clean on the convenient bush of her pubic hair, he said:

"Now that was a proper bottom fuck, Gillian. Any guest would be well satisfied with that. You were fine when you opened up."

"Thank you, Mr Platt... I hope I pleased you."

"You did, girl," he said, patting her upturned bottom with a smile. "You'll be a credit to the Hall pack yet."

Silently Alison withdrew to the office, picking up the papers she had left on Platt's desk, and slipped back out into the yard. She didn't want to embarrass him after all his kindness to her by revealing what she'd seen, especially as her respect for his judgement had just risen another notch.

She'd thought his punishment of Gillian that morning was over harsh, but now it was obvious it had been just what she'd needed. Alison sighed. If only she could learn his secret.

Amber had hoped to talk with Sally Potts during the break between the midday and afternoon pillory sessions, since the barred
doors of their cells opened onto the same corridor, but she'd
only received grunts in reply. Eventually, on a one for yes, two
for no, basis, she discovered Bailey had left Sally gagged as
punishment for whatever backtalk she had given him out in the
yard. Amber had offered her commiserations, but that had been
as far as their interchange progressed.

As Bailey had promised, Sally had been reversed in the pillory for the final session of the day so that her bottom was provocatively presented to her tormenters. The chain of the spiked
ball now ran down the cleft of her buttocks, so that the ball hung
freely between her inner thighs. Amber winced in sympathy.

Fortunately for Sally the two strong-armed young men did
not pay her a return visit, but even so her pretty buttocks and
thatch of pubic hair were thickly plastered with coloured mud
by the time Bailey finally closed the gates. He hosed her down
and returned her to her cell, but once again she was gagged.

This was frustrating as Amber wanted to learn as much about
this bizarre version of England as possible. But it looked as
though she would have to wait until the evening meal when Sally
would have to be ungagged.

It must have been close to eight, for the yard was dark, when
Amber heard a confusion of voices from the front office. Bailey's
rumble rose above those of two other men, who seemed to be
having a rambling incoherent argument. After a few minutes the
communicating door opened and unsteady footsteps sounded
in the passage.

"Gerrof Harry! 'M fine... I tell ya..."

"Yer... we was just havin' a discussion, like."

Alcohol laden breath wafted along the passage. Bailey spoke
disapprovingly: "Your discussion broke four glasses, two chairs
and a table. How you two got yourselves sozzled so early is a

mystery. Pub's not been open two hours." There came the rattle of keys and clank of a cell door. "In there, Davey, and sleep it off. No, you'll be next door, Ted." Another rattle of keys. "You'll have to move out of there, Sally Potts. No, leave her alone, Ted. You just get your head down on that bed. That's better. Along here, girl. You're going to have to double up for the night."

Bailey appeared before Amber's cell door leading Sally by her arm. She had something resembling an old fashioned scold's bridle locked over her head, which held a ball gag firmly in her mouth. Bailey opened Amber's door and pushed Sally inside.

"I'll bring you your food soon as I can," he told them. Sally pointed to her bridle and made pleading noises. Bailey frowned. "All right, but no more of your lip, understand?" Sally nodded vigorously. Bailey removed the device, closed the door, and departed once more.

Sally was scratching her head where the straps of the bridle had rested, shaking her mop of blonde hair loose and running her fingers through it to fluff it up. She licked her tongue over her stretched lips.

"Bloody gag's left me parched," she said. "Can I have some of your water? Thanks." She didn't wait for a reply, but poured herself a mug from the tin jug in the corner, and sat on the bed sipping it, eyeing Amber with casual interest and apparently not in the least abashed by her own nudity.

"Help yourself," Amber said wryly, sitting down beside her.

It was hard not to stare at the girl. Her breasts were large for her build and hung heavy and proud, capped by large pink areolae with neat rounded nipples in their centres. Her waist was slim, with prominent hip bones and a dark blonde delta of pubic hair surrounding a pink-lipped cleft curving away between her thighs. Close to, Amber could plainly see scattered purple and red spike marks about the summits and pale inner curves of her breasts.

"Does it hurt?" she asked hesitantly.

Sally looked down at herself and shrugged. "I've had worse.

You get used to it." She considered Amber thoughtfully: "Your first time?"

"Inside jail? Yes it is."

"You sound like gentry. What did you do wrong?"

"I'm not quite sure myself," Amber admitted. "Got unlucky, I suppose. Kicking Constable Bailey probably didn't help."

Sally chuckled, then shook her head. "You're going to catch it good for that."

"So he told me. I didn't realise they punished people quite so harshly just for being lost and kicking a policeman. You see I'm something of a stranger in these parts. In fact I was wondering if you could fill me in on a few things."

"How d'you mean?"

"Who runs things, how they got the way they are, do's and don'ts, that sort of thing."

Sally shrugged. "Not like I've got anything better to do."

Just then Bailey brought two trays along to the cell. There was vegetable soup, thick slices of bread and cheese. Like lunch, it was good, if basic, food. At least prisoners were fed well enough, Amber decided. She and Sally talked as they ate, and Amber began to learn about the strange society she now found herself in. She also discovered something of Sally's own background.

She didn't seem to have any family, and wandered around the county supporting herself with a series of temporary jobs, mostly on farms, and occasionally prostitution - which Sally was quite open about in a cheerfully mercenary way. She also admitted to a little minor pilfering: eggs and apples and the odd piece of clothing from a line.

"Were you caught?" Amber asked. "Is that why you're in here?"

"Not for stealing nothing." She grinned. "'Least, nothing they could prove. Caught me sleeping in a farmer's barn. Didn't have any money on me to pay a fine, so I was had up for trespass and no means of support. Fourteen days in the pillory."

"That's pretty tough."

123

"'Bout the usual. A village lock up's not so bad, 'specially wintertime. They have to feed you the same, but often can't put you out in the stocks for weeks. Unless you get hired out for the night to some big house party, or they hold a barn show."

"A barn show?"

"Late winter when the barns are getting empty and the weather's still too bad for a proper outside pillory, local farmer might make a few bob by putting up a few ropes and frames in a barn, then having a pay-at-the-door party. He buys a few boxes of pillory shot off the local station and gets the girls free for a night. Course, they usually end up getting a good banging as well, but as long as they're back in their cells the next day and haven't been too badly handled, nobody minds."

The girls might, Amber thought, but obviously that didn't count. "Is it any different in towns?"

"City jails can be tough - they've got indoor pillory halls all year round. No, village ones are best if the local copper's all right, like Bailey. Gives them something to do when it's quiet, and it looks good to have a girl in the yard."

"It sounds like a mutually beneficial agreement."

"What?"

"You both get something out of it."

"Yeah. Trick is not to get had up for anything that gets you a bondslave sentence. Stay on your own ground where you know just what the local bench deals out and you're all right."

"That almost sounds as though sometimes you deliberately let yourself get caught."

Sally was grinning. "Like I say, worse places to be in the winter."

Amber smiled in return. Sally was an engagingly mischievous little vagabond; both defiant and bright, and Amber began to warm to her. Actually, she realised she was beginning to get aroused by her presence and the warmth of her naked body close to hers. There was something especially attractive, she decided, about her pouting lips. Amber considered herself a well adjusted bisexual, and Sally was just the sort of girl she could imagine having a happy time with. But how would she respond to a pass? She was clearly no sexual novice, despite her youth, but what were her tastes?

Just then they heard Bailey returning. Sally made a face.

"Time for his perks. I shouldn't have given him that lip earlier."

Bailey removed the trays, checked the drunks in the other cells were sleeping soundly, then returned with a handful of shackles.

"Now I'm going to teach this saucy piece a lesson," he told Amber. "It'll give you some idea of what you're in for tomorrow, after you've been sentenced."

He made Amber stand with her back to the wall bars beside the cell door, and raise her hands over her head. He pulled them through the bars and fastened her wrists together, forcing her to stand very straight against the cold metal. The tension on her arms stretched and lifted her breasts. Under the thin cotton of her prison shift, her nipples stood up. Bailey noticed and flicked them lightly.

"Does this sort of thing excite you, girl?" he asked with a grin. "We'll see if those teats are as hard tomorrow night, when it's your turn."

Bailey had Sally kneel on the cell's narrow iron frame bed, so that her bottom hung over its foot. He bent her forward so that her face was pressed into the blankets, and pulled her arms underneath her between her knees, cuffing her wrists together, and chained them to the horizontal frame. Then he pulled her ankles wider apart and fastened them to the side posts.

Amber gulped at the sight of Sally so beautifully and helplessly exposed. Bailey ran his hand over the taut pale skin of her proudly raised bottom then down the gaping cleft of her buttocks. Sally shivered as he tickled her bottom hole, then delved into the plump pouch of flesh that hung beneath, and worked his hand to and fro until Sally was gasping and squirming, tugging at her bonds.

Amber was riveted to the spectacle, her breathing quicken-

125

ing. She would have given almost anything to trade places with Bailey at that moment.

He withdrew glistening fingers from Sally's interior and sniffed them with a smile. "The little tart's always ready for it," he said, not unkindly. He held his fingers under Amber's nose, and she could not help inhaling. It was the most heavenly scent.

"Well her hot slit's not going to get her out of trouble this time," he continued, grasping a handful of Sally's hair and jerking her head up. "It's the hole at the other end that you've got to learn to keep closed, girl, not this one."

He dropped Sally's head and looked at Amber closely.

"You like girls? Own a few in your land, perhaps?" He slipped a hand under her shift and cupped her pubic delta. "Yes, you're warming up nicely. Well, you'll have to share a bed tonight, so I'll leave her cuffed for you. Make her squeal a bit if you want. She's here to be punished."

He had brought the long ruler from the station room desk. Now he positioned himself behind Sally, and laid it against the fleshiest part of her out-thrust bottom.

"Are you sorry for giving me lip, girl?" he asked.

"Yes, Constable Bailey, I'm very sorry."

"Do you beg to be taught a lesson?"

"Please teach me a lesson, Constable Bailey."

"Six of the best, then."

He drew the ruler back, then swung it hard across her bottom with a crisp smack. Sally's whole body jerked, shaking the bed, and her face creased with pain. A broad scarlet stripe appeared across her pale moons of flesh and the pouting lips between them. In her doubled-over position, her mound protruded level with her buttocks, and received their share of each blow. Amber found herself unable to look away. She didn't want Sally hurt, even to this relatively mild degree, yet she could not deny that the sight of her, naked and bound receiving her punishment was deeply exciting.

Sally called out: "Oww! My bum! It's too hard... please don't!" And she wriggled her bottom as far as her bonds would allow.

Despite her protests the second blow fell just as hard. Tears sprang into Sally's eyes. "Noo! It hurts, it hurts!"

The third stroke had Sally crying: "Please stop... I can't stand it... fuck me instead!"

Amber looked at the growing bulge in Bailey's trousers and thought that was going to happen anyway.

The fourth stroke: "Oww... use my bum if you like, but no more please..."   The fifth stroke: "Stick it up me, please!"

The sixth stroke: "I'm a bad girl! I'll do anything you want!"

Bailey managed one more stroke before the sight of Sally's gaping inviting cunt below her reddening bottom became too much for him. He threw aside the ruler and unbuttoned his flies, releasing a straining, purple veined cock of impressive dimensions. Clasping Sally's bobbing hips, he rammed it between her thighs and deep into her moist interior.

The bed creaked as Sally's hips lifted with the power of his thrust, her tear-rimmed eyes widening as the breath was forced from her lips in a gasp. Then Amber saw it followed by a quick smile of satisfaction. Aloud she cried out: "Thank you, thank you! Oh... you're so hard. Yes... as deep as you want... Aww... You're stretching me... You're making me come. I can't help it! Please don't stop..."

Bailey bent over her, his hips jerking as he spasmed, and Amber pulled futilely against her own bonds, desperately wishing she could join in. She could only imagine his bliss as he spent himself inside the perfectly bound and presented little tart, who was giving such a convincing display of orgasmic gasps and groans. At that moment she would have traded places with either one of them.

An hour later Amber and Sally were alone, both crammed into the cell's single narrow bed. Apart from a dim night light out in the corridor, all was dark and, except for distant snoring coming from the other two cells, quiet.

Bailey had been as good as his word, leaving Sally with a

parting smack on her bottom and her hands cuffed behind her back. So Amber had bathed Sally's sore bottom and tenderly washed out and dried her still puffy love lips. Now Sally lay under her expectantly, legs spread to allow Amber to rest between them. Their pubic bushes mingled, their breasts flattening together; pairs of hardening nipples pressing into soft pillows of flesh.

Amber had played a few bondage games before, but, as with the boys in the wood, this was different. Sally was a genuine prisoner temporarily at her mercy, neither of them had the key to her handcuffs, and they really were locked in a cell together for the night. It was undeniably exciting, and whatever tribulations tomorrow might bring seemed very far away. Amber gently kissed Sally on the forehead, then on the lips. Sally's mouth was warm and inviting, readily accepted Amber's questing tongue.

After a minute Amber lifted her head breathlessly.

"You really going to make me squeal like Bailey said?" Sally asked.

"Only with pleasure - if you want."

"Doesn't look as though I've got any choice," she grinned. "You go first."

Amber pulled her legs up so she straddled Sally's body, then shuffled forward until she could rest her arms on the iron frame at the top of the bed. She squatted down over Sally's head and lowered her hot, moist cleft onto her face. Sally eagerly nuzzled into her, tongue flicking out busily, licking her rim and probing deeper. The girl was good! Ahh! Sally had moved up to her clit and was working it into even harder arousal. She rode Sally's face, grinding herself into her, revelling in the sensation of the lovely girl trapped between her thighs. She came gloriously, soaking Sally's face with her exudation and almost smothering her between her love lips, so that she squirmed and gasped for breath.

When Amber had recovered herself, she slithered back down until she could kiss Sally gratefully, tasting her own juices smeared across her face.

"Now it's your turn," she said. "Suppose I start with the places Bailey didn't reach..."

She started to kiss her way slowly down Sally's body.

Fifteen minutes later, her legs doubled up so that her knees were almost touching her shoulders and with Amber's face buried between her thighs, Sally had her first genuine orgasm of the night.

16: Through a Skylight

The boys waited in their dormitory for Sister Newcombe to make her final round of the night. The conversation continued on the topic that had preoccupied them for most of the day.

"Look," Jackson said firmly, "if Old Bailey hasn't turned up by now it means she hasn't told on us. It's going to be all right."

"But she saw our faces," said Parsons, "and maybe heard our names. Why hasn't she told?"

"I've been thinking about that," said Jackson. "Remember that pouch of tools we found in her pack. Well I think they're burglars' tools - for picking locks and things."

"So the statuette thing was something she'd stolen?" said Harris.

"It makes sense."

"But why was she going around without any skirt or undies on?" Gosset wondered.

"Woman burglars wouldn't wear skirts," said Bickley. "Not when they're working anyway. They'd get in the way when they climbed through windows or up drainpipes."

"But they'd wear something," Gosset insisted. "Trousers at least."

"Maybe she caught them on some railing spikes, and had to take them off to escape," Parsons suggested, warming to the idea.

"I know - a guard dog tore them off while she was making her getaway," said Harris dramatically.

129

"Whatever happened," said Jackson, "that's why she hasn't told on us yet. She must guess we've got her bag and knows she'll be in even more trouble than she is now if Bailey finds out she's a thief as well."

"But how long will she keep quiet?" Parsons wondered. "It was because of us chasing her that Bailey caught her in the first place. If she finds out what we did to her wasn't quite proper, she may decide to tell Bailey about us to get her own back. She might hope it'll get her a lighter sentence."

"Maybe," said Jackson slowly, "she's hoping we'll do something for her."

As they mused on the possibility, Sister Newcombe entered briskly, neat as always in her starched uniform.

"Come on, boys. Time for lights out."

"Yes Sister," they chorused, removing their dressing gowns and climbing into their respective beds.

She waited until they were all tucked in, then said: "Get a good night's rest. There's still plenty of work for you to do tomorrow. Good night."

"Good night, Sister."

She turned out the light and closed the dormitory door. They waited until the click of her heels faded away, then Parsons whispered: "Are we going over the roof? She might do it again tonight."

"Goss and I are," said Harris firmly. "You three may have had enough, but we missed out on all the fun today, remember."

"We'll all go," said Jackson. "I can do it more than once a day."

Keeping the lights out they dressed quickly, putting on the old jumpers they had worn earlier over their pyjama tops and plimsolls on their bare feet. Going to one of the dark wooden panels that lined the walls, Jackson slid it aside to reveal a narrow gap between it and the underlying rough stonework. Amber's bag was folded into the bottom of this space, together with a home-made rope ladder and a bamboo pole with a hook at one end. Jackson removed these last two items carefully and replaced the panel.

Meanwhile Parsons had seen to the door at the far end of the dormitory. This opened onto the top landing of an external fire escape, which had been added to Cranborough House a few years before. Normally, opening the door would automatically sound the fire alarm, but they had discovered that a matchstick wedged into the switch built into the door frame immobilized it.

They climbed out onto the railed fire escape landing, wedging the door ajar behind them. The night was mild with only a light breeze blowing. In the distance were the scattered lights of Shaftwell, but the grounds at their feet and the rest of the school buildings were still and dark.

Their dormitory being on the second floor, the roof parapet was only some eight feet or so above their heads. Jackson unrolled the rope ladder, hooked the end of the bamboo around the metal bar to which the ladder was tied, and lifted it up to slide through the parapet balustrade. Once it was secure, they swarmed up, climbed over the low balustrade, and onto the roof.

There was a narrow walkway dividing the parapet from the pitched roofing over the attic rooms. They ran along this until they came opposite a large skylight that glowed with light. They scrambled up the heavy tiles and peered down through it.

Below was a small bedroom illuminated by a single ceiling lamp. It was spartanly furnished with an iron frame single bed and side cabinet, a single armchair and a dressing table with small ladder-back chair and three panelled mirror. A dark blue dressing gown hung on a hook behind the door. A circular rug covered the dark polished boards beside the bed, on which was laid out a modest white nightgown. It was in fact the room Sister Newcombe used when the school sickbay was occupied overnight and she had to stay on the premises.

Only a few seconds after they arrived, Sister Newcombe entered.

She took off her studious steel rimmed glasses and placed them on the bedside table. Their removal always made her look younger, causing the boys to re-appraise her familiar features.

Her eyes were a clear cool blue grey, set under dark expressive eyebrows; full by the bridge of her nose and rising to fine tails over the corners of her eyes. Her jet black hair was pinned up into a practical bun. She had a straight narrow nose and neatly pursed lips, with those faint slightly pinched lines around it characteristic of a determined character. Her chin was small but very firm.

Miss Newcombe slipped off her low-heeled sensible shoes and removed the broad uniform belt. She slowly unbuttoned the uniform and stepped out of it, revealing a silk underslip and dark stockings, and folded the uniform neatly over the back of the armchair. She drew the slip over her head and laid it by her uniform. Underneath she wore a bra, suspender belt and panties all black lace trimmed, contrasting with her pale silky golden skin. Her waist was trim, her navel deep and hips wide. She stretched and twisted for a moment, as though glad to be free of the encumbrance of her outer clothes.

On the roof, hands slipped into the folds of pyjama trousers as five young cocks began to rise in appreciation of the spectacle below.

Miss Newcombe sat on the edge of the bed, unclipped her suspenders and rolled down her stockings. They and the belt were laid neatly beside her other clothes. Her tightly filled bra was unhooked to release pale full breasts capped by pink nipples. She cupped and lifted her breasts for a moment, letting the air reach their undersides. They swayed heavily as she moved. Hooking her thumbs about the waistband of her panties she slid them down her legs. For a few seconds as she bent over, her pale full bottom cheeks, still marked with the imprint of her panties, were presented to her secret watchers. Then she stepped out of them and straightened up, revealing thick belly curls trimmed to a prominent oval thatch above bare pubic lips.

Quite naked, she sat at the dressing table, unpinned her tight bun of hair and shook it out in a cascade that fell halfway down her back. She examined her reflection critically in the mirror for a moment, then began brushing her hair with long languid strokes.

Out in the still darkness of the rooftop, five hands busily worked five poles of hard flesh.

Finished with her hair, Miss Newcombe idly drew the bristles of the brush lightly across her nipples, which immediately swelled and darkened, causing her to smile. She sat back on the chair, spread her legs, and gave the dark fluffy tangle between them a few light quick strokes.

On the roof the hands were working faster. There was a desperate stifled cry of: "Do it, do it!"

Miss Newcombe lifted the brush and rubbed an experimental finger up and down the fleshy furrow under her bush. Her eyes half closed and she ran the tip of her tongue around her lips. Very deliberately she reversed the hair brush and slowly slid the handle into her cleft. Its full length vanished inside her until only the head was visible, the lower bristles poking stiffly up between the plump lips of flesh.

Then, with it embedded in place, she tidied her dressing table, the brush head rubbing against her thighs as she moved. She stood up, examining her body in the mirror, giving the brush head an experimental tweak, then walked over to check her clothes were neatly laid out over the armchair, apparently unconcerned by the foreign object protruding from between her thighs.

She drew back her bed covers and rolled onto the fresh white sheets, laying her head on the pillow, her eyes closed. She pulled up her legs, bending her knees until her inner thighs were spread wide and the pouch of flesh between them gaped up at the watchers above like a swollen eye.

Taking hold of the hairbrush she began to pump it steadily up and down. The motion was slow at first, but it gradually increased in speed, the stiff bristles tickling and scraping the tender flesh of her cleft, which began to glisten with the exudation she was bringing forth. Soon she was panting heavily and driving the hairbrush into herself with almost cruel force.

Suddenly her stomach muscles tensed and her hips bucked

frantically. Gasping with pleasure, she clenched her thighs tight about the hairbrush, locking it into place inside her, and rolled limply onto her side.

On the roof above there were stifled groans, and fitful jets of milky fluid splattered the tiles; an impromptu tribute to the most popular matron ever to work at Cranborough House school.

17: Closet Masochist?

Save for the occasional rustling of mice in the thatch, the play-house was dark and silent. Sue had been placed in an upstairs bedroom for the night, and the four younger girls, under Arabella's direction, had made certain their new slave was still going to be there in the morning.

A rubber bar gag had been forced between her teeth, and tied behind her head. She was spreadeagled face down on the old-fashioned webbing underframe of a bed, her wrists and ankles cuffed and chained to the bedposts. In addition a long leather strap ran across the bed frame, crossing the small of her back and pressing her firmly down into the webbing. Her breasts had been squeezed through gaps between the lattice strips and hung heavily, her nipples almost brushing the dusty boards below. Under the place where her golden fuzz of pubic hair sprouted through the strips of fabric was a chipped enamel bowl, ready to catch her water if she had to pee during the night. But the worst indignity was the broom handle.

One end was tied over the footboard of the bed, while the other passed over her spread thighs, between her still flushed and scratched bottom cheeks and plunged six inches deep into her rectum. The slightest movement made her acutely aware of its hard, unyielding presence. Every so often her anal sphincter squeezed about it by futile reflex. It served both to plug her so she would not soil herself during the night and also as a re-minder that she had no control over the use to which the orifices of her body might be put. Arabella had told her that; smiling at the woebegone expression on Sue's face as the handle had been inserted.

After she had been left alone Sue had cried to herself for a while. Partly that had been due to natural disorientation. What had happened after she had used the phallus? It was no exaggeration that she had literally felt the earth move - or rather she had moved... somewhere. How long would it be before she was missed? Not until she was due back from holiday - a week at least. And when a search was started, would it have any hope of finding her? She didn't think so. She felt she was a long way from home.

But her tears had soon dried up as she realised her heart was not in it. She had every right to be appalled, angry and frightened by the incredible predicament she found herself in and the humiliations that had already been heaped upon her. The trouble was she could not sustain any of those responses for very long. Instead, as she lay on the bed, bound, naked and impaled, the insidious feeling crept over her that it was right that she should be where she was. It was perfectly natural to submit to the wishes of somebody with such a dominant personality as Arabella. How easy it would be to accept and embrace her degradation.

The orgasms that had been forced out of her had been the most intense she could remember. If she did not enjoy what was being done to her, why was that?

Then it came to her confused thoughts that she had once been in a similar physical position.

It had been an evening not long after the incident with the scissors. Dave had suggested they try anal intercourse for the first time. She had been apprehensive but he had kept on about it, clearly excited by the idea. He accused her of being a coward, and told her she would enjoy it if she tried. He'd begun touching her, and playfully trying to slide his hand up the back of her skirt, telling her she'd got a beautiful bum, and all he wanted to do was enjoy it properly.

She'd tried to pull away from him, but suddenly he wasn't playing any more.

He dragged her through to the bedroom. She'd genuinely resisted, but her struggles weren't that vigorous. For some reason the fight went out of her very easily when faced with another person's determined will.

This time he stripped her before tying her to the bed with a belt and some of her scarves. She was still protesting feebly, so he balled the remains of her pants into her mouth as a gag. He smeared moisturizing cream around her bottom hole as lubrication and then thoroughly sodomized her, his thick hard cock stretching her in ways she had never known before. Her anus clenched once again about the broom handle as she recalled her shock at the sensation. When he was finished he went down to the pub for a couple of hours, leaving her tied to the bed with his sperm slowly running out of her bottom hole; helplessly aroused but unfulfilled.

When he returned he did the same thing to her again, but more gently, arousing her with foreplay first, and so she finally managed to reach a climax. And he had laughed and told her that he had been right all along, and she had enjoyed it. And of course she forgave him - once again.

But secretly she knew that she should resent such treatment, that Dave was really a good-for-nothing shit. What he'd done to her hadn't been right. He should have accepted her refusal. She knew she seemed to fit the old cliche: the woman who said no when she meant yes, but she really had meant no at the time. The irony was that if Dave had simply been patient he would have won her round. In fact, if he'd really cared for her, he could have done anything he wanted to her. She was looking for love but the search was confused by her weakness for domination. She would probably still be with Dave now if his other failings had not eventually given her the courage to part from him.

But what would happen if she was subjected to such dominance systematically, by somebody who was an expert at training slaves, and where there seemed no limits to what methods might be used? She would protest and struggle against her treatment by reflex, by a sense of convention, but for how long? Was she really a masochist at heart?

Arabella boasted that she would break her totally in a week. Sue was afraid that she might be right, that she might become the helpless slave of this coldly calculating young woman.

Shivering and fearful, Sue tugged at her bonds, only to feel the broom handle impale her a little further. The sensation caused her to lose control of her bladder and she peed into the bowl under the bed. The trickle of water sounded very loud in the silent playhouse.

18: Night Ride

Arabella brought the holly switch down on Melanie's bottom once again, watching it jump and tremble. Here and there the glossy brown flesh was spotted with blood where the spines had torn it.

"Say I am your only mistress," she demanded, but Melanie would not answer. Such insolence, such defiance. She would break her! But instead she found herself licking the blood from those perfectly rounded buttocks and kissing them feverishly. Then she was nuzzling deeper into the cleft between them, tongue desperately probing. No, this was wrong. She would never lick a slave girl's anus!

Then Melanie was lying on her back, stretched out by chains, her cunt lips gaping in invitation. And Arabella found that she herself was now naked, and a hard phallus rose from between her legs and a feeling of tremendous power filled her. Now she would master her. She knelt between Melanie's widespread legs and thrust into her eagerly. But somehow she couldn't find her hole however many times she tried. And then somebody was holding her from behind, and there was a hard shape pushing up between her own buttocks, and she tried to struggle free, but she couldn't move, and somebody had picked up the holly switch and -

Arabella woke with a start.

137

She was in her own bedroom at Markham Hall. The bedside light was still on. The clock showed she had only been asleep for fifteen minutes.

Angrily she felt beneath the tossed bedclothes and withdrew the phallus she had taken from Sue. From her description of its effects she had expected something special, but instead it was cold and dead. She'd actually fallen asleep while trying it on herself and had suffered that odd dream.

Now she would have a miserable night. It was too late to have a girl sent up from the pack. In any case, much of the fun had gone out of it after her uncle had warned her repeatedly about maltreating them.

What was particularly frustrating was that she knew exactly what her uncle was doing at that very moment.

Major Havercotte-gore, dressed in nightrobe and slippers, entered a small chamber that opened off his bedroom and switched on the electric light, illuminating his new brown vixen mounted on the riding machine. He walked around her a couple of times, drinking in the delightful spectacle. She twisted her head as far as her restraints allowed, dumbly following him with wide apprehensive eyes from between the blinkers of her harness. Her teeth showed very white as they clenched about the bit that divided them. He patted her smooth flank reassuringly.

'There, there, girl. You'll soon get the hang of it.'

Melanie was supported by four lightweight tubular rods, rising vertically from slots in the top of a pedestal about a foot deep, four wide and six long. Sets of broad buckled straps secured the rods to the outsides of her arms and legs, so that she could not bend her elbows or knees. These held her with her legs bent at right angles at the hips, so that her torso hung parallel with the ground. In addition the leg rods diverged as they ran down to the base of the device, so that her ankles were spread a good yard apart. Her feet rested in stirrups bolted to the rods a few inches clear of the pedestal top. Set between and slightly behind her ankles was a low wedge-shaped platform, the top angled to face her. Beside this were mounted two long handled levers.

The Major checked Melanie's harness. Apart from the blinkers and bit she was wearing a chin brace. This was a curving tongue made of leather which enclosed a spring steel strip. It clipped onto her own collar and extended upwards, cupping her chin and buckling onto the big snaffle rings that lay against her cheeks. The brace helped support her head in the proper posture, but still allowed her to toss and turn it a few degrees. Reins ran down from the snaffle ring across the supple curve of her back then gathered together to pass through the cleft of her buttocks and hung loose between her thighs.

He ran a hand along the gentle undercurve of her belly, noting the tensing of strong muscles under the soft skin. He cupped her freely hanging breasts, delighting in their warm weight. Large glossy conical nipples, almost maroon in colouring, began to fill at his touch.

He passed round to her rear, and faced the glory of her flawless brown bottom perfectly presented to him. He always thought a girl's buttocks were her most expressive features after her face. So much could be read into them as she moved. The degree of roll could indicate insolence or invitation, they clenched with excitement or trembled with fear, they stretched and swelled as she bent over or mounted stairs. They were the blank canvass on which an owner could leave his mark, whether it was a pattern of lash marks or an imprint such as the one which even now surmounted Melanie's bottom. Gazing at it the Major felt a deep sense of pride and satisfaction at seeing the Markham crest on the skin of such a rare beauty.

And between the fleshy hills there was a dark canyon to explore, holding within it secret delights that only the privileged might enjoy. He lifted the reins aside and gently pried her buttocks apart so that the dark rose hole of her oiled anus glistened in the light. He ran his hands downward, savouring the special humid warmth between her thighs. He tickled the sooty flesh of her swelling cunt pouch, heavy with its own special rewards, bringing forth a shiver from the girl. But it was not that orifice he was going to enjoy now.

"Now, Melanie. Tonight you are my pretty filly. Very shortly I will mount you, and you are going to take me for a ride. You will find this device allows you a certain degree of movement. Push forward with your arms as though you are were trying to straighten your body and you will find out."

Obediently she did so. The rods bracing her legs were mounted on simple pivots, so they would only rock a little way forward and back in their short base slots. The mounts of her arm rods, however, both pivoted and slid forward, running along slots over two feet long. He watched in approval as she pushed her upper body forward, her back dipping, until her arm rods reached the rubber stops at the ends of their slots.

"You feel the resistance of the springs inside the base block?"

Melanie nodded her head.

"They will give you something to work against, and help you regain your starting position from maximum extension. I can adjust the tension with this lever. Now, you will move at three speeds on command. A walk, a trot and a gallop. The second lever here adjusts stops in the forward slots to control the rhythm and length of your stride. You have eight inches of movement for the walk, fifteen for a trot, and maximum extension of thirty for a gallop. I will alter them as required. All that need concern you is to obey your commands quickly and gracefully. When I pull on your reins, you will slow, of course." He gave them a tug, causing the bit to pull at her mouth. Then he took down a riding crop from a hook on the wall and flicked it lightly across her flank. "I will use this only when I want extra effort from you, then you must give of your best."

Melanie nodded again, shivering slightly.

"Good girl. I want to see a good show." He indicated the full length mirrors resting against the walls of the small room in front and to either side of her, tilted so that he could see her face head on or view her side and flanks from his riding position.

The Major removed his robe and hung it up. He was naked

underneath, his manhood already standing rigidly to attention. He might be going a little grey, and have a few varicose veins, but he was still capable of responding properly to the prospect of riding a beautiful woman.

He took up his position on the platform behind Melanie so that his erect prong of flesh lay in the groove of her buttocks, and gathered her reins.

"Walk," he commanded, selecting the first position on the stride lever.

Melanie began to rock gently to and fro, deliciously massaging his erection between the inrolling curves of her buttocks. Slowly he adjusted his position so that his cockhead butted more deeply into the warmth of her cleft, nuzzling her bottom hole each time her hips swayed back into his lap. He felt her tense, and said gently: "Easy, girl. Keep the rhythm. You know you can take me inside you. The probe showed what a fine deep hole you have."

He pressed forward, feeling his foreskin being gently rolled back as his cockhead began to stretch open her anal ring. Half an inch, one inch, two... In a minute the whole head of his cock was being swallowed then expelled by her dusky pit at every stride. He adjusted the control and said: "Trot!"

He leaned forward with her as her arms slid that extra few inches, and allowed her to ram herself back onto his cock. She gave a little choking gasp as his entire length slid inside her. He let her take more of his weight, adjusting the resistance of the springs to compensate, while savouring the bliss of being totally enclosed by the hot tight tunnel of flesh. As he moved within her, he could feel the play of powerful muscles swelling her backside as she obediently maintained her stride. Inches from his face he could see her shoulder blades moving under the skin of her back, and pinpoints of sweat forming in the hollow of her spine.

Looking up he saw her face reflected in the mirror, teeth bared around her bit flashing white against her dark skin, eyes half closed in concentration, as though she was pacing herself.

In the side mirrors he saw the delightful picture of her heavy breasts swinging in time with her stride, nipples now starkly erect.

Reaching out he threw the levers all the way forward for maximum stride and spring tension.

"Gallop!" he commanded, and bent all the way over her, his cheek brushing her thick pony tail of black hair.

Almost his entire weight bore her forward and down, her arm rods thudding into the stops, then rebounding with the force of the springs. She bore him on magnificently, her face contorted with determination, straining to hold the gallop, even though each stride was ramming him up deeper inside her, his balls slapping against her pubic nest.

What a ride she was giving him!

As he felt the supreme moment approaching he gave her straining flank a couple of flicks with his crop, then reached under her to clasp her heaving breasts; squeezing and pinching, lifting them forward, urging her on to one last effort.

"The last furlong!" he cried in her ear.

Melanie managed to thrust forward twice with a final surge of strength before he spouted inside her, his body jerking to its own rhythm, his feet pressing on the angled platform as he pounded against her straining, sweat-streaked buttocks. Gradually his mount rocked to a standstill as his own spasms diminished, breath rasping about her bit. He lay still across her back, hot full breasts still clutched in his hands, savouring her warmth and the clean smell of her sweat, knowing she had to support him for as long as he cared to remain coupled to her.

The clenching and wriggling of Melanie's buttocks roused him. He looked into the mirror to see her eyes were wide and pleading. She was panting not just from the effort she had expended, but from need. Evidently she had been highly aroused by the ride, but had not managed to come before him. Utterly unable to touch any part of herself, she was pleading for relief.

"Does my pretty filly beg a favour from her master?" he

asked.

She nodded her head frantically, whining from behind her bit.

"A finger to tickle her hot little cunny, perhaps?"

She nodded again, humiliated to beg perhaps, but evidently too desperate to care.

"As a reward for a memorable ride, then," he said, running a hand down her belly and into her dripping furrow. He worked her hard bud until she shuddered and groaned, and her discharge wet his hand. He watched her face as she climaxed, and once again felt deeply privileged to own such an exciting and sensuous creature.

19: Working Girls

Morning came to the girlpack yard of Markham Hall.

With a jingle of keys, Alison released the master locks on the bank of kennels.

"Rise and shine, girls," she called out brightly.

Small barred doors were pushed open, and seventeen packgirls, wearing only their collars, crawled out of their tiny sleeping cells. The coconut matting filled with a press of naked bodies, as shapely limbs were stretched and tousled hair was shaken out. Under Alison's watchful eye, they pulled out their blankets and bedding rolls and hung them neatly on the racks opposite. Then in a chattering file, urged along by light flicks of her switch across their bottoms, they passed through into the washroom.

Bells rang in the long narrow sunken-floored potroom behind the wall of the girlpack's ablutions, as numbered buttocks were thrust through the row of small hatches. The head pot boy ran along the line briskly sliding the bolts that locked the girls into place, then stood back to watch as streams of pee hissed from between the lips of their pubic pouches and tinkled musically into the buckets. They were only allowed to pass water on

143

their first visit of the morning. The busy time would come later.

As the streams became drips, he worked his way long the line tearing paper from the dispensers over each seat and wiping the girls dry. Mr Platt was very firm about matters of hygiene, and the boy was thoroughly familiar with the care and functioning of that part of the female anatomy which was his special concern. He took care to press the paper well up into their soft warm cunts and wipe firmly backwards, making sure each was completely clean before she was released. When each was done he pulled back the bolts and sent them on their way with a pat on their rumps, and sometimes a quick pinch and tickle. Then the next set of girls took their places and the process was repeated.

When they were done, the girls crawled out through the flap in the outer door into the exercise yard, and formed up into ranks, shivering slightly in the fresh early morning air. Alison stood before them.

"Hands above your heads and stretch," she commanded. "You can do better than that Molly... now to the sides... and down..."

After five minutes of vigorous bending and stretching, they lay face down for twenty press ups.

"Remember they don't count unless both nipples touch the ground," Alison said. "All together: up and one.... up and two..." Breasts began flattening on the cold brickwork.

When they were done, Alison exchanged her switch for a long carriage whip and she started the pack on laps around the perimeter of the yard.

Through the window of his office Platt heard the slap of bare feet on brick, and looked out with satisfaction on the procession of bouncing breasts, rolling firm-packed buttocks and swelling thighs as it passed by. Even as he watched, Alison flicked the long carriage whip across the yard in gentle warning, laying the tip across a pale bottom.

"Pick your feet up Zoe, there's a good girl!"

Zoe obediently increased her pace to keep up with the rest of the pack. You've almost got it Alison, Platt thought. But if only you could get that extra bite in your tone they wouldn't need tickling with the whip in the first place.

Wheeled wicker baskets began to arrive in the yard and were taken through to the kennel room. Platt went over to check them.

Curled up on blankets within were the girls who had been entertaining guests the previous night, together with any restraints or appliances that had been requested with them. They emerged stiffly, some still bound and gagged and bearing traces of the passions they had aroused. Platt examined them to ensure they had suffered no misuse and to confirm they had given satisfaction.

"Quickly now girls," he said as they stumbled towards the washroom to relieve themselves. "Morning inspection in a couple of minutes." He held Melanie back momentarily, slipping an exploratory finger up her rear. "I trust you pleased the Major last night girl," he said.

Melanie could only blush and mumble: "I... think I did, Mr Platt."

Alison had the rest of the pack, panting and flushed from their exercise, lined up in three ranks in the yard by the time the other girls joined them and found their places.

"Twenty two girls all present, Mr Platt," she reported. "None sick."

Almost back up to strength, Platt thought. Twenty four prime specimens was the ideal pack size. He knew the Major was hoping to pick up the last two in a few daysí time. He smiled at Alison. "Stand them ready."

"Stand ready for inspection," Alison called out

Obediently the pack stood erect with their feet apart so that their toes almost touched, and clasped their hands behind their necks so that their thumbs rested on the upper rims of their collars. Silently, Platt walked along the ranks, looking them up and down, noting the steady rise and fall of their chests, watching forty four nipples crinkling and stiffening both in excitement and trepidation as his eye passed over them. Twenty two different-hued triangles of pubic hair proudly displayed at the apex of swelling thighs, all trimmed back to expose glistening lips protruding from their mossy furrows. Then he returned along the back of the lines, inspecting the row of full, strong, deeply cleft backsides, pinching a couple of buttocks and feeling hard muscle tense under the soft, smooth flesh. That was what he strove for in his girls: a delicate balance between strength and beauty.

"Very good," he said, when he had completed his inspection. He consulted his clipboard. "Work list for the day. All girls who were entertaining last night rest in the pound for the morning. Heavy harness for the rest of you. Numbers one to seven to the gardens. Eight to twenty four: put on flat soles. You'll be hauling branches in the woods. Breakfast in five minutes, then half an hour to wash and harness up. Dismissed."

Melanie found breakfast laid out in the kennel room on the same numbered bowls as the previous day, and again they lined up kneeling in two ranks to feed. Even though their hands were free no one used their fingers, instead eating the chopped egg, bacon and toast compressed into bite-sized balls by delicately picking them up between their teeth as they were accustomed. Several girls made a show of licking the last of the egg yoke from the bowls like dogs.

Breakfast finished the girls scampered back to the washroom. Now bowels loosened by exercise could be emptied. A helper had joined the pot room boy, carrying buckets to the sluice and filling fresh ones. The head boy was kept busy servicing his charges, moving quickly up and down the row of captive yet demanding bottoms, framed between the toilet hatch doors like living sculptures. Hoses were pushed into freshly wiped holes to flush them perfectly clean, bringing forth the usual squeals and gasps from the other side of the wall. Finally, an oil can with a narrow rubber tip was inserted and a measured amount pumped into rectal passages, so they should be ready for whatever use they might be put to that day.

The showers were turned on and soon soapy flesh glistened

through steamy air. Girls who had entertained guests the previous night told of their experiences as they washed.

"....he fell asleep while he was still inside me. My hands were tied to the bedhead, so I had to lie under him all night - and he snored."

Or received sympathy for unusually hard treatment.

"She was pinching my nips all the time I was sucking him off. They're nearly raw... look."

Jill and Gail squeezed their dripping bodies up beside Melanie as she washed herself in silence and looked at her expectantly.

"Well, how did it go with the Major?" Jill asked.

"Yes, was he pleased with you?" Gail added. "I bet he was. He likes girls with nice strong bums."

Melanie stared at them in confusion. How could she discuss something so intimate when she hadn't begun to reconcile her own feelings yet? Despite the virtual demolition of her sense of normality the day before some inhibitions still lingered.

Gillian, who was showering on the other side of her, spoke up: "You don't have to say anything, but we all know what happened. Most of us have been on his riding machine before. I remember how hard it was to talk about that sort of thing when I first came here - even if these two don't because they were born without any shame."

The two girls grinned and stuck their tongues out at her.

"They're only asking," Gillian continued, "because if the Major is content, so is Platt, and he's a bit easier with us. So you see it's not just curiosity, it's self interest."

Melanie managed a smile. "Well... I think he was pleased with me," she admitted. "Afterwards he even... never mind. It was fine."

Satisfied, Gail and Jill departed to dry themselves off and Melanie looked hesitantly at Gillian. After they'd been released from their intimate bondage the previous afternoon there had been no opportunity to talk in private, or at least such privacy as packgirls ever had.

"About yesterday," Melanie began, "what we did together..."

Gillian said quickly: "Don't worry about it. We did what Platt and the Major wanted us to do. If we hadn't they would have cropped us until we obeyed, so we really hadn't any choice. Maybe we should be more like Jill and Gail. They don't seem to mind what they do and actually enjoy themselves most of the time."

"Thanks for saying that," Melanie said. "I feel better now."

Gillian stepped out of the shower, picked up her towel, then turned back to Melanie with a shy smile. "Actually it was fun, wasn't it?" She bit her lip. "And you taste lovely," she added, and hurried away.

The pack milled about their lockers, combing and drying damp hair and tying it back into pony tails or plaits to keep it out of their eyes while they worked. Then they began putting on their boots and harness according to Platt's instructions.

We're preparing ourselves for bondage, Melanie thought as she pulled on her boots with the wedge heels and buckled them tight, yet it seems so routine. The girls who were to work in the woods put on knee boots with thick flat soles, so they could walk upright. Their working harnesses were clearly designed to spread any loads over the whole body. They were made of broad flat rings of leather which lay across the shoulders, bearing two large rings: one hanging over the sternum and the other between the shoulder blades. Pairs of heavy straps ran from these rings down between the breasts and across the back to fasten to a very broad padded belt which buckled tightly over the hips. Large hitching rings hung on either side of this belt.

Their tails, hanging on hooks with the rest of their equipment, went in next. Some girls were reaching behind themselves and slipping them in easily, while others were doing it for each other. Melanie tried but somehow couldn't get the right angle. She saw Gillian looking at her. Without a word she handed her the tail and turned her bottom to her. Gillian deftly slipped the plug into her and wriggled it comfortably into place. For a second her hand slipped between Melanie's legs and brushed across her cleft. Was it accidental - and did it matter if it wasn't?

Gillian gave Melanie her own blonde-haired tail and turned her bottom to her in turn. With trembling hands Melanie inserted the plug end into the tight sphincter and drove it all the way up until the tail bobbed above Gillian's pale buttocks, still marked from yesterday's lashing. Unconsciously Melanie's fingertips traced the line of a raised weal, then dropped aside.

Gillian turned back to her and, smiling, offered her hands to Melanie so she could put on her paws for her. Melanie did so, fumbling slightly as she buckled them into place. Alison, who had been watching over them, fastened Melanie's paws in turn.

"The Doctor will be coming to check you over this morning," Alison told her. "I'll be taking you to the examination room later."

The pack was properly harnessed. Melanie and the other excused girls went to the pound, while the rest went back through to the yard. Alison leashed the girls chosen for garden work and led them out of the stable court, around the side of the Hall and through a side gate to the sheds and greenhouses. Here she handed them over to Mr Wainwright, the head gardener, who soon had a couple fastened between the shafts of barrows hauling newly dug weeds to the compost heap. The others were chained to the traces of the large garden roller, the seat of which Wainwright himself would take to steer them carefully around the Hall's broad lawns; spending a pleasant morning riding behind three pairs of straining thighs and taut backsides.

Meanwhile Platt divided the rest of the girls into three groups, cuffed their hands behind them, and fastened their harnesses to wooden crossbars trailing lengths of heavy chain. In the company of a couple of groundsmen, he led them off towards the woods.

The Markham Hall pack had been put to work.

"Amber Jones," the Clerk of the Court intoned solemnly. "You are charged with illegal entry into this country, being without a passport or any identifying documents, being without gainful employment or having sufficient lawful funds to support your-self independent of trade, being without fixed abode, vagrancy, unlicensed public exposure of the person, and finally assaulting a police officer, namely Constable Bailey, during the execution of his duty. How do you respond to these charges?"

Shaftwell's tiny courtroom was adjacent to the town Hall. The sessions had begun at nine o'clock. The two drunks Bailey had brought in the night before had already received fines and been bound over to keep the peace for three months. Now it was Amber's turn before the bench. She was standing in the tiny wooden-railed dock, dressed only in her flimsy prison shift, her hands cuffed behind her back and a chain running from her collar to a padlock on the railing. Bailey was taking no chances on her escaping from custody.

"Look, I came here by accident and didn't mean to break any of your laws," she said, trying to sound reasonable. "And I'm very sorry for kicking the constable."

"Ignorance of the law is no excuse," said Major Havercotte-gore from his position of eminence on the judge's bench.

"Can I claim extenuating circumstances?" Amber asked hopefully.

"We shall decide that," said the Major. "A response of Not Guilty shall be recorded. Constable Bailey, will you please take the stand..."

Bailey gave an account of his encounter with Amber on the Boxley road and her arrest, confirming the details in his written report. He mentioned Sister Newcombe's sighting in the woods as likely corroboration of Amber's story of masked abductors. As there were no other witnesses and the basic facts were not in dispute, Amber was then invited to speak for herself before sentence was passed. With a sinking feeling she realized she could not escape some sort of punishment, but it was not in her nature to go down without a fight.

"For a start I challenge the charge of vagrancy. If it means the same as where I come from, I am certainly not idle or normally disorderly. I'm perfectly willing to work if given the opportunity. And when I kicked the Constable - which I'm really sorry for because I know he was just doing his duty - I was not being disorderly. I was still shocked by what had happened and wasn't thinking straight and reacted in panic to a strange situation.

"As for being without a fixed abode, I was arrested when I had been in this country less than an hour, so I could hardly have found a place to stay so soon. You cannot assume that I would not have done so, had I been given the chance.

"And if 'exposure of the person' means I was starkers from the waist down, then that was certainly not by choice. I would have covered myself up if I could, but as the Constable will confirm my hands were tied behind my back at the time, so I can hardly be held responsible for that.

"As for not having a passport or identity papers, that's simply because I didn't mean to come here. If I had, do you think I would have come as badly prepared as this?"

The Major had been looking at her with a slight smile, as though impressed by her spirited defence. He now said: "The fact remains that you have entered this country by some irregular means." He consulted Bailey's report. "Your explanation seems a little vague. Can you give us any more details?"

Amber hesitated. She didn't want to say any more about the 'statuette' both for personal reasons and in case her bag containing it and the lockpicks subsequently turned up, leading to further awkward questions.

"No. Sorry."

He frowned. "Have you anybody who will speak up for you, or confirm any other part of your story?"

"No."

151

"Do you know anything of another stranger who appeared in mysterious circumstances on my estate yesterday - a woman evidently of African descent?" He said in an aside to the court recorder: "She sensibly volunteered for bondservice, saved a lot of fuss. I have filed the papers on her."

Amber kept her face straight and tone exactly level. "You mean a black woman? No, nothing."

The Major conferred with the Clerk of the Court in whispers for a few minutes, then he turned back to Amber.

"The charges of vagrancy, being without fixed abode and unlicensed exposure will be set aside. The more serious charges of assault and illegal entry cannot be ignored, despite your apology and plea of mischance. I suspect you are not telling us all you know about the manner in which you came here. However, I am satisfied you intended no deliberate harm by your actions.

"I direct Constable Bailey to pursue the men who waylaid you on the matter of harbouring and failing to report an illegal alien."

"Not rape?" Amber said.

"If they caused you unreasonable physical injury during the process, you could bring an action against them on those grounds. Do you wish to make such a charge now?"

Amber sighed. "Don't bother."

"Very well. Meanwhile, I am glad to know you are willing to work, because that is what you will do. I sentence you to six months bondservice to follow an open auction. This to take place after serving three weeks in the public pillory, and ten lashes for the assault on Constable Bailey."

"Ten lashes!" Amber said, aghast. "Just for a little kick. That's not fair!"

"And another five for speaking out of turn and questioning the judgement of this court."

Amber choked back her next retort and subsided into numbed silence.

The Clerk stood up and said: "Amber Jones. Being of suitable age and fitness, you have been sentenced to licensed public servitude and shaming. Your rights of self determination are hereby revoked. You may now be freely subjected to all duties, functions, restraints and punishments permitted under the Female Public Servitude Act."

And with that, Bailey stepped up to Amber and stripped the shift from her, leaving her completely naked. Even though she knew it was coming her sudden exposure numbed her mind. This can't be happening! she thought.

The occupants of the public gallery looked on with interest. A couple of ribald comments were made about what they would do to her in the stocks. Shivering, though not from cold, Amber tried to shrink down below the railing, only to have Bailey pull her straight by the hair.

"Now you'll learn to behave, girl," he told her.

An official brought over a numbered red enamelled metal collar similar to Sally's, and it was exchanged for her temporary police issue one. It felt very heavy about her neck.

As though in a dream, Bailey led her out of the building and down the street, receiving looks of mild contempt or covetous appraisal from passers by, who took in every detail of her body. There was nothing she could do to stop them. The public humiliation had begun. The image of the pony girls pulling the vicar's carriage came into her dazed mind. Now she was properly licensed to satisfy the vicar's sense of propriety, was that how she would end up?

Miss Newcombe cycled up the Hall drive, through the archway of the stable court and dismounted nimbly. Wheeling her bike, she made her way through to the pack yard where she knocked on the door of Platt's office. Alison answered.

"Good morning, Miss Chalmers," Miss Newcombe said briskly. "Doctor Gideon is rather busy today, and, as I was passing the Hall anyway, he asked me if I could check your new girl over for the records."

"That's very good of you, Sister. I've just put her in the Examination Room. If you'd follow me."

153

Melanie, wearing only her collar, was standing beside the examination table, her hands cuffed over her head to a bar suspended by a chain from the ceiling.

"My, we don't usually see many girls of her colour outside the cities," Miss Newcombe observed, putting down her medical bag and unclipping her cape. "Very striking."

"I think she's going to be one of the Major's favourites, even though she's an outsider." Alison confessed. "He's going to time her on the track this afternoon."

"Well I'd better do a thorough job on her then. I'll call if I need anything."

Alison departed and Miss Newcombe began the examination; testing the joints and muscles of Melanie's arms and legs with practised hands.

"Don't worry, girl. This is just a routine check for your records. What is your name, by the way?"

"Melanie Kingston, Miss."

"And apparently you're an outsider."

"Somebody called me that. I don't really know what it means."

"They're usually young women who appear from nowhere in a confused state. They tell odd stories about coming from an England with very different ways than ours."

"That's me, then. Parallel worlds or something science fictional. I don't really understand."

"It must be difficult - especially if you've left people behind who will miss you."

"There's nobody special, but I will be missed soon. You see, I'm in the police force. I had a few daysí leave owing..."

As Miss Newcombe checked Melanie's eyes, ears and throat, ran a stethoscope over her chest and pushed a thermometer up her rear, she poured her story out. It was easier talking to a nurse - another professional in a uniform who was used to receiving confidences.

The external examination concluded, Miss Newcombe unclipped the ceiling chain from the cuff bar and had Melanie sit on the examination table. She swung her legs around and began to strap them into the stirrups.

"Must you do that?" Melanie protested.

Miss Newcombe smiled coolly and finished securing them anyway. "You are a bondslave, and it is convenient that I strap you down for the purposes of examination." She took hold of the cuff bar, pulled it over Melanie's head and fastened it to the top of the table. The tension made Melanie's back arch, lifting her breasts. "It is the way things are done here."

She snapped surgical rubber gloves on and inserted her fingers into Melanie's gaping vagina. After a minute she withdrew and said: "No trouble there." A finger slid up Melanie's anus, causing her to shiver. "Or there," the nurse said, after feeling around. "I would say you are in perfect health. The Major will be pleased." Her cool grey eyes narrowed thoughtfully. "How do you feel in yourself?"

"Confused," Melanie admitted in a small voice. "I've only been here a day, but it seems like forever. Everything is so much more real, more intense. I can't believe what's happened. The things I've done..."

"You're appalled but also stimulated, despite yourself," Miss Newcombe diagnosed, a knowing smile playing about her lips. "Even your position right now excites you. I can see you're lubricating and your nipples have risen. You know anybody might walk in and see you like this, perhaps even touch you, and you would be absolutely helpless to stop them."

She had stripped off her rubber gloves, and now she ran her bare fingers through Melanie's wiry black bush, then over her quivering stomach to squeeze a heavy brown breast.

"The Major won't begrudge me a little feel," she assured Melanie as she pinched a hard nipple. "After all, you are a fine piece of female flesh, here to be appreciated and enjoyed."

Melanie closed her eyes and shook her head.

"Don't fight it," Miss Newcombe said, bending over her so Melanie could feel her warm sweet breath on her cheek. "You must learn to let your true feelings through. Perhaps you belong

155

here after all. At least you're better off than the other outsider right now."

Melanie's eyes blinked open. "Who?"

"Another woman arrived here in mysterious circumstances yesterday. She also had an encounter with an oriental box. She was in court this morning, and at midday she's going be lashed in the police yard."

Grasping the cell bars for greater leverage, Bailey drove his hard swollen prick deeper into Amber's hot grasping cunt and watched her face contort once again as the force of his thrust drove the breath from her. The chains of her wrist and ankle cuffs rattled as she was lifted off her feet, the flesh of her buttocks bulging through the bars as she was ground against them. He withdrew a few inches and she slid back down, tossing her head and gasping for breath. For a moment her eyes locked with his. They were wide both with raw animal desire and lingering anger. An interesting type, he thought as he rammed into her again; half fighting it, half loving it, rather like Sally Potts. She'd never be tamed, but she could be taught a lesson.

Then he came, pulses of sperm blossoming within her. She gasped raggedly as her backside was drummed rapidly against the bars in time with his spasms.

He rested his weight against her for a few seconds, enjoying the resilient warmth of her captive body and the rasping of her breath, before he pulled out of her and rebuttoned his flies. Her head dropped onto her heaving chest and she sagged forward, her wrist cuffs sliding down until stopped by a cross bar, leaving her hanging from her upward stretched arms, her trembling legs splayed wantonly apart, knees bent. He smiled at the glistening swollen lips of her cunt, framed by a tangled nest of brown hair. Slowly fluid began to drip from the bottom of her cleft onto the stone cell floor.

She raised her eyes to him, needful and angry. He had finished before she had come herself. Well there would be other opportunities. For the next three weeks he had sole charge of her. He grasped her hair and pulled, so that she had to struggle upright.

"That's the first lesson, my girl," he told her. "Bondslaves are for use - whenever and however needed, not for their own pleasure. Understand?" She tried to nod, her hair still in his grasp. "My job is to soften you up, see, so that when you go for auction your new owner gets value for money. But before that you're going to give a lot of pleasure to the local folk. People like to see somebody worse off than themselves; somebody they can take out their little frustrations on. It's the only entertainment some of them can afford. And it all starts at twelve with your flogging - and I'm going to make sure you put on a good show."

He poured a mug of water from the jug in the cell and held it to her lips. She was thirsty and gulped it down gratefully. When the mug was empty he refilled it and offered it again. Frowning she drank it more slowly. At the third mugfull she turned her head aside.

"Thank you, I've had enough - ahhh!"

He had pinched her right nipple between thumb and forefinger and twisted.

"It don't matter whether you want it or not, girl. You'll drink it because I tell you!"

With tears in her eyes she forced the water down, almost choking over the last mouthfuls.

"That's better," he said, consulting his watch. "Now it ís about time I was taking you outside."

He released Amber from the bars, clipped a leash to her collar and dragged her into the front office, keeping her head low so she had to shuffle along in a crouch. From a cupboard he took out a pair of wide cuffs, padded inside with felt and bolted to the ends of a six inch steel bar with a heavy ring welded to the middle. The cuffs were locked by wing nuts which Bailey tightened until Amber's wrists were clamped immobile before her.

Similar cuffs, with loose rings dangling from them, were fastened about her ankles. He pushed a hard rubber bit between her teeth and tied its cords behind her neck.

"You'll need something to bite on," he explained, "unless you want to risk your tongue or cracking a tooth." He saw her nipples were standing up in thick rounded cones, looking very large against her neat breasts. He flicked them sharply until she squirmed. "Getting excited, are you? Thinking of all those people outside waiting to see you get a smacking. Some girls can't help make an exhibition of themselves. Well you've come to the right place for that."

He led her out into the punishment yard. There was the sound of a gathering crowd coming from outside the gates. Sally, splattered with multicoloured mud, was restrained in a pillory in a corner of the yard. She flashed Amber a sympathetic smile as she was dragged across to the whipping stand.

A gibbet-like frame was mounted on a raised wooden platform, dangling a hook and chain from its outstretched arm. Below this was a box which Bailey stood on, pulling Amber up beside him. He lifted her arms above her head and passed the ring of her cuffs over the dangling hook. He stepped down from the box and pulled it out from under Amber's feet, leaving her swinging and kicking in mid air, supported only by her wrist cuffs.

"That's a pretty dance, my girl," he observed, "but I need you to keep still if I'm going to hit the target."

He grasped her flailing legs and pulled them apart, picking up chains bolted to the top of the platform and snapping them onto the rings of her ankle cuffs. Then he stood back to admire his handiwork.

Amber now hung in an inverted 'Y'. Her straining arms lifted her breasts, and their hard tipped nipples, high. It stretched the skin taut over her ribs, framing the soft swelling pad of flesh about the her navel, which rose and fell tremulously. The tendons at the back of her knees stood out as she pulled against her ankle chains. Her toes wriggled and curled tight. And all to no avail. She was absolutely helpless and perfectly presented for her punishment.

"Right, open the gates," Bailey called out to old Tom Soams, who had been sitting in his usual chair beside the crates of pillory shot.

The crowd paid their money and surged into the yard, pressing against the rails surrounding the whipping stand on three sides jostling to get their preferred vantage points. Some to see her rear as the blows fell, others to watch her face as she reacted to them.

Bailey removed his jacket and rolled up his shirt sleeves, then mounted the platform. He was carrying a three foot length of narrow springy cane. He took up position beside and behind Amber, careful not to obscure the view of the crowd, and rested the cane against Amber's back, as though to measure his swing. The crowd became very silent, tense with expectation. Amber stopped struggling and screwed up her eyes.

Bailey drew back his arm and swung. There was a swish and then the sharp ringing crack of compressed female flesh as the cane struck just under Amber's shoulder blades, the tip curling around her ribs. A red stripe appeared on her clear skin. She managed to stifle her cry of pain. It hurt, but it was not as bad as she had feared.

The second stinging blow struck where her waist was narrowest. Again Amber controlled herself. It was no harder than the first.

After a half a minute five almost parallel stripes crossed her spine, decorating her back like animal markings. Amber began to relax, as far as her position allowed. She'd get through the ordeal without making a peep. That would show them.

Then the sixth blow fell squarely on her buttocks, this time driven by the full force of Bailey's brawny arm. It was as though a red-hot poker had been laid across her skin.

Amber screamed from behind her bit in sudden agony and jerked convulsively, her back arching in reflex, thrusting her hips forward. And, just as Bailey had planned, the shock made her lose control of her very full bladder. A clear jet of urine burst from between her cunt lips and splashed onto the platform.

The crowd laughed and cheered the degrading discharge. This was what they had come to see: the thorough shaming of a pretty young woman.

Amber tried to hold back the flow as the seventh blow fell. She lost control again and more water spurted out. It was as though Bailey was driving the pee from her. By the tenth stroke she was past caring about her dignity, too preoccupied with the fire burning across her arse cheeks. So, as the weals multiplied across her bottom the pool between her splayed legs spread.

By the time the last blow was delivered Amber's rump had become one continuous blotch of scarlet, as blatant as any baboon's, criss-crossed with deeper red and purple lines. The crowd applauded Bailey, while Amber hung limply from her aching arms, breathing raggedly around her gag, her eyes wet with tears. Dazedly she realised how cleverly Bailey had used her, revenging himself for that kick and reminding her once again of her utter helplessness.

Bailey dragged the whipping stand round on its casters so that Amber faced the crowd square on.

"Right, ladies and gentlemen," he announced. "I'll leave her up here for an hour. You'll never get an easier shot at her."

Coins clinked into old Tom's palm as the crates of shot rapidly emptied.

Amber had just managed to blink her eyes clear as the first missile smacked wetly into her smooth stomach and burst, sending a bright red stream trickling down into her pubic hair. The stinging impact was mild by comparison with the blows of the cane, but she still squirmed at the sudden spray of cold mud across her flesh. If only, she thought despairingly, a little could reach her burning bottom!

"As a matter of fact, I judged another outsider girl in court earlier," Major Havercotte-gore said lightly, as he finished lunch. "Two appearing in one day must be something of a record for any county." He didn't notice Arabella's sudden start and then the look of intense interest she directed at him from the other end of the dining table.

"But how do they get here, that's what I want to know," one of his house guests said.

"Who cares?" another opined. "They don't do any harm, and seem to make rather good bondservants. Tried one out myself at Charnley's place a few months ago. Very eager to please and quite delightful."

"This one was as vague as all the rest on how she arrived here," the Major said. "Bright creature though, spoke up for herself well. I gave her to three weeks in the pillory and six months servitude. I might bid for her myself if I haven't got the pack up to strength by then."

"When will we be able to see this girl of yours run?" the first asked. "And is she really as fast as you say?"

The Major smiled. "She was certainly nimble enough when she tried to escape from us yesterday. Depending on her trials this afternoon, I might put her in the hunt. I'll certainly be showing her at the Ball."

Arabella had been silent through this exchange, thinking hard as though in two minds about something. Now she spoke up with uncharacteristic meekness.

"May I watch her run, Uncle? And you can tell me more about this other outsider at the same time."

The rest of the girlpack had returned to their work, leaving Melanie alone in the grassy pound with Una, who was keeping to herself in the far corner of the yard. Melanie had noticed a few suspicious bruises on Una's back when they were eating lunch, and suspected some other members of the pack were taking their revenge on her for past ill-treatment. Melanie knew she would have to reach some understanding with Una sooner or later, but for the moment she was preoccupied with her own thoughts.

According to Sister Newcombe another outsider girl had appeared at almost the same time as she had. It had to be Amber Jones. She had escaped her only to suffer much the same fate as her own, it seemed. How ironic! She was in jail and Melanie could do absolutely nothing about it. But should she tell anybody what Jones was?

Her speculations were interrupted by Platt, the Major and Arabella entering the pound. Melanie quickly rolled onto her knees and assumed the sejant position, wiggling her bottom to set her tail wagging. Una did the same. A tingle of anticipation passed through Melanie as she watched the Major approach. The man who had ridden her, the first man to broach the virginity of her anus, the man she had begged to masturbate her. What did he plan for her next?

Una shuffled quickly forward and rubbed her cheek against his leg, and he patted her head and ruffled her hair in return. Instinctively Melanie copied Una's gesture and received the same attention. She told herself she was just doing it out of self interest to keep the Major happy. That of course did not entirely account for the unexpected warm glow his touch kindled within her.

"And how is my pretty brown vixen this morning?" the Major said, smiling down at her with kindly eyes. There was no sense of him gloating over his mastery of her the previous night, just genuine interest and appreciation. Melanie said nothing, but smiled and wagged her tail harder. Una glared at her angrily.

"Sister Newcombe came in to check her over, sir," Platt said. "Says she's in perfect health."

Arabella was giving her the same impatient, hungry look as she had the previous day, but this time tinged with annoyance. "She seems to be learning fast," she observed.

162

"Yes, she's a bright creature," the Major agreed. "Let's see how she does on the track."

Platt unlocked the rear gate of the pound and they passed through into the paddock beyond.

The paddock was ringed by an oval four-lane grass running track, slightly banked at each end. Inside this was a sunken garden laid out as a miniature assault course. Low wooden footbridges crossed over the obstacles and linked the opposite sides of the track.

They halted by the trackside and Platt said: "Tails." Una bent over, legs spread, paws resting on her knees, presenting her bottom to Platt. Melanie copied her and Platt quickly removed their tail plugs.

"Boots," Platt ordered.

Shadowed by Melanie, Una rolled onto her back and extended her legs into the air, clasping her arms behind her knees to support them. Of course, Melanie thought, no owner bends down to remove a slave's footwear when she can raise them conveniently to him.

When their feet were bare, Platt said: "Training halters."

Una and Melanie scrambled upright and stood with their arms lifted and pawed hands folded across the backs of their heads. From a bag he was carrying Platt produced items made of broad black straps and cord woven into a one-inch mesh. As her halter was fastened about her, Melanie felt her breasts lifted and squeezed by the mesh until they stood out proudly and firmly from her body. The broad shoulder straps and a secondary flat ring collar spread their weight with surprising comfort, even better than her sports bra, though they did nothing to conceal them. She trembled momentarily as Platt automatically tweaked her nipples to check they were protruding freely through the surrounding mesh. At least there was no danger of them chafing, she thought ruefully.

When both girls were kitted out, they were positioned on staggered starting lines chalked across the running track, with simple wooden starting blocks placed behind them. There was a curious arrangement of waist-high posts set on the side of the track beside each starting point, linked by wires and pulleys to a lever mounted on a small plinth. Each post carried a long hinged arm which could be swung out to reach the appropriate lane. Mounted on the end of each arm was a flat strip of thin wood, like a long ruler, glistening with bright blue paint and connected to some kind of spring arrangement. Below it was a small curving piece of tubing that ended in a rising tip that pointing up the track.

The mechanism's purpose baffled Melanie until she saw Una, crouching down on the blocks, calmly back herself against the tip of the curving arm. Platt rested a hand on the small of her back and guided a couple of inches of the arm tip into her bottom hole. With a sinking feeling, Melanie grasped the function of the devices, even the wet paint on sprung strips of wood. Of course, if the dignity and comfort of the runners was not important, they made perfect sense - and it was one way of checking there were no false starts. With a sigh of resignation, she took up position on her own blocks and allowed Platt to impale her as he had Una. The tip inside her felt like greased rubber, and unlike her tail plug, was tapered so it would slip out easily.

The Major took up position by the control lever and spoke to them. "You will both run one circuit as fast as you can, do you understand?"

They both nodded. Una looked across at Melanie, a cold smile on her lips. This is where I show you who's the best, she said without words.

Platt had taken out a large stopwatch, while the Major positioned himself by the trackside lever. Melanie looked only at the track ahead. Despite her humiliating stance she felt quite calm. This was a test she understood. She would show them how well she could run. Her nipples, she realised, were hard with anticipation.

The Major jerked the lever, releasing the starting bars which smacked across their bare buttocks, imprinting stripes of blue paint on them. Bottom holes contracted, expelling the probes

164

that had held them in position. Thigh muscles swelled under cream and brown skin as they sprang off their blocks. Taut breasts bounced within the tight mesh of their halters.

Una was lean and strong and used to the strange starting arrangements and running on grass. Melanie was used to synthetic tracks and advanced running shoes. Una was also running her hardest to make a point. She crossed the line half a yard ahead of Melanie, but from the look she flashed her it was evident she had hoped it would be more.

Platt was showing the Major and Arabella the time he had recorded as they returned to kneel before them.

"A fast time. Competition standard," the Major exclaimed, beaming and twirling his moustache. "With both she and Una on the team, perhaps we may be in for a place at the games this year?"

"Could be, sir," Platt agreed. "I'd like to try her again to be sure."

The marker paint was wiped from their bottoms and the start was set up again. But Melanie was beginning to get the measure of the conditions and there was nothing to separate them as they crossed the line the second time. On the third run they were directed to make four circuits of the track. Una fought hard but Melanie came in two clear yards ahead of her.

Melanie jogged to a halt, breathing heavily but feeling joyously alive.

To run virtually naked, unencumbered by clothing, exposed to the flow of air across her skin, to feel the ground under her bare feet, suddenly seemed perfectly natural. Even the sting of the starting bar played its part, giving that extra thrill of anticipation to the race. Was the mild pain stimulating the production of her body's natural hormones, such as adrenalin, that bit sooner? Whatever it was, she felt wonderful, and gave a surprised Una a quick hug. "I'm actually beginning to enjoy this," she whispered.

For the first time, Una smiled back uncertainly in return. "You're fast," she admitted grudgingly.

"You're no slouch yourself."

Even the cautious Platt looked down at Melanie with approval as she and Una knelt at their feet, sheened in sweat and breathing deeply. "Excellent time, Sir," he said. "Una improved on her own personal best as well."

The Major beamed and patted their heads.

"So she did, but Melanie is going to be the champion on the track," he said.

"Are you going to try her out on the hunt course now, Uncle?" Arabella asked. "I want to see what her endurance and agility are really like."

"It's always the hunt with you, Arabella," the Major said.

"It's the real test of a girl's character. But we saw her run in the rough yesterday. Suppose we make it more of a challenge. A tail plugging chase, say, with Una as prey. Melanie can run with her paws off as compensation."

The Major nodded. "That might be interesting. Fetch a pricker, George."

While Platt went back to the harness room, the Major removed

Una and Melanie's halters and Melanie's paws. They were allowed to splash their faces over and drink from the small trough at the side of the paddock. Melanie flexed her fingers. She had no idea what they intended.

Platt returned carrying something she had no time to make out, because the Major said: "Melanie: spread!"

She assumed the position quickly, staring up at the sky trembling with anticipation, but unsure of what would happen next. Platt knelt between her widespread thighs. She gasped as he pushed a plug with a long stem into her anus, even as something larger parted her labia and slid into her. It was some sort of phallus, tapered so that the automatic contraction of her vaginal muscles tended to pull it deeper. She looked down at herself. She was now wearing a seven inch black rubber dildo, secured in place by the plugs inside her that extended from the lower end of its shaft and angled together. The device was rampant, standing erect and close to her lower belly.

"Stand," the Major commanded, and Melanie obeyed cautiously. The dildo even had false testicles attached to its root that swung realistically between her thighs, while the ribbing on top of the shaft teased her clitoris as she moved. It was so absurd she had to suppress a giggle. What must she look like!

"Una will have a ten second start, and you must follow her route exactly," the Major explained. "The chase will end when you plug her rear."

Melanie blinked at Una, but the other girl showed no surprise at the objective of the race. Evidently it was just another way slave girls entertained their masters.

Platt led them down to the start of the obstacle course, while the Major and Arabella looked down from the footbridge that spanned the sunken garden. As Una stood ready she flashed Melanie a fierce proud smile, as much as to say: You won't catch me this time.

Platt slapped Una on the rump and she dashed off, leaping the first of a set of low wickerwork fences gracefully. Melanie took her place, her eyes on Una's tawny buttocks as she scampered away. Platt counted the tenth second, another slap, and Melanie was away in pursuit, the dildo bobbing absurdly in front of her.

The three wicker fences were close set, allowing only a stride between them. As she landed the dildo bounced and the head slapped against her stomach. It was terribly distracting. She misjudged her stride and scraped her inner thigh on the last fence, banging the false testicles swinging below it. How did men manage? She stumbled as she landed and splashed through the water jump that followed instead of clearing it. Una was two obstacles ahead of her and moving easily. Determinedly Melanie leaped and ducked through an array of poles, ran across a narrow log over a mud bath and zig-zagged through a closely set clump of shoulder high besom 'bushes', that scraped and grazed her flanks and bare breasts. Una was still pulling away from her. Melanie crawled through a two foot wide pottery pipe, scraping her knees and elbows. Beyond was a five bar gate too high to jump which had to be half climbed and straddled over, which she did, catching the dildo yet again. She scampered over trunk-stump stepping stones and dived under a net crawl, her breasts flattened on the ground as she squirmed through: driving the large plug deeper into her cunt and making her feel as though she was trying to plough the ground! She scrabbled up and over a sequence of humped earth banks and dashed past the Major and Arabella on the footbridge, completing her first circuit.

But Una was already half way round her second. She must have run this course many times and knew every twist and turn. Melanie gritted her teeth. The only way to catch her was to wear her down by sheer persistence. She would not give up.

Besides, the bobbing dildo was beginning to excite her, despite its inconvenience. She began to feel motivated in a way she never had before.

Round and round the two girls went, breasts bouncing with every stride. The mild afternoon grew warmer as the clouds became sparser in the sky. Sweat ran from their bodies, plastering their hair down to their heads and dripping from their pubic curls. For eight circuits Melanie made no impression on Una's lead. Gradually they both began to tire. Melanie no longer tried to jump the water, but splashed heavily through it. Her throat was raw, her whole body ached. She was scratched and grazed all over. But she was determined not to give up. The base of the dildo was wet with her juices. Slowly she began to cut down Una's lead, and her eyes fell more often on Una's dancing buttocks and the deep dark cleft between them. There lay the reward for her exertions and relief from the knot of pleasure tightening low in her stomach. But she had to catch her soon or else she would orgasm while she was still running.

On the fifteenth circuit Una slipped off the log bridge and landed in the mud bath below with a splash.

She scrambled unsteadily to her feet and remounted the log with a tremendous effort, but she could not get a grip with muddy feet and paw-sheathed hands, and had to crawl the rest of the way over, losing precious seconds. She was only at the besom thicket when Melanie stumbled across the bridge. Una was dragging herself out of the pottery pipe as Melanie entered it. She half-fell over the five bar gate, leaving muddy smears on its rails, as Melanie pounded up. She stumbled over the stepping stones with Melanie, equally unsteady, only yards behind. They were both under the crawl net together, Melanie reaching out trying to grab Una's scrabbling feet. Una staggered up the first of the earth banks, sinking onto her hands and knees. As she crested the top, Melanie made a desperate lunge, caught hold of her ankle, and together they rolled down into the hollow beyond in a tangle of trembling limbs.

Melanie came out on top, grasping the back of Una's neck and pushing her face into the grass. She heaved Una's long legs wide, kneeling across their backs as she pried apart the firm, dirt-smeared, sweat-streaked buttocks to expose the dark crinkled pit of Una's anus. Unhesitatingly she hunched over and guided the tip of the dildo against it, then thrust with her hips.

Una gasped as she was stretched and penetrated by the rubber intruder. Melanie slid her arms under Una's body and lunged again, using the girl's rear as a fulcrum to work the plug ends of the dildo back and forth inside herself. She grasped Una's breasts, squeezing and kneading the fleshy hemispheres. Through the mounting waves of pleasure she realised she was riding Una almost as the Major had ridden her. And Una was responding - pushing her bottom back to meet her thrusts. It felt like a perfectly natural culmination of their chase. What better prize could there be than this?

She climaxed in an explosion of intense pleasure and blissful release, then slumped exhausted across her prey.

For a minute neither girl spoke. Una's hot sticky body lay limply under Melanie's, and she could feel the thudding of her heart. For a moment Melanie was assailed by guilt at the thought of the outrageous thing she had done to the girl. Then slowly Una twisted her head and looked her in the eye.

"Best... out of.. three?" she panted hopefully.

Melanie began to laugh, still gasping for air. She had never

169

felt so alive. Una joined her. They clung together: two vital young women elated by the shared joy of intense physical exertion.

Dimly they became aware of hands clapping. The Major and Platt were standing over them, the Major applauding, Platt nodding in silent approval, Arabella's eyes drinking in every detail of their coupled bodies.

"Bravo!" the Major exclaimed. "Don't know when I last enjoyed a pursuit as much. Two splendid runs by two gallant bitches. What sport you're going to give us this summer."

Hearing his words of heartfelt praise Melanie found a glow of satisfaction spreading within her. Here sex and sport were one - raw, uninhibited, simple and intensely rewarding. Here her ability was appreciated without reservation, her skin colour a curiosity, nothing more. Had Sister Newcombe been right? Was this where she belonged?

22: A Private Inquisition

Sue had spent the morning on her hands and knees scrubbing the floorboards of the playhouse. Blinkers and bit assured her silence and concentration on the area of floor immediately in front of her. A rod, running up from the ring in the middle of the bar that kept her ankles spread, plunged into the deep cleft between her fleshy buttocks, replacing the broom handle that had occupied her rear passage the previous night. Not only did it prevent her from straightening up to ease the ache in her back, but every time she moved the buried rod worked back and forth, reminding her she no longer had any control over what was inserted into her most intimate places.

Arabella had found an old oval galvanised bucket, designed for dunking long mop heads, which she had chained by its handles under Sue's chest. It meant Sue's large breasts were never less that half submerged in increasingly dirty water. Grimy tide marks began to ring the pale heavy globes, and she had to scrape the brush past them each time she dipped it into the bucket. To move she had to straighten her arms and lift the whole bucket, setting the water lapping at her bobbing breasts. One further humiliation grinding down the few remaining shreds of Sue's instinct to resist. How much easier to accept that this was her rightful place, to submit totally and utterly.

By the time Arabella returned to the playhouse it was mid afternoon. She was in an impatient mood; wanting to oversee the next stage in Sue's training personally, but with other matters on her mind.

"Right," she told the girls briskly, after inspecting the results of Sue's cleaning, "This afternoon you will see how slaves can be used for games. Bring her out into the garden and wash her down."

Sue was released from her harness, taken outside and put under the garden pump. Meanwhile Arabella took a mallet and four stakes from a sack she had brought with her and hammered them into the grass in a square. A heavy coil spring and leather cuff were fastened to each stake. Sue, still dripping from her dousing, was spread-eagled on her back between them.

"Secure her right arm and left ankle first," Arabella directed the girls, "then let the springs stretch her out... that's better."

Sue was staked out in a cross; taut, pale and vulnerable on the grass, eyes wide, the wedge of golden curls between her legs glistening. Arabella looked down on her and felt a warm swell of delight within. What a lovely creature to master and possess. What trials and delights she still had in store for her!

Arabella took out a thin black bakelite face mask from the sack. It had fully contoured features, but it was only pierced through at the nostrils. A wooden pin some six inches long protruded from its hard lips like a fat cigar. On the inside of the mask's mouth was a rubber ball gag. This she forced into Sue's mouth, securing the mask in place with wire loops that hooked around Sue's ears.

171

"Now she's blindfolded," she explained to the fascinated girls, "she will not be able to anticipate what is happening, so her responses will be more pronounced."

She brought out two more wooden pins, this time fitted with coiled springy wire cones about five inches across at the base. These she began screwing onto Sue's soft breasts, bringing forth whimpers from behind the face mask. Arabella continued, forcing folds of pale flesh out from between the turns of wire, until Sue's breasts were fully enclosed and squeezed into upthrust cones and the pins stood up from them like parodies of enormous nipples. Lastly Arabella drew out a pin attached to a dildo by a swivel joint. At either side of the joint were a pair of heavy, wide-jawed spring clips. Holding the clips open, Arabella knelt between Sue's spread thighs and slid the dildo into her, closing the clips on her plump outer lips to hold it in place. Sue's hips jerked and there came a muffled yelp from behind her mask. Arabella adjusted the pin until it stood up vertically, like some strange growth erupting from Sue's golden pubic bush.

Arabella stood up and took out a dozen flat wooden rings from the sack.

"Now she's ready for hoopla. A living target is so much more fun to play with."

She stepped back a few yards and tossed a ring at Sue. It fell neatly over her mouth pin, striking the hard mask with a rattle and making Sue jerk her head back in alarm.

"She doesn't know when you're going to throw or at what pin, so she's very alert."

She threw another ring. It caught the pin rising from Sue's right breast, setting it bouncing to and fro as it spun about it, pinching the rolls of flesh trapped between the coils of wire, before dropping down over the tightly-bound mammary. Arabella's third shot clipped the top of the cunt pin and struck Sue's smoothly rounded stomach, leaving a slight red graze.

"She might pick up a few minor bruises during the game if you miss the target," Arabella said, taking aim again, "but nothing serious. They only show she's being fully used."

Her fourth ring caught the cunt pin firmly and dropped down to hang between Sue's thighs. The pin trembled on its fleshy mount as Sue's buttocks twitched and squirmed on the grass and a squeal came from behind her mask.

"Of course hitting the target can also be painful for her," Arabella observed with a smile, "but she must learn to get used to it."

She handed the remainder of the hoops to the girls. "You might paint some numbers on her beside the pins for scoring. There are many other target games you can play with slaves. They're useful practice for real hunts. If you're good I might let you join one someday. Now, have fun with her. Belinda, come with me. We're going to the village."

Jackson rested amongst the lower branches of the poplar tree on the edge of the little copse beside the police station road. From there he could see not only the inside of the station's punishment yard, but also the side door of the building and the barred windows on the cell block. With the stub of a pencil he sketched the layout in the back of his pocket diary.

He was not the first to make use of this convenient vantage point. The bark on the branches around him was polished by the bodies of local boys who, with catapults and pea shooters, had over the years added their own private torments to the legally sanctioned sufferings of the yard's occupants. Jackson could also see Amber and Sally bound to a pillory frame, but with an effort he ignored their naked bodies. He had more immediate things on his mind.

The sketch completed, he climbed down and brushed the smudges of mould from his trousers. Now if the others would only follow the plan through properlyÖÖ...

"Hallo, Anthony," came a familiar voice. "What are you doing here?"

He spun round guiltily to see Miss Newcombe wheeling her bike towards him over the little patch of grass that skirted the trees.

173

"Uh... I was just going to the tuck shop, Sister," he blurted out. "You said we could as long as we were getting on with our work properly."

"So I did, but this isn't the way to the tuck shop, is it?" She raised an eyebrow. "Unless Constable Bailey has started selling sweets in the police station yard." She smiled coolly at the look of consternation that crossed his face. "You'll have to learn to tell a more convincing lie to fool me. You wanted to see the girls in the pillory, didn't you?"

Jackson swallowed and then nodded dumbly. To his surprise her smile softened.

"I would have been angry if you'd tried to deny it. Don't worry, you won't get into trouble. It's quite natural that you're curious. The girls are there to be looked at and shamed, and you're seventeen; old enough to appreciate them."

Jackson managed an embarrassed smile.

"But you'd better be careful," Miss Newcombe continued sternly. "This is just the sort of behaviour that got you and your friends into trouble before. If you're going to spy on girls at least do it sensibly..." Jackson went very still, acutely aware of his burning cheeks. Fortunately Miss Newcombe seemed not to notice. "... and be ready to take the consequences if you're caught. If you want to indulge in adult pleasures, you have to take adult responsibilities. Do you understand?"

He nodded again. "Yes, Sister."

Her penetrating grey eyes flashed at him, and she appeared suddenly thoughtful. "You know, I think I should talk to all of you properly about this sort of thing."

"About what, Sister?"

"You know what I mean, Antony; sexual desires and preferences. Not merely simple biology, but more complex subjects as well. I was meaning to raise the matter with the Headmaster next term. I think sixth formers should leave school with a better understanding of certain facts of life. It might avoid much misery later. What do you think of the idea?"

Jackson was spared the need to reply by the sight of Arabella

Westlake and Belinda Jenkins making their way briskly along the road. The two girls did not notice them standing under the trees. Miss Newcombe watched them pass as well, and raised an eyebrow as they turned into the police yard gate.

"Now I wonder what she wants in there?" she murmured, half to herself. She glanced at Jackson. "You don't care much for Arabella Westlake, do you Antony?"

"No, Miss Newcombe," Jackson said with feeling.

"Well I'm sure she'll get her comeuppance someday. That sort always do."

Inside the yard gate, old Tom Soams protested feebly. "But I'm not supposed to leave the yard while the Constable's out, Miss."

"It's almost the end of the afternoon session," Arabella said impatiently. "Close the gates early."

"Don't know if I can do that, Miss," Tom mumbled. "It's me job to see folks get a fair go at the girls."

Arabella scowled. "How many pillory shots have you got left... a box and a half? I'll buy them all." She produced a note from her pocket. "Here's a pound, and you can keep any change. Now, you might as well close because you've got no shot for people to throw. It'll only be for ten minutes - twenty at the most."

"Well... put it that way, Miss." Tom took the note. "I suppose I could go back home for a cup of tea. As long as the girls aren't left unattended."

"They won't be," Arabella promised.

Tom slipped out through the gate and closed it behind him. Arabella and Belinda walked over to the pillory device that held Amber and Sally.

The platform on which Amber's pillory rested was built on a rotating mount. A beam projected from one side with a pony collar bolted to its end. This collar was strapped over Sally's shoulders, confining her to her hands and knees and forcing her to follow a circular path around the platform, turning it as she crawled along so every aspect of Amber was presented to her tormentors. Each rotation caused a counter attached to the base of the platform to click over, keeping a record of her efforts and ensuring she reached a set quota.

Sally was forced to hold her head high by a gag connected by twin chains to a spring fastened to a rubber rod embedded in her anus. The upper end of the rod, held aloft by the tension of the spring, flattened into a thin disk about six inches across that stood out from Sally's buttocks like a tail. The disk, like the twin hills of flesh below it, was well splattered with shot. Every missile that struck it would have twisted the rod painfully within Sally's tender interior as well as giving her gag a sudden painful tug.

As Arabella and Belinda approached, Sally shuffled to a halt uncertainly, allowing them to inspect Amber.

Amber was bent forward at right angles from her hips across the middle of a six foot long horizontal plank supported at each end, with her arms outstretched sideways and secured by wrist straps. Her breasts dangled through two holes in the plank and were secured by a figure-of-eight double noose of wire strapping that pinched them so tightly that they ballooned out below it. Despite her posture Amber's head was held high. She had no choice in this as her chin rested in a groove in the top of a wood block screwed to the front edge of the plank. A ball gag filled her mouth. Her ankles were clamped in a second plank chained at each end to the platform, so that they were spread a good yard apart. This forced her to hold her legs straight and thrust her bottom out. Mounted on the platform between her legs was a sprung rod ending in a fan-like blade of rubber with a serrated edge. This had been positioned to nestle between her labial lips. An accurate pillory shot would make it sway to and fro, scraping and stimulating the fleshy slot.

The villagers had taken full advantage of this tempting target, and her buttocks and thighs were well plastered with pillory shot, the most recent still dripping from her tangled pubic wick. Her face and imprisoned breasts had received almost as much attention, and her hair was a caked mess. Only her eyes shone out bright and clear from the mask of mud.

Arabella walked around the pillory thoughtfully and the imprisoned girls looked anxiously back at her. Then she said to Belinda: "There's a tap and bucket in the corner. Fill it and bring it over."

As Belinda obeyed, Arabella took off her jacket, hung it carefully on a hook in the wall, and rolled up her shirt sleeves. Taking the bucket from Belinda, she stepped up to Amber and threw the contents into her face. As Amber snorted in shock, Arabella gave the bucket back to Belinda for refilling. The second load she threw over Amber's hindquarters. Muddy water streamed away over the platform and onto the bricks of the yard.

"That's better," she said, putting the bucket aside. "I couldn't see what sort of creature we had under all that mud." She stepped onto the platform, grasped Amber's mop of short wet hair and twisted her head from side to side, examining her closely.

"Yes, quite attractive really," she pronounced. She pulled the gag from her mouth. "What is your name, girl?"

Through numbed lips Amber said: "Amber Jones."

Arabella slapped her cheek. "Amber Jones, Miss Arabella Say it!"

"Amber Jones... Miss Arabella," Amber choked out.

Arabella reached down and cupped Amber's taut, mud-streaked and constricted breasts in her palms and kneaded them expertly, feeling her nipples begin to swell. Then, looking Amber straight in the eye, she transferred her grasp, pinched each hardened bud of flesh between her nails and twisted. Amber gritted her teeth, stifling a gasp of pain, and returned Arabella's gaze.

"You're a determined one," Arabella said. "It would be such fun breaking you in. Maybe later."

She released Amber's nipples and stepped round to Amber's side, drawing her fingers down the hollow of her spine, then reaching under her to feel the swell of her belly which tightened at her touch. Moving round further she stood between Amber's spread legs and ran a hand between her thighs, stroking the damp

177

tangle of her pubic hair. Amber stiffened. Arabella worked the fan blade of the teaser to and fro a couple of times, then pushed it aside and

slid a forefinger into Amber's slit and began to work it about the fleshy grotto within. After a few seconds it had warmed and become slick with an oily exudation. Amber tugged at her restraints and gave a tiny throaty gasp.

"Belinda, stand before her and describe the expression on her face," Arabella commanded.

"Her eyes are half closed... she's chewing her lip with her front teeth... and she's breathing fast."

"Would you say she's enjoying herself?"

"Yes, she is."

Arabella shook her head, still working her finger back and forth inside Amber. "It's always the same with you jail sluts," she told Amber. "You take more pleasure than pain from your exposure, however you're shamed. The pillory is too easy. I think we should be stricter and more direct." She gazed down at Amber's bottom cheeks, which still displayed the scarlet weals of her public lashing. "At least Bailey did a thorough job there. Still tender, I suppose?"

She suddenly withdrew her teasing finger, clasped handfuls of buttock flesh in both hands, dug her nails in hard and twisted. Amber yelled out loud.

"Do you want me to find out just how tender?" Arabella said.

Amber, caught off guard by the sudden switch from pleasure to pain, choked out quickly: "No, Miss Arabella!"

"Good. Because there's a question I want to ask, and if you do not wish to learn how much more pain I can inflict, you will answer it promptly and truthfully. Do you understand?"

"Yes, Miss Arabella."

"Then tell me how many of you outsiders came here yesterday?"

"Uh... the Magistrate said something about another girl in court. I don't know about any others."

"But might there be more? Four of you, perhaps?"

"I really don't know, Miss Arabella. Honestly!"

"Do you think she's telling the truth, Belinda?" Arabella asked her companion, who was still watching Amber's face.

"Well, every time you squeeze her bottom you can see the tears in her eyes. I think she's too afraid of what you might do to her to lie."

"Very well." Arabella released her hold on Amber's abused flesh. She stepped round to Amber's head and rammed the ball gag back between her teeth. "We should leave her as we found her. Bring that open box of pillory shot over here, Belinda."

Amber watched anxiously as the box was brought over. Arabella selected one of the wrapped balls of soft mud and pushed it firmly into Amber's face. The wrapping burst, releasing a sticky blob of yellow tinted mud, which she worked well in as Amber snuffled and screwed up her eyes. Arabella then ran her muddy hands through Amber's hair until it stood up in spiky ridges.

"Two more please, Belinda," she said, smiling at Amber's discomfort.

These she pressed against Amber's pinioned breasts until they also disgorged their contents, leaving one hanging mammary thickly smeared in bright red mud, the other in green.

"Nipples still hard, I see," Arabella observed as she worked the mud in. "You really are a hot little slut. You'll get excited over anything."

Arabella walked round to Amber's rear, followed by Belinda with the box of shot. "A blue bottom, I think," Arabella said.

She rammed the shot into the cleft of Amber's buttocks against the pucker of her anus, where it burst and oozed sensuously out from between the firm moons of frantically clenching flesh. She smeared each cheek with streaky lines, then stepped back to admire her handiwork.

"Good. But she's still too clean down there."

She cupped a shot ball in her palm and rammed it up into Amber's bush. Amber gasped as her outer lips were parted and some of the syrupy thick mud squirted up into the channel of her vagina.

"I think we've found a new sport," Arabella said. "Another shot, Belinda."

Amber bucked her hips frantically, but she could not prevent Arabella grinding a second shot into her, pinching her thick swollen outer lips closed about it so that some more of its contents was driven upwards.

"Can I have a go?" Belinda asked.

"Of course," Arabella said with an approving smile. "That's right, force it into her. Fill her passage. Don't mind the noise she's making. She's here to be punished, and there are a lot worse things she could have put up her than nice clean mud."

Amber's back was dipping and arching, her knees flexing, turning inward and outward as far as the ankle block allowed. She was being driven to a frenzy of arousal and resentment at the stimulation she was being forced to endure. But the hands pressed up into her burning cunt, rolling her labia and clitoris around and around as they drove more of the cooling, maddening, mud inside her.

With a convulsive shudder Amber spent herself, her contractions expelling a thin stream of mud and shreds of paper from her gaping nether lips to splatter onto the platform. Then she slumped in the pillory frame, knees splayed in ungainly fashion, chest heaving, eyes closed in her mud-caked face.

As Arabella wiped her hands over Amber's naked hips, she said: "I'll try to persuade my uncle to bid for you when you come up for auction. Then we can try this again."

They stepped off the platform. As Arabella passed Sally she slapped the disk on the end of her tail rod, bringing forth a muffled grunt of pain.

"Lazy slut - keep her turning!" she commanded.

Sally began shuffling round once more.

Arabella and Belinda washed their hands under the yard tap. Arabella put her jacket back on and they left, looking as prim and proper as when they entered. Half a minute later Tom Soams slipped back into the yard. He checked the imprisoned girls over quickly, retrieved the box of shot, and, with a sigh of relief, resumed his regular seat.

23: Plans in the Dark

The springs of the riding frame creaked under Melanie's straining body as the Major, his cock embedded deep within her bottom, rode her at a gallop.

"That's it, girl... the last furlong... ahh!"

His hot sperm filled her bowels, even as she reached her own climax. They shuddered and bucked together, then slowly rocked to a halt.

For several minutes he lay across her back, still coupled, savouring the animal warmth of her body and idly fondling her freely hanging breasts. Then he said: "You know, my dear, the day after tomorrow is the last hunt of the season with the hounds. After your fine performance today I think you could run as a vixen. Platt agrees with me. Normally I wouldn't put an untrained girl up so soon, but I think you're an exceptional case. But I'm allowing you the choice. If you doubt you're up to it, I won't force you. Well?"

Melanie hardly hesitated. A hunt had to mean more uninhibited running of the kind she had done that afternoon, and she desperately wanted to experience that joyful sensation again as soon as possible. She nodded her head with a jangle of harness. The bit in her mouth made speech difficult, and in any case she knew he preferred a mute response.

"Splendid," he said, stroking her hair. "I was sure you would want to. Tomorrow I'll take you round the woods so you can learn the lie of the land, and explain the rules of the hunt. You understand I want you to give my guests the best of sport. You won't let me down, my pretty Brown Vixen, will you?"

She shook her head firmly. She felt excited, wanted, valued, happy. Somewhere through the day her inhibitions had simply melted away. It was all outrageous madness, of course, but she didn't want it to end.

She also felt the Major's cock hardening inside her once more. He cupped and squeezed her breasts encouragingly.

"Do you feel up to going for another canter?" he asked.

She smiled as well as her bit allowed and nodded.

The bedroom of the playhouse was lit by the soft shimmering light of a single oil lamp. The mattress webbing creaked as the half moons of Arabella's naked bottom rose and fell over the apex of Sue's spread thighs as she lay on her back, wrists and ankles secured to the bedposts. From under the bed came a regular scrape of wood caused by the end of the broom handle working an inch or so backwards and forwards over the floorboards. The handle itself rose up at a shallow angle through webbing and, as on the previous night, stopped Sue's bottom hole.

As Arabella fucked her, Sue dutifully repeated aloud the words she had been taught: "I am your slave - use me, Mistress... I have no other desire but to serve you... my body is yours to do with as you wish..."

With a grunt and spasm of rapid hip thrusts, Arabella orgasmed, and then lay limply across Sue, breasts flattened against breasts, mats of pubic hair intertwined. After a minute she lifted herself off Sue, withdrawing the glistening shaft of the thick double-ended dildo she was wearing from between her slave's cunt lips.

Arabella's body was slender but full-hipped, her stomach taut, her buttocks firm. Her breasts, capped by nipple-cones of flushed pink, were heavy but neatly rounded, and they rose well from her shapely ribcage. In the soft lamplight her skin was creamy golden. Sweat shone on her breasts, stomach and thighs from the fleshy friction with Sue's body. She unbuckled the supporting belt and withdrew the other end of the dildo from herself, filmed with her own exudations which darkened the narrow line of honey-blonde hair that fringed her deep cleft.

She had kept her calf-length boots on while enjoying Sue.

Now she slipped on a soft white shirt and ankle-length skirt. Over these she threw a dark hooded cape. As she was tying it in place she looked down at Sue, who was following her movements with wide pleading eyes but tightly pressed lips. She had already learnt when to speak and when to be silent.

"I finished before you had a chance to come yourself, didn't I girl?"

Sue nodded desperately, straining to lift her tightly bound body towards her for the final touch that would bring relief. Arabella only gave her a cool pitying smile.

"Perhaps I'll bring you off tomorrow - if you're good." She reached under the bed and tugged at the end of the broom handle until it came free from Sue with a soft sucking pop. "Meanwhile we'll have this out so you can't work yourself off on it." She frowned. "How much more convenient if I could keep you in my room at the Hall instead of sneaking out like this. Maybe that will be possible very soon."

Arabella threw a blanket over Sue, then snapped on a pocket torch before blowing out the oil lamp. The light disappeared down the stairs and Sue was alone in the darkness. She listened for the click of the lock on the front door, then dropped her head back on the bed. Her Mistress had left. Tomorrow morning she would be awake and anxiously awaiting the same sound that announced Arabella's return, even though it would herald another day of degradation, pain and servitude.

Sue knew Arabella was totally controlling and shaping her life, but she could do nothing to prevent it, either physically or emotionally. She was being submerged by the sheer force of Arabella's will.

"I am your slave, Mistress," she said in the darkness. "I have no other desire except to serve you..."

In a few days she would believe that totally. But it wouldn't matter if only Arabella would say that she cared for her. Or ever thanked Sue, just once, for the pleasure she had given.

The Cranborough House boys waited for the sound of Sister

Newcombe's footsteps to die away before slipping out of bed. But they were not going up on the roof to spy on her tonight. They dressed quickly, putting on the old dark clothes they had been wearing while clearing out the old stable block. As a final precaution they smeared black shoe polish onto their faces. Ready-packed rucksacks were pulled out of lockers and slung over shoulders.

Jackson tested his pocket torch. He had pasted a piece of card over the lens with a small hole punched through the centre, so that the torch now emitted only a pencil beam of light

He took a deep breath. "Ready?" he asked softly.

The others whispered back: "Ready!"

They carefully opened the fire escape door and stole out into the night.

24: Jailbreak

Amber woke with a groan.

She'd been sleeping face down on her cell bed because her bottom still burned after her caning and Arabella's attentions. The position hadn't helped her back and shoulders, which ached from the pillory, and did nothing for the lingering soreness in her vulva from the vigorous shafting Bailey had given her before locking up for the night.

What had disturbed her?

"Hsss!"

She blinked about at the darkness of her cell until her eyes found the window. The faint barred grey rectangle of moonless night sky was broken by the bobbing outline of a head. The hissing came again, followed by a whispered: "Wake up... we've come to get you out of here!"

Hugging her blanket to her, she climbed stiffly out of the bed and shuffled over to the window.

"What did you say?" she whispered back.

"We've come to get you out of here."

"And who's we?" She could just make out three shadowy figures clustered about the other side of the window.

"We caught you in the woods, remember."

"Oh yes! Jackson, Parsons and Bicks - gang bangs a speciality. And you also mentioned a couple of friends - Harris and Gosset, I think. Are they here as well?"

She heard a second voice mutter anxiously: "She's sharp. She remembered all our names!"

"They're keeping lookout," Jackson admitted.

"I see. And what brought on this sudden desire to break me out of jail?"

There was a slight hesitation, then: "Well, we do feel responsible for chasing you into Bailey's arms like that -"

"So you should."

"But then you shouldn't have run away from us in the first place. You're an outsider and we had caught you fair and square. You really should still belong to us."

"So you want to break me out just to make me your pet - that was what you had lined up for me originally, wasn't it? Why will I be better off with you than serving my time in here?"

Actually Amber had no intention of accepting her sentence so meekly. Being in the pillory was a peculiar sort of turn on, but after meeting Arabella she realised just how vulnerable it made her. And she certainly wasn't going to risk being sold to Arabella's uncle in auction. But what the boys offered wasn't much better.

"I could have given Bailey your names and descriptions, but I didn't," she pointed out. "So if you can get me out of here you'd better do it and forget any ideas about 'pets' - unless you want me to change my mind."

"If you did tell on us, we could show them your bag with that statue in it and those burglary tools, and then you'd be in even more trouble," came the unexpected riposte. "Of course, if you agree to coming with us, you can have the tools right now."

The words startled Amber. They had the phallus! And if using it had got her here, then it might also be her way back. But to

185

have a chance of getting it she would have to submit to the boys first.

"If I agreed, how long would it be for?" she asked cautiously. "I'm not planning on being your slave for life."

There was a whispered conference outside the window. "Until the end of this term," Jackson said. "We couldn't keep you over the summer anyway."

That wasn't as long as her official sentence. She could survive that if she had to and they could hardly treat her worse than a legal owner. They were bound to get careless after a while and she could slip away. And if the phallus didn't work, by then she would have learnt enough about local customs to blend in.

"If you want to keep me healthy it'll have to be somewhere warm and dry, and I'll need decent food and drink and the means to keep clean."

She felt a momentary sense of unreality as she realised she was negotiating the terms of her sexual slavery. Her stomach did a little flip flop, even as a familiar tingle of anticipation grew in her loins.

"I promise we'll take proper care of you," Jackson said. "We'll be... responsible."

He sounded sincere. "About the kind of things you expect me to do -"

"You do whatever we want whenever we want," Jackson said firmly. "And we can punish you if you don't please us, or if you're disrespectful, or if we catch you trying to escape. That's how all bondslaves are treated. Everybody knows that."

"All right - but I don't promise not to escape if I get the chance."

"You won't get one," Jackson replied confidently. "We won't make the same mistake twice."

Amber took a deep breath. "OK, I agree. You've got yourselves a pet slave. Now, where are my tools?"

Her pack of lockpicks was pushed through the bars. She clutched at it eagerly.

"Give me ten minutes. I've got to get through a few doors

186

and collect my shoes and top from the station room."

"Come out the side door into the yard," Jackson told her. "We've got a way over the wall at the back."

It took Amber less than thirty seconds to pick the lock of her cell door. She swung it open very carefully to avoid any squeaks, then padded silently down the dimly lit passage. Outside Sally's cell she hesitated, then pressed against the bars, peering into the gloom.

"Go on, get out of here. I won't say nothing," came Sally's voice.

"You heard?"

"Most of it." Sally slipped out of her bed and came over to the other side of the bars. "These the ones you told Bailey had you in the woods?"

"They are, but don't let on. Do you want to get out as well? I think you'll be OK. It's only me they want."

"Thanks, but I'm getting out in a couple of days anyway and I'm too well known round these parts to want the coppers chasing after me. You get going."

"Sure you won't get into trouble? Will Bailey believe I could slip out of here without you knowing?"

"Doesn't matter. I won't tell..." She hesitated. "'Course, for a few bob I could tell him anything you or your friends want."

Amber grinned and patted her naked thighs. "I seem to have come out without my purse. But maybe... hold on."

She picked the lock on Sally's door and stepped inside.

"You're real good at that," Sally said admiringly.

Amber moved to the window and called softly: "My mercenary friend here is open to bribery in a good cause. How much are you willing to pay to have her say it was two or three hulking great men who sprang me?"

It worked out at ten shillings, to be paid to Sally on the day of her release at an agreed rendezvous outside the village. Ten minutes later, Amber now wearing her tee-shirt and trainers recovered from the locker in the station room, was binding Sally securely to her bed with a selection of police restraints. In the dim light she worked mainly by touch. Sally's flesh was warm and pliant - it was not an unpleasant task.

"Next time you see me," Amber whispered to her, "I'll probably be trussed up like this, so be kind."

"Give 'em a little of what they want and you'll have 'em twisted round your little finger before you know it."

"I hope so." She held a rubber bit and tie ready to serve as a gag, bent down quickly and kissed Sally. "It's been fun. See you soon, I hope."

"Good luck."

Amber put the gag in place, then covered her with a blanket. She re-locked the cell doors, and went to the end of the passage to the yard door. It was bolted and locked. Right, she could fix that. She opened it silently and stepped out into the cool night air. They were waiting and caught hold of her as soon as she emerged.

"Not so fast!" she hissed.

Pressing the largest probe in her kit against the frame beside the bolts she pulled the door shut on it, indenting the wood and making it look as though the bolts had been forced from outside. Removing the probe she then locked the door.

"OK. I'm all yours."

They took her lockpicks away and, holding her firmly by the arms, hurried her across the yard to the back wall. She could just make out a rope ladder hanging against it. Hands clasped her naked thighs and buttocks and half threw her up the rungs. A folded blanket cushioned the worn and rusted spikes topping the wall, allowing her to swing her legs over and climb down the other side where two more boys were waiting.

She had hardly set foot to ground before they caught her arms and forced her face down onto the cold dew-wet grass. One sat astride the small of her back, pulling her arms up behind her, while the other held her legs. They waited until the others joined them, retrieving the ladder and blanket and packing them away. Amber lay still, only shivering slightly as the dew soaked her tee-shirt. This was what she had expected, and in a way she admired the evident thoroughness and planning.

Her face was pulled up from the grass and a handkerchief gag tied across her mouth. Her wrists were crossed and bound tightly behind her. She was lifted to her feet and more ropes were tied about her waist, with boys holding their trailing ends.

Jackson whispered in her ear: "There'll be two of us holding you; one in front, one behind. Don't try running away this time or you'll get hurt."

He tugged the rope looped about her waist by way of demonstration, and Amber felt it tighten alarmingly. They really were learning fast.

For twenty minutes Amber trotted obediently along in the middle of the file of boys. Silently they crossed a strip of common ground that skirted a row of back gardens, squeezed through gaps in hedges, across a couple of lanes and then through a stretch of woodland. The boys seemed to know the way well, with Jackson only occasionally checking the path ahead with his torch.

Finally they came to a high chainlink fence which cut across their path. They jogged along beside it for a few yards until they came to a place where the wire mesh hung away from its support post and squeezed through. Beyond was a thin belt of trees skirting an open stretch of ground, on the far side of which loomed the bulk of some large building. They moved along the edge of the trees, walking on close-cut grass, until they reached a smaller single storey structure. The boys led her around the back, opened a door and ushered her inside. Hands grasped her shoulders and pushed her to her knees. She felt wooden boards under her. There came a clink of glass on metal, the scrape of a match, and an oil lantern flickered into life.

Amber blinked. She was in some sort of storeroom. Bundles of nets, kit boxes, folded canvas sheets and marker posts rested against the walls, together with a white line painting machine and stacks of folding wooden chairs. The only item out of place stood in the clear space in the centre of the room. It was a large wooden 'A' frame stand of the sort that used to carry blackboards when they stood freely in the corner of schoolrooms.

But this frame was tied about with many short lengths of rope, their loose ends hanging ready for use.

Amber swallowed and looked up at the ring of excited polish-smeared faces that surrounded her. The success of their bold coup was evidently just sinking in, and they were admiring the prize they had won as she knelt bound and half naked before them, her nipples standing up through the damp clinging material of her tee-shirt. Amber felt her love lips becoming slippery, preparing themselves for the inevitable. Her body knew what was coming next.

They pulled her to her feet, loosened the ropes and stripped her top off, then lifted her legs and removed her trainers and socks. Now she was completely naked, surrounded by a press of young male bodies. She felt the hard bulges of their erections rubbing against her through their trousers, even as curious hands stroked and pinched her. Fingers roughly probed the moist warm nest of her cunt, discovering its secret anatomy. They were withdrawn slippery and glistening to be sniffed deeply, the rare perfume savoured to the full.

"That's her pre-come," said Jackson. "It means she's ready to be had."

She'd better give them a little of what they wanted as Sally had suggested, she thought. She was aroused anyway, so she might as well enjoy the sensation of helpless vulnerability. From past experience it would be over quickly enough - these young cocks had hair triggers. Maybe this time, with five of them she'd have a chance to orgasm herself. She half twisted, as though trying to pull away from them, and let her eyes widen in apparent apprehension. They immediately clasped her even tighter, laughing as they discovered what fun it was to hold a naked struggling young woman in their arms.

"Gosset and I get to have her first," a ginger haired boy said, breathing heavily. "To even up for you lot having her the other day."

"No. First she's got to be punished," Jackson said, "for es-

190

caping after we caught her."

This time Amber started in genuine alarm as she watched him take a cane from behind the bundle of marker posts and swish it experimentally through the air. "It'll teach her to be better behaved in future. Tie her to the stand bottom out."

Amber was shaking her head frantically and trying to speak. Jackson untied her gag.

"Not on my bottom, please!" Amber gasped. "It's still raw from the beating Bailey gave me."

Still holding her tightly, they bent her over and examined her bottom; bringing the lantern closer so they could see every stripe and weal, feeling the warmth of her abused flesh.

"It is very red," Parsons agreed. "It must be jolly tender."

"But she still deserves six of the best for escaping," Jackson insisted. "She'll have to put up with it, that's all." His eyes narrowed and he suddenly grinned. "Unless she can suggest somewhere else she'd rather take it - somewhere that's right for a girl to be caned."

Amber gulped, and said faintly: "My breasts... you can cane my breasts - but lightly, please! They're much more delicate than bottoms."

The boys stared at her neat firm mounds. They were still ringed about with the lingering purple indentations of the wire straps that had secured them in the pillory, but at least the skin on them was unbroken. She realised her nipples had hardened even further at the thought of what was going to be done to them. One way or another, this was going to smart! Jackson cupped and squeezed her breasts as though assessing their texture.

"Are you sure?' he asked her.

"Yes."

"Rather than your bottom?"

"Yes - it's really still too painful."

"Then beg."

"What?"

"Tell us you want to be punished and how. Do it properly, or

191

else you'll get it across the bottom even if it is sore."

Amber gulped again. They were learning the game much too fast. They really were going to make her suffer - and in a dark way, she knew she would enjoy it.

She said in a small girl voice: "Your pet knows she's been naughty and begs you to punish her. She wants you to tie her to that frame over there and give her six strokes of the cane across her pretty breasts to teach her to behave better in future. Then she wants each of you to push his cock up her hot wet hole as deep and hard as he likes until he comes inside her - "

Before she had finished speaking they had picked her up bodily and carried her across to the 'A' frame. They pressed her back against it, drew her arms up over her head and spread her legs so they lay along its splayed front struts. With trembling fingers they wrapped and knotted the ropes about her wrists, upper arms, across her chest, about her waist, around her thighs above her knees and around her ankles, until she was lashed so tightly to the frame she could hardly move.

Jackson positioned himself before her, drew back the cane, and swung. It caught her just below the nipples with a crisp smack, setting her pliant breasts bouncing. Two thin upward curving red lines appeared on her clear flesh.

Amber gasped and yelled loudly.

Actually the blow hadn't hurt as much as she had feared, but she wasn't about to let them know that.

"Gag her again," Jackson said anxiously. "She mustn't make too much noise."

Before Amber could protest the gag was stuffed into her mouth again. Jackson drew back his arm and swung, decorating her breasts with another pair of curving red lines even as she screamed through the cloth wadded into her mouth. She jerked and strained against her bonds, making the frame creak and putting on a fine show of helpless suffering. The last stroke of the cane caught both erect nipples squarely, bringing forth a genuine stifled yelp from Amber and filling her eyes with tears.

But now the punishment was over and she found herself

tingling expectantly. Maybe she was developing a taste for bondage, because she was seriously excited and desperately needed
to be filled.

The boys did not keep her waiting long.

They folded the back strut of the frame flat and laid it and
Amber onto a bed of folded canvass tarpaulins. The ginger-haired
boy pulled down his trousers and pants, releasing a fine erect
cock, and knelt between her bound and spread legs. He thrust
into the depths of her gaping cunt, squashing her smarting breasts
as he almost fell on top of her.

Roughly, without any thought for her comfort or pleasure,
he
repeatedly rammed his rod into her, until hot sperm blossomed
within her and he came with a shudder. Breathing heavily he
pulled himself free and rolled aside. Immediately Gosset took
his place.

Amber's cunt eagerly sucked him into her.

Whether it was due to the tight biting ropes that bound her,
the stinging of her breasts or the procession of hard young cocks
that were remorselessly reaming her out she did not know, but
Amber felt herself building to a tremendous orgasm. Her only
fear was they would finish before she was ready.

She just managed it. The boys watched in fascination as she
spasmed wildly, eyes rolling then screwing shut, straining at her
bonds, gasping and moaning inarticulately through her gag, her
cunt tightening desperately about Jackson's cock, the last inside
her, milking it for all it contained before it withdrew. The scent
of her discharge mingled with the heavy musk of freshly spilled
sperm that filled the air of the storeroom.

Sweaty and trembling, she lay limply in her bonds, sinking
into the glorious afterglow of her climax. Sticky fluid began to
ooze from between her engorged cunt lips and drip onto her
makeshift canvas bed.

"Did we do that to her?" Parsons said, wonderingly.

"Is she all right?' Bicks asked.

"Of course - that's just how girls come when they're really

193

excited," Jackson said confidently.

They exchanged embarrassed but also slightly smug glances.

"I want her again," said Harris.

"No. Only once each tonight," Jackson said, checking his watch. "We've got to get some sleep. Tomorrow we'll work out a rota. We've got to feed and exercise her as well, remember. We should be able to slip away from work for half an hour at a time easily enough. That way we can each have her two or three times a day. More if we can manage it."

Amber, who was slowing recovering from her blissful exhaustion, sore but extremely satisfied, suddenly blinked as the implication of what she had heard sunk in. Fifteen or more fucks a day! They'd wear her out! She looked up anxiously but they were preparing to leave. Surely they weren't going to leave her tied to the frame all night - her arms and shoulders were already beginning to ache. She started to struggle as they pulled another sheet of canvas over her.

"You'll be safe enough here," Jackson told her, ignoring her muffled protests. "We'll bring you some food and water in the morning."

Then the canvas covered her head. She heard the rattle of the oil lamp being extinguished, then the storeroom door being closed and locked.

Had she managed to jump out of the frying pan into the fire yet again?

25: Displeasure

Constable Bailey was whistling cheerfully as, balancing a tray of morning tea in one hand, he opened the door of the cell block.

"Stir yourselves, girls. It's going to be a busy day -"

He stopped as he saw the door of Amber's cell at the end of the passage standing open. With an oath, he ran to it as fast as his bulk allowed, spilling the tea. Amber's blanket and pillow were strewn across the floor, while on her bed lay her open collar. But of Amber herself there was no sign.

He lumbered back to Sally's cell. At least there was still a body under the blankets. Then it squirmed urgently and he heard muffled grunts and whines. Hastily he opened the cell door and tore the blankets aside.

Sally lay bound up like a Christmas turkey, her eyes glaring up at him over the gag strap that covered her mouth.

He pulled the gag free. She licked her dry lips, then said angrily: "Why ain't there ever a copper around when you need one?"

The showers were a press of naked soapy bodies and the air was filled with steam and the excited chatter of packgirls. Melanie saw Una looking at her expectantly and nodded.

Una stepped over to her and said clearly: "Can I wash your back, Melanie?"

"Of course you can, Una," she replied loudly.

Washing the back of the First Girl was usually something of a privilege amongst the pack, Melanie had discovered. When she had been first girl, Una had turned it into a chore, or to demonstrate her favouritism. Melanie decided to put the ritual to better use, and had arranged this little show the previous night.

The chatter muted as the rest of the pack realised what was happening. Undeterred, Una soaped and scrubbed Melanie's smooth back meticulously, surreptitiously slipping a finger down the cleft of her buttocks as she did so, which made Melanie squirm and smile. When she was done, Melanie said: "Now let me do yours."

And she returned the service, including a quick tickle with her finger about Una's bottom hole. Meanwhile Gillian had been standing close by, waiting her cue. When Melanie had done, Una said: "Would you like me to do you as well, Gillian?"

"Thank you, Una," Gillian said. "I'd like that."

By the end of the ablutions Melanie could sense a much more relaxed atmosphere amongst the rest of the girls, knowing their two strongest members were reconciled. Now they could turn all their attention to tomorrow's hunt.

Miss Newcombe sat at the head of the only table laid up in the otherwise empty dining hall while the boys served the porridge, tea and toast they had prepared, then took their own places. It didn't take her long to notice they had a rather distracted air about them, at the same time eating as though they wanted to finish breakfast as soon as possible.

"You seem in rather a hurry to get on with your work today," she observed.

The boys exchanged anxious glances. Jackson said quickly: "We thought we'd make an early start, Sister. Get as much done as we could."

"Very commendable, I'm sure," Miss Newcombe said. 'But there is no need to bolt your food quite so fast. Giving yourselves indigestion will do nobody any good.'

Somewhat sheepishly the boys slowed down. After a minute, Miss Newcombe asked: "Have you thought any more about what I said yesterday, Anthony?"

Jackson blushed slightly. "Well... yes, Sister. A bit."

"And do you think you should be taught about sexual attitudes and behaviour at school? What about the rest of you?"

There was a mumbled chorus of agreement. Miss Newcombe smiled reassuringly. "If there's anything you want to ask me - about women or sex, for instance - don't be embarrassed."

After a moment Parsons, evidently screwing up his courage, said: "We did wonder... when girls, or women, are put in the pillory for shaming... do they secretly enjoy it?"

"Do you think men sent to hard labour camps or road gangs enjoy that experience?" she replied. They shook their heads. She continued. "But you wonder, because women are put on public show, and actually give pleasure while they are being shamed, that they might get some in return?"

They nodded, and Jackson said: "Some women do sell themselves into bondage, don't they, so they must like it."

196

"Yes, some adventurous women may do so for the thrill of it," Miss Newcombe agreed. "Or they may have chosen bondservice as the least onerous option available. Others, who have simply fallen foul of the law, learn to accept their punishment and make the best of it. The majority, I would think, are genuinely shamed by their treatment - which is meant to be a deterrent after all. The answer is that women are as varied in their tastes as men - something you should always remember."

Blushing, Parsons asked: "Do you think it's right that women bondslaves can be used by their owners for... you know, having sex with?"

"Whether it makes their subjugation more or less pleasant would depend, once again, on the individual and her circumstances," said Miss Newcombe. "Certainly it's been an accepted part of bondservice for two hundred years or so. Women have had the opportunity to influence the law for rather less time than that, but still very few try. Perhaps the majority realise it is the safest way of accommodating mostly male, sexual needs and desires. And if women make use of bondslaves themselves, they can certainly not complain."

"Maybe they never believe it'll never happen to them," suggested Harris.

¡Very possibly," agreed Miss Newcombe. "All we can say is that the system seems to work. But remember this. Whatever the reason a woman might have become a slave, she deserves to be treated fairly by her master or keeper. They can be strict and demand any lawful service from her, but they must never inflict cruelty for its own sake. That's where people like Arabella Westlake overstep the mark." She fixed them with a very penetrating gaze. "I hope you never give cause to be compared with her."

The boys were suddenly very silent.

Sue had been harnessed to an old four-wheeled play cart. On her hands and knees she fitted neatly between the shafts, fastened by the rings of a broad belt that took the place of a horse's collar, while there was just room for one girl at a time to squat in the cart behind her. Reins had been fitted to her bridle and bit, while Arabella had plugged a horse hair tail into her bottom.

Jemima, Ernestine and Penelope were taking turns driving Sue round the playhouse garden, under Arabella's watchful eye. Belinda, usually the most eager of the four girls to help with Sue's training, had not yet arrived. Just when Arabella was beginning to wonder what had delayed her, she appeared looking flushed and excited.

"Arabella!" she said breathlessly "That outsider woman we questioned in the police yard yesterday, she's escaped!"

"What do you mean?"

"During the night somebody broke into the police station and took her away. Constable Bailey's hopping mad, of course, because they did it right under his nose. He's already out looking, but they've had hours to get away."

Arabella looked thoughtful. "What about the Potts girl who was serving time with her?"

"Oh, they tied her up and left her. That's how they know what happened. Two or three men wearing hoods, maybe the same ones they say chased Jones the day we found this one." Her eyes widened. "Oh... they must have been in the woods all the time we were. They might have taken one of us!"

Penny and Ernestine, who were hanging on Belinda's every word, squealed. Arabella quashed their horrified delight at the idea.

"Do be quiet," she said sharply. "Perhaps I should question the Potts girl about the escape."

Belinda looked eager to accompany her once again, but instead Arabella's eyes fell on Jemima, who was riding in the cart. Currently the cart was stationary and Jemima was holding the whip limply in her hand while staring in apparent fascination at Sue's pale, crimson-striped bottom.

"Why did you allow her to stop?' Arabella asked.

"I think she's tired," Jemima said, looking suddenly embarrassed and tearing her eyes away from Sue's posterior.

"She's here to obey your commands whether she feels tired or not. You're much too soft on her, Jemima. Or are you still worried that she's not legal?"

"Uhh... perhaps I am," Jemima said uncertainly. "Sorry, Arabella."

"Then you'd better come with me and see how a common criminal is treated."

If Tom Soams was surprised to see Arabella back again so soon he made no mention of it. Nor did he protest when another pound note changed hands. It was nearly time for lunch anyway, and without the attraction of Amber in the pillory, the yard had not been busy. Bailey was out searching the local area and might not be back for hours.

Sally Potts, only lightly splattered with pillory shot, was strapped to a plain upright wooden board, her arms and legs spread wide so that her feet did not touch the ground. Foot long brackets projected from the board on either side of her torso level with her breasts. Mounted on the ends of the brackets were two short wooden arms, hinged in the middle so they could swing from side to side like weather vanes. On the outer ends of the arms were standard six inch target disks, while the inner ends had rings screwed into them from which ran taut chains that circled Sally's breasts like nooses.

Sally eyed Arabella and Jemima anxiously as they approached.

Arabella halted in front of Sally and looked her up and down for several seconds before speaking.

"You remember me from yesterday, girl?' she asked brusquely.

"Course I do," Sally said.

"You will address me as Miss Arabella."

"As you like... Miss Arabella," Sally said flatly without any hint of deference.

Arabella's lips pinched. "You've been up before my uncle several times. You're a cheap little tart who'll do anything for

199

money."

Undaunted, Sally replied: "I'm a fair priced tart who does just what she wants for money... Miss Arabella."

Arabella's nostrils flared slightly, but she continued icily: "You will tell me everything about the escape of the Jones woman."

Sally shrugged as well as her bonds allowed. "Like I told Bailey: middle of the night I was woken up by somebody opening my cell door. Thought it was Bailey himself at first, coming in for some late perks. But then two men grabbed me, stuffed a gag in my mouth and strapped me up tight. As they were finishing I thought I heard Jones being dragged along the passage. Gagged as well by the sound of it. The men left, locking up behind them, and that was it 'till Bailey found me in the morning."

"I see. And you heard no names spoken? There was nothing out of the ordinary about the men? Think hard. I can persuade you to remember if necessary."

"You can do what you want but there isn't anything else... Miss Arabella."

Arabella's eyes narrowed. "I see. Then I have no further questions. Now, how shall I punish you?"

Sally looked confused. "What? But I told you everything I know."

"This is for insolence. When you speak my name in future you will do so with proper respect."

"You can't. You shouldn't be talking to me like this anyway - not without Bailey's permission."

"But the constable's not here, is he? And even if you complain to him, I doubt if he'll take the matter any further."

"If your uncle hears about it -"

"I can handle my uncle."

Sally's jaw set defiantly. "Well stuff all the pillory shot up my slot you want - see if I care."

"Stupid girl. It won't be shot up your cunny. I'm sure it is quite accustomed to all kinds of rough use. No, I think those rather full breasts are your tenderest spot."

She slapped one of the target disks with the palm of her hand as a shot might strike it. The arm swung back, pulling the chain trailing from the other end, pinching and jerking Sally's soft breast up and outwards. Sally yelped. Arabella slapped the disk on the other side with the same result.

"Is that all they do?" Arabella said. "That's not severe enough. Bailey would get far better results if the chains were connected differently. Such large nipples must be quite sensitive. And I happen to have brought something along with me that will just suit them." She took a small device from her jacket pocket.

For the first time Sally looked alarmed. "No... not that, not my tits, please!" She tugged futilely at her straps, but the only effect was to set her breasts trembling.

"Ahh, a little less brazen now, are you? But it was too late. You must be taught a lesson. No respite until you beg, using my name properly. Jemima, watch this closely.'

Under Jemima's horrified yet fascinated gaze, Arabella placed a metal ring over each of Sally's nipples and tightened the screws with the butterfly heads that were set in each one. The shallow pointed screw ends bore down on the crinkled bulbs of flesh, pressing them against the inside of the rings, which were finely ribbed to prevent slippage.

As the screws pressed harder, Sally began to gasp. "I'm sorry I was insolent, Miss... Miss Arabella. I didn't mean to give any offence... No, please stop!"

"Not sincere enough, girl," Arabella said, continuing to tighten the screws until their ends had dug deep and the rings could not possibly pull free. Now each nipple was joined by the short length of chain that connected the rings, in the middle of which hung a small metal box with a key set in its side.

Jemima was goggling at Sally's nipples. Their broad pink areolae were flushing and darkening under the unwelcome stimulation. She looked into the girl's pain-creased face and swallowed heavily.

"Arabella, I don't think we should be doing this," she said in

201

a tiny voice. "You're hurting her."

"She's here to be hurt," Arabella said, "because she's a thieving little slut who deserves everything she gets. Isn't that right, girl?"

"Yes, yes!" Sally gasped. "I'm a thieving little slut who deserves everything she gets! I'm sorry I spoke out of turn, Miss Arabella, and I promise never to do it again!"

"Still not enough feeling," said Arabella. She turned the key on the box reeling in the chains, pulling the rings with their imprisoned nipples towards each other against the resistance of the heavier chain nooses. The skin about the nipples stretched as Sally's breasts were dragged through the nooses after them.

Sally let out a fresh yelp of pain. "No... please! It hurts... You're tearing my tits off!"

Arabella turned the key further. The two distorted pink balloons met and began to form a cleavage as they were pulled together. Her areolae had become stretched cones of scarlet flesh. Another turn and the nipple rings were almost touching.

Sally shrieked: "I'm a stupid girl who doesn't know any better... please stop, Miss Arabella. I beg you, I beg you! Ohh!"

A stream of pee jetted fitfully from between her pink cunt lips, and Arabella had to step quickly aside as it splattered to the ground. Sally's chin dropped to her chest, and tears ran down her cheeks.

Arabella smiled in cool satisfaction, released the tension on the chain, and freed the rings. Sally's breasts swung loose, her nipples purple with deep indentations in them where the screws had bitten in.

"Thank you, Miss Arabella..." Sally choked out brokenly.

Arabella looked at Jemima. "You see how a little firm handling improves a girl's disposition. You must practice more. Meanwhile we're done here. This baggage can't tell us anything useful."

Sally looked up only after she heard the click of the gate latch. Blinking back her tears she scowled. Sometimes you had to put on quite show, she thought, then shuddered at the needle

202

tingle of returning feeling to her nipples. Not that it had required much acting.

The insulting thing was Arabella had only seemed mildly amused. What did it take to please her? There was something very wrong there, Sally thought, something really mean. If Amber doesn't get even with you first, Arabella Westlake, I will. And she spat onto the brick floor of the yard.

26: School Pet

It was an hour after breakfast before Miss Newcombe rode away from the school. Leaving the others working on the old stable block, Jackson and Bickley immediately went to the cricket pavilion.

Inside the storeroom they pulled back the canvas covers and lifted the frame to which Amber was bound upright. She groaned and glared at them through bloodshot eyes. Jackson pulled out her gag and fed her some water from the flask he was carrying. After a minute she was able to speak.

"Don't you ever, ever, leave me like that again! I can't feel my arms - oww!"

Jackson twisted her left nipple, still tender from the previous night's caning, between his thumb and forefinger. When he had her undivided attention, he said earnestly: "I'm sorry we left you tied up too long and I promise we won't do it again. But you can't speak to us like that. You belong to us, that's what we agreed. You can ask, but do it properly. Do you understand?"

Amber nodded. Jackson released her nipple. She said carefully: 'Your pet is sorry for speaking out of turn. She begs you to release her so she can get some blood back into her arms before they drop off!"

They untied Amber, standing ready in case she tried to escape. But Amber was quite incapable of anything so energetic. Her numb legs bent at the knees, and she slid gracelessly down onto the canvas sheeting, then toppled forward onto her face, arms still crooked above her head as they had been tied. Her flesh was marked by the rope, and also the imprint of the stand where it had pressed against the backs of her legs and across the upper slopes of her bottom. She gasped in pain as she tried to straighten her arms.

Bickley chuckled at her helplessness. "Well it's a good lesson for her," he said, nudging her stiff body with the toe of his shoe.

Though he knew they'd been thoughtless, Jackson had to agree. It was exciting to look down at Amber's naked body and know she belonged to them and to think of the many ways they could make use of her during the months ahead.

"Your pet begs you to help her, or else she won't be able to move," Amber said faintly.

They knelt beside her and massaged her flesh, working the circulation back towards her extremities. Her buttocks received more attention than they strictly required, which caused the two boys to grin at each other, but slowly the deep imprints of the ropes reddened and began to fill.

"My shoulders, please," Amber said. 'Ohh... that hurts... but it is good."

They rolled her over and began working on her front.

"Please, if you could massage my pectorals a bit," Amber begged. "Those are the muscles under my arms and breasts... I'm sure you'd like that... yes... my tits were cold anyway... that's right."

Her crinkled and shrunken nipples began to fill out.

They worked on her arms until she could bring them down to her sides in a more relaxed position. "That feels better," she said, flexing her fingers. "Rope can get really mean after an hour or so."

Jackson was looking at her intently. ìI know you didn't like being left overnight, but you did enjoy what we did to you before that. I mean you did come, didn't you?"

Amber managed a weak smile. "That was a giveaway, wasn't it. Yes, that sort of session can be fun."

"Even the caning?"

"Yes as long as it's mixed in with the sex... and I get a chance to get off at the end. I'm not deeply into S and M, but I play occasionally."

"S and M?" Bickley asked.

"Sado-Masochism... maybe you don't have the phrase here. Inflicting and receiving pain for sexual pleasure... the sort of thing you did to me last night." She turned her head stiffly and looked at the bulges in their trousers. "Only please, before you have me again, can your pet be exercised? I really need to pee badly."

They put the slip-knot leashes they had used the night before around her waist and coiled the ends of the ropes securely about their fists.

"Stay on your hands and knees," Jackson warned her. "Don't try to stand up."

They led her out of the back of the pavilion and into the belt of trees and bushes that ran along behind it. Reaching a suitable spot, Amber looked up at her captors.

"I don't suppose I get any privacy?"

They grinned and shook their heads. Her bladder was too full for her to care, so she squatted like a dog and relieved herself on the grass. The boys watched the hissing stream emerge with undisguised fascination, bending down to look more closely.

"Do you think we could charge to watch her pee?" Bickley wondered.

"That's an idea," said Jackson, grinning. "How about a penny a time?"

"Where exactly does it come out of anyway?"

"We'll find out later," Jackson said, causing Amber a renewed shiver of alarm and anticipation.

Amber wiped herself dry with a handful of grass, then looked about her. She could just see the top of a large building through the trees. "Can I ask where we are?"

"Cranborough House School," said Jackson. "We board here, we're in our last year."

205

"It's still the Easter holiday," said Bickley, with a scowl. "We shouldn't be here really - except we got into trouble."

Jackson said: "We can't stay outside talking. Let's take her back inside and feed her."

"Food!" Amber exclaimed. "Yes please. Your pet is hungry."

"We shouldn't leave her untied for too long," Bickley said to Jackson. "Remember what happened last time."

"I'm not going to run away if you're going to feed me," Amber promised them. In fact she was not going to run away until she found where they had put the phallus, but they mustn't know that.

They sat her in one of the folding chairs and tied her wrists and ankles to it securely, but not as tightly as the previous night. She was quite comfortable as long as she didn't struggle. They had a paper wrapped bundle of assorted sandwiches, cheese and an apple, which they fed her by hand.

"What sort of trouble did you get into?" Amber asked between mouthfuls. From the expression on Bickley's face she suspected they were angry about something, and she was ready to lend a sympathetic ear if it made her time with them a little easier.

Jackson grimaced. "It's all the fault of somebody called Arabella Westlake."

Amber almost choked. "She paid me a visit yesterday while I was in the pillory. Nasty piece of work."

The boys nodded and Amber knew she'd said the right thing.

Jackson continued. "It was the end of last term. We'd heard a story that Arabella and these four girls who follow her around, 'Snooties' some of the village boys call them, were going to a place in the woods where there's this old ring of trees. They were dancing there like Greek maidens - sometimes with not many clothes on."

"So you thought you'd take a look yourselves," Amber said. "Perfectly natural. Go on."

"Well, the five of us, we share the same dorm, went to the ring one Sunday. The weather was fine and it seemed a likely time. And they were all there sure enough, except for Arabella. So we kept out of sight and watched. They were wearing sort of Greek costumes - just a few gauze scarves wrapped around them, really. They laughed and giggled, daring each other on, then began dancing."

"And you got an eyeful. And then?"

"Somebody, we couldn't see who, started firing a catapult from the bushes at the girls. They all screamed and ran away into the trees on the other side of the ring. We ran too because we didn't want to be seen there. But the next day the headmaster called us in and said he'd received a complaint about us spying on the girls, and accused us of firing a catapult at them, then stealing their clothes and scattering them all over the woods, so the girls had to go home wearing nearly nothing."

"Let me guess - the complaint was made by Arabella."

"That's right. She says she was making her way to the ring when she saw us going through the woods carrying bundles of clothes. She was backed up by Belinda Jenkins, who said she saw us as they ran away from the catapult attack. But we were too well hidden. She couldn't have done."

"So you think Arabella set you up. What happened next?"

"We all got six of the best and letters were sent to our parents saying we had to come back early from Easter hols. Old Speers, that's the headmaster, has done that sort of thing before. Missing hols is really mean, and he gets the boys to do work around the school. He says it's constructive punishment and good for our characters. Actually the school isn't doing too well, and he likes to save money on odd jobs when he can. It's a pity because it's not such a bad place most of the time."

"But you're not here by yourself?"

"No. There has to be at least one member of staff on the premises. Speers himself usually takes charge - he's got a house in the grounds. Only this time he had to go away, so Sister Newcombe, the Matron, is standing in for him. She has a little cottage by the front gates and she wasn't going anywhere over Easter. She's been quite decent about it really. As long as we get our work done, she leaves us alone." He grinned. "It gave us a chance to plan our revenge on Arabella."

"So that's what you were doing in the woods when I turned up. You were waiting for her to come along."

"That's right. We knew she and the Snooties sometimes picked flowers there ñ itís right next to Markham Hall where she lives. Except she didn't show up, and you did."

Amber nodded in the direction of the 'A' frame. "And you had that waiting for her?"

"We were going to give her six of the best, just like we got. That only seemed fair."

"You think you could have got away with it?"

"We had masks on, and we would have blindfolded her. She might have guessed who we were, but she couldn't prove it. Afterwards we would have released her back in the woods again well away from here. Just in case, we had the alibi of doing our work around the school. If we timed everything right, Sister would say we were working here all the time."

"But instead you ended up with me." She looked at them closely. "Apart from the caning, did you ever think of doing to her what you did to me, if you'd had her at your mercy?"

The boys blushed slightly and looked troubled.

"Well... we were tempted," Bickley admitted. "But that would have been going too far. It's not done."

"You did it to me, and I hadn't treated you like Arabella had."

"Oh, you're heaps nicer than Arabella - it's just different with outsiders."

"So I can tell," Amber said with feeling. "And what other delights have you got in store for me? What was that about charging to watch me pee?"

"We thought, when the rest of the school gets back, we can charge the rest of the senior boys for using you," Jackson explained.

208

"We owe ten shillings to that Potts girl, and we may not always be able to sneak food out for you when the cooks are back, so we'll have to buy it in the village."

"Don't price me too cheap," she said faintly. Hell, the whole sixth form was going to go through her at this rate. Evidently she was going to be a working pet and be expected to earn her keep. She took a deep breath. She'd just have to see what she could do about that later.

"OK, you've been very patient," she said brightly. "I can see you want to have me again. But please, let's keep the frame for special occasions only. If I'm going to get visitors all through the day, I need something more comfortable."

"But you've got to be properly secured," said Bickley. 'We're not going to give you a chance to run away again."

"I'm sure we can work out a compromise," Amber said, looking around her. Now I'm organizing my own bondage, she thought - this is seriously weird. "Look, you've got lots of rope, and there are those bundles of posts..."

Around the edge of a bed-sized 'mattress' of folded covers, they lashed together a rectangular frame of marker posts, then tied Amber to it with her legs spread wide, but her arms stretched straight out from her shoulders, making the position more comfortable. At her direction they used several turns of rope about her wrists and ankles to spread the pressure and prevent her being marked again.

"I'd like to have a wash sometime today," she said as they tied her down. "You'll enjoy me much more if I smell nice. Shampoo might be a good idea too. And do you think I could borrow a toothbrush?"

"We'll arrange something," Jackson promised, sounding a little impatient. The boys were beginning to realise that keeping a slave was more complicated than they thought. And Amber intended to remind them of their responsibilities at every opportunity. When they were done, Amber tugged and pulled at her bonds to convince them she was secure. She was and she began to feel the lips of her pussy lubricating in anticipation. Then

209

Jackson got out the cane and swished it through the air.

"What's that for? I've already been punished," Amber said anxiously.

"You said you liked it. And we like seeing you jerk about and make a noise," Jackson said.

"Oh all right." She had no choice and in any case it had been surprisingly exciting. "But kiss me first - both of you." They looked down at her in surprise. "Go on, you'll enjoy it. Let your pet know you like her. What? Embarrassed at the thought of a little kiss - after what you've already done to me? And what youíre going to do." She smiled up flirtatiously.

They grinned nervously at each other, then knelt beside her.

Of course, kissing could be far more personal and intimate than simple fucking, as Amber well knew. She could tell immediately the boys hadn't been kissed seriously before, and surprised them with what could be done with tongues.

Then she put on a fine show of helpless writhing under a dozen hard slashes of the cane across her breasts and stomach.

"Ohh! Your pet is ready now... Ouch! Please have me... look I'm wet...Ahh! My pussy's dripping... Ohh - that stings! Aren't my legs wide enough apart for you... Ahh! I can't open them any wider... do me now, please!"

And she was promptly ravaged twice in quick succession.

Afterwards, as they lay beside her breathing heavily, Jackson said: "You didn't come yourself."

"It doesn't happen every time with girls," Amber reassured him. "Even two of you are a bit too fast. But I still enjoyed it." She dropped into her little girl voice. "Did their pet please her masters?"

They were quite sweet really, she thought. Maybe she could twist them round her little finger as Sally said.

Parsons visited her an hour later, followed shortly afterwards by Harris. Gosset paid his respects just before lunch. Fortunately they all came quickly so they didn't exhaust her, and none could be away from their work long enough to try twice in succession.

By careful timing, she was able to ask each of them to 'exercise her' before they coupled, and behaved like a very obedient bitch on a leash. They were all fascinated to see her pee. Clearly there was something about watching water spouting from a hidden orifice that particularly intrigued them. Maybe they should charge tuppence for the privilege. She also ensured each of them learnt what fun it was to kiss her, and found out their first names in the process.

In between fucks she thought intently.

She wanted to know where the phallus was, but didn't dare ask yet, for fear of letting the boys know it was important to her. She'd just have to be patient, that was all.

Then there was the matter of constable Kingston. It had to have been her that the Major and Arabella mentioned. She must have used a phallus and followed her here. A genuine case of hot pursuit! Apparently she'd chosen 'bondservice' with the Major. That sounded daring, but then Amber had thought there was something special about her from the start. Well, at least it would keep her out of the way.

Meanwhile how could she, a captive sex slave, arrange circumstances more to her tastes? It was a challenge but there were some interesting possibilities. Somehow she had to make the boys work for her. They had to have a goal in common. But apart from enjoying mutual kinky sex, what was there? Well they all disliked Arabella.

It was a start. And there was something that Arabella had said to her during her impromptu interrogation lurking in the back of her mind. Something that didn't make sense. What was it? Of course! And suddenly Amber saw a whole scheme unfolding before her.

"Put her in that," Arabella told the girls, indicating the small clothes trunk she had dragged out of a dusty cupboard. She had returned to the playhouse after lunch in an evident mood of frustration following her interrogation of Sally Potts. The girls had watched her uncertainly, wondering what fresh torment she would subject Sue to. Now she seemed to have reached a decision.

"She'll hardly fit," Jemima said.

"Make her!" Arabella said simply. "I'll be back soon."

And she strode out of the playhouse door.

Alison led Melanie out of the girlpack yard into the stable court. Melanie was walking upright in flat-soled shoes. Her paws were clipped together behind her back and a long chain was fastened to her collar. Through the gates of the adjacent yard Melanie saw men unharnessing a coach. Her nipples stood up as she felt their eyes upon her.

How different from the first time she had walked through here. Had it been only two days before? Then she had been ashamed of her bondage and nakedness. Now it was as though a switch had been thrown in her mind. She stood erect and proud, her sheathed and chained hands lying easily in the hollow of her back, resting on the full swell of her haunches. She was not unconscious of her enforced exposure, but now it gave her a dizzy sense of elation. She had never felt so alive.

"More guests for the hunt," Alison said, looking at the coach. "I hope you'll run well tomorrow, Number 9."

Arabella appeared. She paused for a moment to stare at Melanie, then crossed to the stable yard. In a couple of minutes she emerged again driving a dog cart and passed through the arches out into the central court.

There came the clop of hooves Melanie had been waiting for. The Major rode up.

212

"I see my pretty Brown Vixen is ready for her tour of the grounds," he said with a smile.

Melanie beamed and nodded eagerly.

Alison handed over Melanie's leash and the Major led Melanie out of the yard. Her tail, curving out and upwards, wagged merrily with the roll of her buttocks.

Sue was packed into the trunk like a sardine in a can. Her legs were doubled up so that her breasts were flattened against her knees, her head was bowed over and her arms were strapped straight down her back. Her mouth was filled with a ball gag so that her eyes rolled up mutely at Arabella.

Satisfied, Arabella closed and latched the trunk lid, then, with the help of the other girls, carried the trunk out to the dog cart and loaded it onto the back. As they tied it in place Penelope asked: "What are you going to do to her? Can't we see?"

Arabella looked at Belinda and hesitated, then shook her head. "Not this time, but soon, maybe. While I'm away think of something amusing to do to her tomorrow."

She climbed into the front, took up the reins and set off along the path that curved around to rejoin the main drive. At the Hall gates she turned towards Lower Boxley.

***

Melanie trotted happily along beside the Major as he explained the rules of the hunt, which would be run across the Hall estate itself and two adjacent tithe farms. That encompassed several square miles, and since the packgirls would be given a head start it seemed they had a good chance of evading capture. Except that they would be tracked by dogs, just as in a real fox hunt.

"Don't worry, girl," the Major assured her. "They're very well trained animals. They won't harm you, just flush you out. We want to make the capture ourselves."

They passed through a glade of trees on the edge of the strip of woodland bordering the boundary wall. Suddenly the ground

213

seemed familiar to Melanie. This was the very spot she had first encountered the Major's party. That laurel bush under the elm was where she had dropped her pack. Yes, she could see it. And inside would be the phallus that had brought her here...

Suddenly she felt dizzy. What was she doing? She wasn't a slave! She had another life... What sort of spell had been worked upon her?

The Major noticed her expression and halted, following the direction of her gaze. ¡Hallo, what's this?" He dismounted and picked up her pack, examining it curiously. "Is this yours?" he asked.

She nodded, her eyes suddenly brimming with tears.

With unexpected perception, he asked gently: "Does this remind you of your home? You may speak."

"I have duties there, Master. And people will be looking for me by now. I... I must go back!"

"Do you know if that's possible, girl?"

Melanie thought of the phallus. Was she sure it could get her back? "No, Master."

He looked about him for a moment to get his bearings, then led his mount and Melanie through the wood until they came to a tiny glade formed by a fallen tree. He tethered his horse, sat back against the mossy trunk and indicated Melanie should kneel before him. She did so, squatting back on her heels with her widespread thighs open towards him so that her intimacies were not hidden from his eyes.

"Tell me what you do in your world and how you came here."

He really wants to know, Melanie thought. "It's complicated, Master..."

And she told him everything.

It was mid afternoon when all the boys came into the storeroom. They all made a point of kissing Amber and giving her breasts a quick squeeze, as though showing off their confidence in handling her, then sat around her on the folding chairs looking tired but satisfied.

214

"We've finished clearing the old stables," Jackson explained. "Miss Newcombe's ticked it off her list, so we've got a few hours free before supper."

"So we thought we'd all have you together so you'd come again," Bickley said brightly.

"Because you can't come as easily as we do," Parsons added, "which doesn't seem fair."

"Then you can have a rest for a few hours, and we'll come down again tonight after lights out," said Harris.

Amber blinked. They really thought they were doing her a kindness. She was touched, in a weird way. "That's... really very sweet of you," she said. "But listen, there are things we've got to think about. First, what's the reaction to my escape?"

"I went down to the village just before lunch," said Bickley. "Bailey's going around asking if anybody has seen three big men, probably not locals, hanging around in the last couple of days." The boys laughed. Gosset went on: "Anyway, he's put the word out and now he's checking any places they might be hiding you."

"Such as school cricket pavilions?" Amber said meaningfully.

The boys suddenly looked anxious. Amber stepped in and took the initiative.

"Exactly. You'll have to find somewhere safer than this to keep me, at least for a few days. What about inside the school itself?"

"No, Sister lives in while we're there," Jackson said. "She does her rounds very thoroughly - she'd be bound to find you."

"We need somewhere that looks secure. What about these outbuildings you've been working on?"

Jackson's face suddenly brightened. "There's two largish rooms on ground level, one for horse stalls the other for tack. Above them is a loft which you reach through a trapdoor. I think it must have been used to store feed. It has a row of low wooden partitions and two smallish windows at each end."

"The loft sounds promising," said Amber. "Has it got water?"

"There's a tap in the corner of the stalls."

"Electric lights?"

"Yes."

"Is the place sound and can it be locked, especially that trap-door to the loft?"

"It's solid enough," said Jackson, "and we've got a set of keys for all the locks."

"I'd like to see it. Where's Sister Newcombe now?"

"Down at her cottage."

"No time like the present then."

"It seems to me," the Major said after Melanie had finished her tale,
"that your qualities were not properly appreciated in your world. Yet your conscience still troubles you because you feel you must make every effort to return."

He looked at the phallus he had taken from her pack. "Perhaps this will take you back. I wonder if other outsider girls came by similar means? Your girl thief was certainly here, but she has slipped away from us again. I knew she had spirit - like her hunter. Well, you'll have your chance to pick up her trail again."

Melanie's eye widened.

"After you have served the duration of your time with the pack," he continued. "You should know I will not let a prize specimen like you go one minute sooner than I must. That is my right by law. And since that is a fact beyond your power to change, do not let it trouble you further." He smiled. "For now, just answer this. If there was no obligation upon you, where would you rather be?"

She could not abandon all thoughts of home. One day she would have to satisfy the obligations of her duty. But she knew now where she was truly valued.

"Here, Master."

The Major looked relieved. He closed Melanie's pack and

216

hooked it over his saddle. "This will be put with your clothes in Platt's care. I promise you will have it back when you have served your time. Talking of which..." He took out his watch. "I must be getting back shortly. Can't have guests arriving without being there to greet them, especially as Arabella seems to have taken herself off somewhere." He smiled at Melanie. "There will be no girls for our pleasure tonight since you must all rest to be fresh for the hunt, and tomorrow night you'll be somebody else's prize. So I must make the most of you now."

Melanie beamed in delight and her nipples stood up.

"That's more like it, girl," the Major said, approving the display.

He motioned her to her feet and had her lie across the fallen trunk, her stomach resting on a padding of moss and lichen. He took out her tail and put it between her teeth to hold, then stroked and patted the firm, nutbrown cheeks of her rump. Automatically she spread her thighs a little wider so he could slide his hand down to tease the moistening peach of her mound.

"Ready for the off, eh? A little more encouragement, perhaps?"

He stepped back and swung his riding crop hard enough to make her bottom quiver.

Melanie gasped, jerking forward, the bark chafing the undersides of her breasts.

But how different from her switching in these very woods just a few days before. This excited her, like the smack of the starting arms on the race track. She squirmed in delight, opening herself to the crop, spreading her legs even wider and turning her feet in to expose the tender inner flesh of her thighs and bottom cleft.

Half a dozen more blows and she was wiggling her haunches in urgent need.

The Major unbuttoned his flies, releasing his cock. Clasping her hips he drove it into her dark glistening bottom hole and the hot succulent tightness beyond.

Between thrusts he said: "This is where you belong, girl...

217

where your talent can bloom... you'll be such a worthy prize... make me proud of you!"

Melanie gasped and moaned. Through her clenched teeth she said: "I will, Master."

As far as Sue could judge from within her cramped and stuffy trunk, the cart journey lasted about half an hour. Then the cart came to a halt. There were muted voices from outside. The cart rocked as Arabella climbed down and Sue heard the click of her boot heels recede. For a couple of minutes there was nothing, then more footsteps returned.

"...I have another job for you." Arabella was saying. "Payment as before."

"Always willing to oblige you, Miss Arabella," a man's voice replied.

"And you will be discreet, remember."

"We knows how to keep our mouths shut, ma'am," said another voice.

Sue's trunk was lifted from the cart and carried off. The other voices faded. She heard the creak of hinges, a few more steps then she was set down. A door closed.

"Tip her out," said Arabella

The trunk was turned onto its side and the lid opened. With a shake, Sue was rolled out onto a floor of dry soft earth mixed with shards of straw. Groaning, she lay in the same doubled over position as in the trunk, too numb and stiff to move.

She was in a barn, with just a few bales of straw stacked to one side, illuminated by fingers of sunlight reaching through chinks in its boarded walls and sparkling off floating dust motes. Two large men in their twenties were grinning down at her. One had red hair, the other was dark. They wore leather jerkins over loose shirts with rolled up sleeves, exposing sun-browned brawny arms, and had gaiters round their ankles.

Arabella stood opposite them. "Pick her up," she commanded, "and take the straps and gag off her."

They hauled Sue to her feet, their hard, work-roughened

hands feeling like sandpaper against her soft skin, and released her bonds. She hung limply between them, trembling as the circulation burned back into her limbs, sick fear knotting itself in her stomach.

Arabella looked Sue's pale body up and down, then said: "Use her in any manner you like. Don't be gentle. I want to see her struggle and suffer." And she made herself comfortable on a straw bale and prepared to watch Sue's violation.

Sue looked up into the grinning faces that loomed on either side of her and knew she could expect no mercy. She received none.

A large hand closed over her right breast and twisted and squeezed the gland, even as stiff fingers were rammed up between her cunt lips and into the tunnel beyond. Sue screamed, fluttering between the men like a trapped butterfly. They gave her a shove that sent her sprawling flat, her numbed legs unable to support her. As the men laughed at her helplessness, she began to crawl away on her hands and knees. They grabbed her thick mane of hair and, as she was held tight, crouched down and slapped her pendulous breasts from side to side so hard that they rebounded from one another.

Still holding her hair they dragged her through the dirt back into the centre of the barn. Fear loosened control of her bladder and a tremulous fountain of urine splattered over the dirt.

"Look - she's wetting herself!" said Dark Hair with a chuckle.

They dropped her to the ground and stood over her. As she looked up at them through tear-streaked eyes, they unbuttoned the flaps of their flies and released two thick hard cocks.

Red Hair caught Sue by the scruff of her neck and pulled her to her feet. Keeping her bent over he thrust her at his friend who caught her flailing arms and pulled them up behind her and. Sue opened her mouth to scream and found it instead filled with a rod of swollen flesh.

"Suck it good, bitch!" Dark Hair commanded.

Even as she choked and gasped for breath, Red's hard fingers dug into her fleshy buttocks and he drove his cock into her slit. Penetrated fore and aft, her knees threatened to buckle under the assault, but they were supporting her weight between them so she was not allowed to collapse. With brutal force they rammed into her, first front, then rear, handling her as though she was a toy, a doll of flesh they were playing with between them.

Then the shameful, wonderful, humiliating response took over Sue's mind and body as need replaced revulsion. She was being defiled and yet raw pleasure was coursing through her.

She sucked desperately on Dark's cock even as her channel contracted about Red's member and tried to squeeze the life from it.

Dark's hot sperm spouted into her throat and Sue swallowed it thirstily, even as Red's seed blossomed deep in her vagina.

They had come yet she was still in need of release! Was this the ultimate torment? But they were still hard and had not done with her yet.

Red lay back on the ground, pulling Sue with him. Dark knelt down before her, hooking his arms under her knees and wrenching her legs apart. With a heave he lifted her up and dropped her onto Red's erection. Her buttock cheeks parted, exposing her crinkled sphincter to the intruder, and her own weight impaled her.

She gasped. Even her broom handle-stretched anus was not prepared for this. Red's cock was too thick, it would split her in two! Then it was wholly inside her and she was filled to perfection.

Dark hunched over and thrust into her already used and lubricated front passage, the force of his entry making her ride up the piston of flesh in her rectum. Red's hands on her shoulders pushed her back again. She was the squirming fleshy filling of a carnal sandwich, crushed and ground between the two powerful bodies; skewered by two cocks trying to meet inside her. She had felt nothing like it in her life.

"Harder... please... harder!" she yelled.

There was an explosion of pleasure within her.

She shrieked and bucked and kicked... and fainted.

The first thing she saw when she came to was Arabella.

Still seated on the straw bale she was staring at her intently with those cool sharp eyes. Sue realized her hair was being tugged lightly. The men, crouched over her, were wiping their cocks clean on it. She found she was pleased that they had made use of her, even while unconscious. It was good to be soiled a little further.

When they were done, with sperm oozing from every orifice of her body, Sue crawled through the dirt and kissed Arabella's booted feet. Arabella lifted Sue's chin with her toe.

"That was quite pleasing, girl," Arabella said, smiling slightly.

Sue's heart surged with hope. It was the nearest thing to a compliment she had yet given. Now she understood a little more. Her mistress wanted more than just simple obedience from her slave. She wanted submission to the idea of suffering, a willingness to undergo torment for her amusement, a show of futile resistance. It was a cruel path, but this time Sue would follow it to its end, to find if that was where love, and her own salvation, lay.

"Please, Miss Arabella," Sue begged, "have them do it again..."

The boys carried Amber over to the stable block wrapped in a groundsheet. Thinking of Cleopatra she had suggested the method and they had agreed without question. She meant to do that at every opportunity, so they became used to following her directions.

They unrolled her in the stall room, which was just as Jackson had described. Putting on her leash, her hands still bound behind her back, they helped her up the steep stairs to the loft.

It was a dusty but dry room about thirty five feet long, with a low sloping ceiling of exposed rafters carried by solid struts and beams. A secondary framework of lighter posts and crosspieces supported the planking sides of half a dozen waist high open-ended bays that ran down one side.

Jackson led Amber along to the far end where she peered through a grimy, cobweb-filmed square window. One corner of the main school building was about twenty yards away. On the other side was a belt of trees.

"That's our dorm at the top," Jackson said. "We've fixed it so we can get out down the fire escape without anybody knowing."

She realized they were waiting on her approval. She made a show of looking about the loft thoughtfully. "You'll have to find something to cover the windows, so the lights don't show at night."

"We bundled up some old sacking downstairs," Gosset said quickly.

"Great. Can you find a hammer and nails to put it up?"
"Yes."

She walked back to one of the low bays so that Jackson had to trail after her, holding the end of her leash like a train.

"Can you put a few more nails, or screw-in eye rings if you can find some, in the sides on this?" she asked Gosset.

He nodded.

"Good. Then your pet'll have somewhere secure to sleep where you won't worry about her escaping."

From the expression on their faces it was evident she had delighted them with her unexpected co-operation. They cheerfully brought up the cover they had carried her in, and with some more sacking, built a rough pallet in the bay. Gosset found the hooks and rings could be removed from the walls of the tack room downstairs, and he industriously hammered and screwed them into the sides of the bay. Ropes were threaded though them ready to fasten Amber in place. Buckets of water were brought up for drinking, washing and sanitary purposes, together with an old towel and a roll of school issue toilet paper. Amber praised their efforts generously, sitting down to test her new bed. As their eyes fastened upon her splayed legs they were reminded of what they had planned to do to her before the sudden move to

222

new quarters. Amber felt her stomach do a little flip flop at the prospect of another gang-bang as she saw their trouser fronts begin to bulge. She could only influence them a little before they took what was theirs by simple right of possession, enforced by the ropes that bound her. She had no choice in the matter; she was their helpless plaything. She shivered at the darkly exciting thought, and said quickly:

"Now, you've got this nice roomy loft but only one pet to keep in it. How would you like two?"

The boys looked at each other uncertainly, then back at Amber. "That would be terrific," said Jackson, "but where would we find her?"

"I think Arabella Westlake is secretly keeping an outsider girl." Now she had their full attention. "How many outsiders have appeared around here in the last few days?" she continued. "Myself and a black girl Major Havercotte-gore has taken, right? You'd have heard if there had been any more." They nodded. "Well then, why did Arabella take the trouble to come to the punishment yard and ask me if there might be four of us? Not three, please note, but four!"

"You mean," said Jackson slowly, "she's already got one herself?"

ìThat's right. And, like you, she can't be holding her legally. So, if some enterprising young men were to find where this outsider girl was being kept and took her for themselves, it would seriously annoy Arabella, yet there would be absolutely nothing she could do about it!"

She saw smiles spread over their faces as they began to appreciate the possibilities.

ìIt's just an idea," she said. ìThink about it and we'll talk more later." She took a deep breath and surrendered to the inevitable, smiling seductively. "Meanwhile, shall we try out the, er, new facilities? I'm sure you can think of a good use for all these lovely beams and posts." Something made her add: "By the way, my bottom feels a lot less sore now. I'm sure it could stand a little punishment as well as my tits. What do you think?"

They strung her up under one of the beams. And Amber noted approvingly how they were handling her with growing confidence. For good measure they pulled her feet apart and secured her ankles to ropes running from the bases of the support posts.

"Of course if you get me really excited I might make a lot of noise," Amber said as they stretched her wide, feeling her juices begin to flow. "Perhaps you'd better gag me just in case - but kisses first, please."

Learning fast, they each kissed her as a slave should be kissed: fondling her buttocks even as they enjoyed her lips and hot darting tongue, and finishing with a squeeze and pinch of her moist pussy. Then the gag was pushed into her mouth and firmly tied in place.

They stood back for a moment and feasted their eyes on their pet slave, displayed before them in her perfect helpless nakedness, ready for their use and pleasure. Hard nipples trembled on firm high breasts, while tiny dewdrops of excitement glistened on pubic fur.

As she felt their gaze devour her, for first time Amber herself realised how intense her own arousal was as she contemplated what was to come. Despite her schemes and manipulations she really was at their mercy, to do with as they wished. She was their slave and they her masters. What could be more natural?

Amber jerked as the cane swished through the air and made her bottom cheeks shiver. A pleasant stinging blow that warmed her flesh, but they needn't be that gentle with her. The last few days had taught her to accept far worse than that. Perhaps even to want far worse?

She twisted her head around and gazed imploringly, challengingly, at Jackson. Harder she begged mutely.

He must have understood because the next blow was much more severe - and much better, setting a fire burning deep in her buttock flesh.

The boys took it in turns to use the cane, slashing at her front and back. The tops of her thighs and the flat of her stomach received their due attention, while her breasts were made to shiver and jump. She was a naked pinioned target. All of her was at their disposal, to serve and to suffer for their pleasure.

Amber yelped and moaned through her gag, tugging at her ropes, helplessly, happily giving her young masters what they wanted, what they were forcing out of her. In return, five young hard cocks would soon be reaming her insides out while pumping their bolts of hot sperm into her. Then she'd have a few hoursí rest tethered in her cubicle before a second, midnight visit. She could see a steady cycle of restraint and sex and punishment, pleasure and pain, mixed with a little intrigue, stretching into the days ahead and merging into one perfect whole.

As she writhed and swayed in her bonds, feeling her desire rising, Amber thought of the chained female figure carved into the base of the phallus she had used. That was her now. She had submitted to the puzzle box's spell and had found a strange but wonderful new life for herself.

Now the adventure could really begin.

THE END

Will Amber's plan succeed?
Can the boys steal Sue from Arabella before she has been totally broken in?
How will Melanie fare in her first girl hunt and will she ever catch Amber?
Will our three heroines ever return home, or has the Girlspell claimed them for good?

Find out in part two of THE GIRLSPELL.

And now for the opening of next months title "INSIDE THE FORTRESS" by *John Strenes*

CHAPTER ONE
THE LADY ON THE TRAIN

The young officer strode briskly along one of the platforms of the St.Petersburg Station in Moscow. He was an impressive sight in the uniform of the Tsar's Lifeguard, and drew admiring glances. The white tunic and close-fitting breeches were topped by a lancer's cap, whose black shine was matched by his riding boots. His luggage had been loaded into the rear van, and he was looking for a first-class carriage. There was a hiss of steam from the great locomotive and the railway guard raised a whistle to his lips.

The officer gestured him to wait, and the man obediently dropped his arm. Without hurrying, the lieutenant walked along the train, tapping his stick in his hand and idly scanning the first-class compartments. If he could find an empty one, he would be spared the tedious duty of having to make conversation with his fellow travellers. Suddenly his eyes met those of a woman, gazing back at him. That gaze seemed to have possibilities, he thought, and without a flicker of hesitation he opened the carriage door and entered. Before shutting it behind him, he gave a curt nod to the guard, who blew on his whistle.

As the train began to move, he turned to his travelling companion. She was a good-looking woman, perhaps in her late twenties - some years older than himself, anyway. She was smartly dressed in the height of fashion: a greyish beige skirt and jacket, unbuttoned to show a lace-trimmed blouse. From the hem of her skirt peeped delicate, well-made boots and she had laid her hat on the seat beside her. The delicate smell of her scent filled the compartment.

Her hair was brown, drawn back into a small bun with a few curls on either side of her face, which was attractive rather than beautiful. She was regarding him with an amused twinkle in her eye.

"Isn't it considered impolite to enter a lady's compartment without asking her leave?" She addressed him in French, as any Russian aristocrat would.

"I have to admit it is, dear lady," he drawled "but the train was about to leave and I thought it worse manners to keep you waiting." He placed his shiny cap and stick on the opposite seat and sat down.

She smiled at this obvious lie, holding her head to one side, coquettishly. "Well, lieutenant, this is the express to St.Petersburg. The only stop is for lunch at Bologoye, so we have each other's company for at least four hours."

"Indeed, madam, and perhaps for the rest of the journey also. I am glad to have such a charming companion on what might otherwise have been a dull journey." This was untrue, as he had tucked a slim volume of French pornography into his tunic with which he had hoped to while away the time. He stood up. "Perhaps I should introduce myself?"

"Really, lieutenant, that is not correct etiquette. You must know that a gentleman can only be introduced to a lady by a mutual friend." Her eyes had a sparkle of amusement.

He gave a slight bow. "Well, shall I just say I am an officer of the Tsar's Lifeguard?"

"So I see". Her eyes ran down his uniform. The officers of the regiment prided themselves on the tightness of their breeches. The lieutenant had made his tailor use a slightly stretchable material - a cad's trick, the other officers thought, but now his breeches fitted as tight as a skin, without a crease or wrinkle. Of course, he could wear nothing beneath them, and the bulge of his genitals was prominent beneath the snow-white material.

She stared fixedly for a moment, then swallowed hard. As he sat down on the seat opposite her, her gaze did not leave the front of his breeches. He sat with his legs slightly apart to give her a better view.

228

"Lieutenant, a lady alone in a railway carriage with a strange man may think herself in danger."

"Danger? What danger can you fear, madam?"

"Why, violation."

"Do you think violation is likely?"

A curious eagerness came into her voice. ""Oh yes, indeed. I heard that on this very line, not a month ago, that a young working girl got into a third-class compartment with five soldiers, and by the end of the journey they had all raped her several times."

"Several times?"

"Yes, and in different ways. I believe, for instance, that one man was using her mouth while another entered her from behind."

"How remarkable!" To hear tales of sex from the lips of an attractive woman was far more entertaining than any pornographic book. Already his penis was beginning to swell and straighten in his breeches, and he knew she could not help but notice it. "Do you know any other details?"

"Yes. Apparently she struggled at first, but they were too many and too strong. Two held her back against the seat while two others pulled her legs apart. The fifth man penetrated her, and when he had finished, one of the others took his place."

His penis slowly uncoiled and hardened beneath his breeches. "How do you know of this? I don't remember seeing any such thing in the newspapers."

"Oh no, the girl wouldn't dream of reporting the rape. The shame of other people knowing would be worse than the ordeal."

"Then how do you know about it?"

"Ladies talk of these things, naturally. Gossip is sure to get round."

"Well, madam, nothing you would not wish can happen to you. You have the protection of an officer of the Tsar's Lifeguard."

For a full minute she stared at the long, hard outline push-

229

ing out the material of his breeches. She ran her tongue quickly round her lips.

"The Tsar's Lifeguard is always smart, but I think such tight uniforms must surely be uncomfortable."

"Not always, my dear madam. But when an officer meets an attractive lady, sometimes it happens that he finds his breeches growing too tight. It is the way of the world, as I'm sure you understand." She nodded.

"Yes, that must be inconvenient" she murmured, her gaze never leaving the massive bulge. There was silence in the carriage, the rumble and clatter of the train partly muffled by the expensive velvet upholstery.

She spoke again. "Lieutenant, it is very rude of me to see you so uncomfortable while doing nothing to assist you. If you should wish to rearrange your clothing, I would raise no objection".

"Madam, you are very kind. I was hoping you would be so gracious."

Slowly he undid his breeches. The flies were fastened with small, flat buttons which were carefully concealed to avoid spoiling the smooth outline. He reached inside, and drew out his erection. It was very long and thick, and stood stiffly upright from his body, a drop of clear fluid gleaming at the opening of its purplish head.

She contemplated the uprisen sex thoughtfully. The train clattered over some points. They must be on the outskirts of the city by now.

"It's so big," she murmured.

With a moment's hesitation, she reached down to the hem of her skirt and pulled it up to her lap. With a rustle of petticoats, she exposed first her buttoned boots, then black silk stockings and finally a pair of close-fitting, lace-trimmed drawers of fine white cotton. She moved her thighs apart, and he could see that the centre seam of the drawers dimpled into the soft outline of her vulva. Almost as if in a trance, the lady's hand stole between her thighs. Her middle finger began gen-

230

tly to stroke the cleft between her legs. Her eyelids fluttered for an instant.

For a moment, both sat silently contemplating each other. The lady cleared her throat. Then she spoke, and her voice was shaking slightly.

"If you are to take me, captain, it must be by force. You must overcome the resistance I will put up, with all the violence you consider necessary. A lady of my breeding cannot consent willingly to such an assault, but must defend herself, even if she suffers injury."

He could not have been given a clearer invitation. Slowly he stood up, his member seeming to tower over her. She had gone very pale, and her breath was rapid and shallow. Then abruptly he sat down next to her, and reached his hand between her thighs. Violently, she shoved his hand away, and made as if to slap him. He grabbed her wrist and twisted it, seizing a handful of her hair with his other hand. He hauled her towards him, releasing his grip to punch her shoulder. Then he shoved her backwards, sending her sprawling along the carriage seat.

Quickly moving to sit on her stomach, with one hand he held her wrists above her head, while fumbling to unbutton her blouse with the other. He tore it open roughly, sending a button skittering across the carriage. She only wore a corset beneath, which he quickly unclasped to release her breasts. They were quite small but firm to his hand, as she writhed soundlessly under him. He smiled down triumphantly at her helplessness.

Then swinging himself round, he sprawled on top of her, the gold lace and buttons of his tunic digging into her exposed breasts. Forcing his knees between hers, he prised her legs apart. His hand fumbled up between her thighs, feeling through the thin fabric of the drawers for the mound of her sex. Her eyes were screwed tightly shut, but she tried to jerk him off her body. A sudden punch in the stomach made her go limp.

231

His questing fingers found the cleft they were seeking, and he noted that it was moist beneath the cotton. For a moment he caressed her there, then dug his fingernail into the seam of the undergarment, bursting the stitches. He was able to introduce his finger, and tore the crotch of her drawers open.

With his free hand he introduced the blunt head of his member into her, nudging apart the lips of her sex. She flinched at its touch. Slowly he began to push himself into her. She gave a gasp as the full length of him suddenly rammed into her body. Then he withdrew, so that only the tip of his phallus remained inside her, and then rammed in hard again. Slowly but mercilessly he drove in and out. The woman lay quite still beneath him now, making a little moaning sound at each thrust.

He quickened his pace, slamming his hard shaft into her again and again, as if it were a weapon with which he was beating her. Then, gasping, his orgasm swept over him, his final thrusts pumping his sperm deep into the passive body beneath him.

He lay without moving for a while. The clickety-clack of the train seemed suddenly louder. Then he slowly climbed off her. As he withdrew, semen ran from the swollen lips of her vulva and dribbled onto her petticoats.

He slumped, breathing heavily, onto the seat opposite her. He made no effort to put his sex away, but sat with his legs apart, his wet member hanging out of his breeches. She sat up, and smoothed down her skirts. Matter-of-factly, she refastened her corset and did up her blouse, tutting quietly at the missing button. She reached for her travelling bag. Her face was flushed but she acted nonchalantly. She took out a mirror and checked her hair, tucking it back into place where his rough hands had disarranged it. Without taking her gaze from the mirror, she broke the silence.

"Is this not remarkable? Twenty minutes ago we had not met. Now here I am, full of your semen." The woman put away the mirror and regarded him.

"Were you not taking a dreadful risk just then? You are

232

young, and a scandal could ruin your career before it has started. What makes you trust me not to report this to the police?"

"Dear lady, I am, as you say, only a young lieutenant, but I flatter myself that I know enough of human nature - indeed, of feminine nature - to know how far I may go."

"Am I so easily understood, even by a lad?" She smiled sadly to herself.

"No, madam. As I say, I consider myself an acute observer of human character. No, don't think I am boastful - my senior officers think so too, and that is why I am posted to St.Petersburg." He paused. "But enough of that. It is better that we remain strangers."

By now his penis had softened, and he tucked it back into his breeches. She watched closely as he buttoned his flies. Then she took a needle and thread from her bag and began to sew a button onto her blouse to replace the one torn off during the assault. It was rather awkward for her, and he watched her with a lazy interest. He yawned. She sat back in her seat and gazed at him reproachfully.

"Now you've had your pleasure, you want to sleep, I suppose."

There was a hint of disappointment in her voice, but he could not deny she was right. "Just a few minutes repose, madam, and I shall be a man renewed." She tied the thread of the button and trimmed it off.

"Come then, lie along the seat here and lay your head in my lap. I shall be your pillow."

He came across to her side and stretched himself out. As he laid his head on her lap, he could feel on his cheek the warmth of her thighs through the fabric of her skirt. She gently caressed his hair.

"So young, and so vicious," she murmured softly. He slept.

When he opened his eyes, he saw she was reading a little novelette which she must have taken from her bag. He got up and stretched himself. They were passing through open country, the empty birchwood landscape beyond the city. She smiled up at him and put her book away. He sat down opposite her.

"Lieutenant, have you ever committed rape before?"

The officer was startled and a little disconcerted by this abrupt question, but tried to recover his poise.

"Rape, madam? Well, I really..."

"Don't be alarmed, lieutenant, I promise I will never betray any confidences. It is just that I think you must have often taken a woman by force."

The captain hesitated. "Well, perhaps ... perhaps on occasions it might have been considered rape."

Her eyes glittered and she sat forward eagerly. "Tell me about them'" Her hands were clasped together tightly in her lap. He swallowed hard, but then decided that this opportunity to brag of his sexual adventures to a well-bred lady was too good to miss.

"Most were only peasant girls or serving maids, you understand. On my family's estate."

"Where is that?"

"Let us just say it is deep in the country, many days journey from Moscow."

"Tell me about the first one."

"Well, I had arrived back home from the academy for the summer vacation. You must know that an all-male boarding school is full of dirty talk and wanking. I was growing less and less satisfied with that. I wanted a real screw, and I wanted it soon."

"And you didn't much care how you got it?"

He smiled. "Perhaps. I admit I was hot for sex and to my astonishment, when I got into the house, I met a new housemaid - one of the prettiest I'd ever seen. She was very young, younger than me even, and before she had carried my bags to my room I had made up my mind to fuck her."

"How long did it take?"

"It was the next evening. I was going upstairs to change for dinner, and I met her on the landing. She stood aside to let me pass, but I stopped in front of her. I praised her beauty and said that such a pretty girl must have many lovers. She blushed, and said she had none.

I pushed my hand against the front of her apron, feeling her crotch through her clothes. She begged me to stop, and said she was afraid someone would come. I told her to come to my room, and that nobody would disturb us there. She was clearly frightened, but I knew she wouldn't dare to disobey the young master. After all, she and her relatives depended on being employed by my family."

"So she followed you?"

"She had no choice, really. She was pale, though, and looked terrified when I locked the bedroom door behind us. She stood helplessly with her hands by her sides in the middle of the room. I exposed my cock to her - it was the biggest hard-on I'd ever had. Then I told her to lift her skirts. She hesitated, and I had to order her again. She was reluctant, but did as she was told. She began to cry."

"To cry? Did you pity her?"

"Not at all, in fact I began to feel the spur of cruel pleasure. She was at my mercy, and my prick grew even harder."

"What did you do?"

"I grabbed her by the hair and forced her down onto the floor. She was sobbing and begging me not to, but that only made me more determined. I pulled up her clothes. She wasn't wearing any drawers - few country girls do. I got my cock to the opening of her cunt and rammed myself into her. She was tight and dry, and it was not easy. She gave a cry as I pushed in, but I told her to be quiet in case anybody heard.

The actual shagging only lasted a few seconds. I was so keyed up that my orgasm exploded like a bomb, and I must have pumped about half a pint of hot spunk into her."

The lady smiled at the thought of all that adolescent semen. "And then?"

"Then I told her to get out, and not to let anyone see she had been crying. I dressed for dinner, and joined the others downstairs. It was pleasant to be served at the table by the red-eyed maid, knowing that my sperm was inside her."

"You men have no conscience." She said it sadly, as a fact of life. "Aren't we women silly to desire you so much?"

"And do you?"

"Alas, too much. It has been the pleasure and the pain of my life. I have always been obsessed by men."

"And by a particular part of their bodies?"

She nodded. Describing the rape of the servant girl had given him an erection, and her eyes lingered on the long bulge in his breeches. He stood up and slowly undid himself, pulling out his shaft. The head of it bobbed a few inches from her face. She gazed at it admiringly.

"It's magnificent."

She moved forward on her seat to bring herself closer. She reached out with both hands and gently stroked the hard shaft, her fingertips tracing the veins that stood out from its rigid surface. Then she guided it to her mouth. She parted her lips and took the massive erection in. Her soft mouth closed round it and she began to suck. Soon she was working her head back and forth with a rhythmic movement, her cheeks sucked in to grip the shaft. Her soft tongue caressed its hard length. The member nudged the back of her throat and her nostrils flared as she struggled to breathe.

He looked down with a smile of satisfaction: she was certainly an experienced fellatrice. He stroked her hair as she rocked her head back and forth. Soft wetness engulfed his prick. The swollen shaft glistened with her saliva as it slid in and out between her lips. Her free hand slid up the back of his thigh and began to caress his buttocks.

Gradually his muscles began to stiffen and his breathing grew more rapid. She felt his tension rising and quickened her rhythm, her lips gripping his cock just below the head. Her other hand reached up between his legs to squeeze the bulge of his testicles. Just then he groaned, and suddenly jet after jet of hot semen was spurting into her mouth. She coughed and gagged, having to swallow the sticky flood to keep from choking.

Panting, he withdrew his sex from between her wet lips. Expertly, she squeezed the shaft to catch the last dribbles of his sperm in her hand to prevent it dripping on her skirt. Swallowing the last gulp of the semen, she licked her fingers clean.

He slumped back down on the seat opposite, and there was silence for a while as his breathing became slower. She had produced the mirror again and was wiping away a dribble of sperm from the side of her mouth with a tiny lace-trimmed handkerchief.

"There now. I hope you won't consider me rude, lieutenant, if I suck a pastille. I confess after all these years I have never grown used to the taste."

"Not at all, madam. Please feel free."

She took a small enamelled box from her bag and popped a lozenge into her mouth.

"Did you find that pleasant, lieutenant?"

"Indeed, I cannot say I have even been more expertly sucked off. I wonder where you came to be so skilful in that ladylike accomplishment."

"Why, at the Smolny Institute. As you know, it is the most select girls school in the empire. Young ladies of gentle birth are expected to receive a good education, and an important, if unofficial, part of it is how to cope with the demands made upon a young lady by a young gentleman." She smiled a little mockingly.

"You mean ..."

"But of course. I had not been there a fortnight before the older girls had told me all about those important matters concerning men and women. They told me of the pain and also, I am glad to tell you, of the pleasure. But whatever pleasure we took, we had to ensure that we stayed virgins. Young girls of our class must marry, and marry well."

To be continued........

The cover photograph for this book and many others are available as limited edition prints.
Write to:-

Viewfinders Photography
PO Box 200,
Reepham
Norfolk
NR10 4SY

for details, or see,

www.viewfinders.org.uk

TITLES IN PRINT

Silver Mink

UK £4.99 except *£5.99 --USA $8.95 except *$9.95

All titles, both in print and out of print, are available as
electronic downloads at:

http://www.electronicbookshops.com

e-mail submissions to:
Editor@electronicbookshops.com

TITLES IN PRINT

Silver Moon

ISBN 1-897809-16-6   Rorigs Dawn *Ray Arneson*
ISBN 1-897809-17-4   Bikers Girl on the Run *Lia Anderssen*
ISBN 1-897809-23-9   Slave to the System *Rosetta Stone*
ISBN 1-897809-25-5   Barbary Revenge *Allan Aldiss*
ISBN 1-897809-27-1   White Slavers *Jack Norman*
ISBN 1-897809-31-X   Slave to the State *Rosetta Stone*
ISBN 1-897809-36-0   Island of Slavegirls *Mark Slade*
ISBN 1-897809-37-9   Bush Slave *Lia Anderssen*
ISBN 1-897809-38-7   Desert Discipline *Mark Stewart*
ISBN 1-897809-40-9   Voyage of Shame *Nicole Dere*
ISBN 1-897809-41-7   Plantation Punishment *Rick Adams*
ISBN 1-897809-42-5   Naked Plunder *J.T. Pearce*
ISBN 1-897809-43-3   Selling Stephanie *Rosetta Stone*
ISBN 1-897809-44-1   SM Double value (Olivia/Lucy) *Graham/Slade**
ISBN 1-897809-46-8   Eliska *von Metchingen*
ISBN 1-897809-47-6   Hacienda, *Allan Aldiss*
ISBN 1-897809-48-4   Angel of Lust, *Lia Anderssen**
ISBN 1-897809-50-6   Naked Truth, *Nicole Dere**
ISBN 1-897809-51-4   I Confess!, *Dr Gerald Rochelle**
ISBN 1-897809-52-2   Barbary Slavedriver, *Allan Aldiss**
ISBN 1-897809-53-0   A Toy for Jay, *J.T. Pearce**
ISBN 1-897809-54-9   The Confessions of Amy Mansfield, *R. Hurst**
ISBN 1-897809-55-7   Gentleman's Club, *John Angus**
ISBN 1-897809-57-3   Sinfinder General *Johnathan Tate**
ISBN 1-897809-59-X   Slaves for the Sheik *Allan Aldiss**
ISBN 1-897809-60-3   Church of Chains *Sean O'Kane**
ISBN 1-897809-62-X   Slavegirl from Suburbia *Mark Slade**
ISBN 1-897809-64-6   Submission of a Clan Girl *Mark Stewart**
ISBN 1-897809-65-4   Taming the Brat *Sean O'Kane**
ISBN 1-897809-66-2   Slave for Sale *J.T. Pearce**
ISBN 1-897809-69-7   Caged! *Dr. Gerald Rochelle**
ISBN 1-897809-71-9   Rachel in servitude *J.L. Jones**
ISBN 1-897809-72-2   Beaucastel *Caroline Swift**
ISBN 1-897809-73-5   Slaveworld *Steven Douglas**
ISBN 1-897809-76-X   Sisters in Slavery *Charles Graham**
ISBN 1-897809-78-6   Eve in Eden *Stephen Rawlings**

*UK £4.99 except *£5.99 --USA $8.95 except *$9.95*